Transactional Analysis
Approaches to
Brief Therapy

Brief Therapies Series

Series Editor: Stephen Palmer
Associate Editor: Gladeana McMahon
Focusing on brief and time-limited therapies, this series of books is aimed at students, beginning and experienced counsellors, therapists and other members of the helping professions who need to know more about working with the specific skills, theories and practices involved in this demanding, but vital area of their work. Books in the series include:

Bill O'Connell *Solution Focused Therapy*
Gertrud Mander *A Psychodynamic Approach to Brief Therapy*
Berni Curwen, Stephen Palmer and Peter Ruddell *Brief Cognitive Behaviour Therapy*
John Sharry *Solution Focused Groupwork*
Ian McDermott and Wendy Jago *Brief NLP Therapy*

Transactional Analysis
Approaches to
Brief Therapy

or

What do you say between
saying hello and goodbye?

edited by
Keith Tudor

SAGE Publications
London ● Thousand Oaks ● New Delhi

The authors and publishers wish to thank Methuen Publishers
Limited and Suhrkamp Verlag for the Bertholt Brecht poem
from '*Brecht Poems (1913–1956)*' that appears on page 132.

SAGE Publications Ltd
1 Olivers Yard, 55 City Road
London EC1Y 1SP

SAGE Publications Inc
2455 Teller Road
Thousand Oaks, California 91320

SAGE Publications India Pvt Ltd
B-42, Panchsheel Enclave
PO Box 4109
New Delhi-100 017

British Library Cataloguing in Publication data

A catalogue record for this book is
available from the British Library

ISBN 0 7619 5680 8
ISBN 0 7619 5681 6 (pbk)

Typeset by M Rules
Printed and bound in Great Britain by
Athenaeum Press Ltd., Gateshead, Tyne & Wear.

To everything there is a season, and a time to every purpose under
the heaven:
A time to be born, and a time to die;
A time to plant and a time to pluck up that which is planted;
A time to kill, and a time to heal;
A time to break down, and a time to build up;
A time to weep, and a time to laugh;
A time to mourn, and a time to dance;
A time to cast away stones, and a time to gather stones together;
A time to embrace, and a time to refrain from embracing;
A time to seek, and a time to lose;
A time to keep, and a time to cast away;
A time to rend, and a time to sew;
A time to keep silence, and a time to speak;
A time to love, and a time to hate;
A time for war, and a time for peace.

Ecclesiastes 3.1–8

If it were done when 'tis done, then 't were well
It were done quickly.

William Shakespeare (1623) *Macbeth* 1.vii

The goal of transactional analysis is to cure as many patients during
the first treatment session as is possible. This means that the aim is
100% success and any failure to achieve this percentage is viewed
as a challenge.

Eric Berne, Claude Steiner and Jack Dusay (1973)

As soon as you're born they make you feel small
They give you no time at all instead of it all

John Lennon (1970) *Working Class Hero*

Time is what you make it

Swatch advert (2000)

Keith Tudor is a qualified social worker and UKCP Registered Psychotherapist, Group Psychotherapist and Facilitator. He is in private practice offering indivvidual and group counselling, psychotherapy and supervision, and is a Director of Temenos, Sheffield. He is also author of over 30 articles and three other books.

To my transactional euphemeri,
colleagues and friends –
with thanks

and with fond memories of
Sue Fish
(1946–2001)

who taught so many
how to say hello and goodbye
and how to live life to the full in between

Contents

List of Contributors

Barbara Ann Allen was, untill her death in 2000, a Psychotherapist, Family Therapist, mental health planner and human ecologist. A graduate of the social work program at Fordham University and the University of Southern California, she then helped found the Gestalt Institute of Dallas where she was an original Teaching Member. She had an active therapy and consulting practice in Oklahoma City and Tulsa, Oklahoma. Following her retirement, she established a crisis intervention centre and three community mental health centres in Tulsa and was a Clinical Associate Professor of Psychiatry and Behavioral Sciences at the University of Oklahoma Health Sciences Center.

James R. Allen is a Psychiatrist, Gestalt Therapist, Family Therapist and a Teaching and Supervising Transactional Analyst (Clinical). His formal training was at the University of Toronto, McGill University, Baylor Medical School, Harvard Medical School and the Hampstead Child Therapy Clinic, London. At present, he is Professor of Psychiatry and Behavioural Sciences, Rainbolt Chair of Child-Adolescent Psychiatry, and Director of the Child-Adolescent Psychiatry Fellowship at the University of Oklahoma Health Sciences Center.

Steve Dennis works as a Psychotherapist, counsellor, trainer and supervisor. He originally trained as a Dramatherapist and practised in Social Services and adult training settings. He is a Certified Transactional Analyst and a Provisional Teaching and Supervising Transactional Analyst. His specialist area of work is counselling in organisations and working with people who have experienced post-traumatic stress and PTSD. He currently works as the Welfare Officer for Dorset Fire and Rescue Service. He is a trained Critical Incident Debriefer and is a regular contributor to counselling training courses.

Helena Hargaden is a Teaching and Supervising Transactional Analyst and is in private practice as an Integrative Psychotherapist in London. She is a Tutor on the MSc in Transactional Analysis Psychotherapy Course at the Metanoia Institute in West London. She is the author of several articles on therapy and the co-author (with Charlotte Sills) of

Transactional Analysis – a Relational Perspective (to be published by Routledge). She is particularly interested in exploring the use of the therapist's subjectivity in the service of the therapy and also in how we explore and understand the social/political context of our own lives and those of our patients.

Adrienne Lee is accredited by the International Transactional Analysis Association and the European Association of Transactional Analysis (EATA) as a Teaching and Supervising Transactional Analyst. She is a UKCP registered psychotherapist and a Master Practitioner in Neuro Linguistic Programming. Adrienne has been a University teacher and a psychotherapist for more than 25 years. She is a Founder Member and past Chair of the UK's Institute of Transactional Analysis (ITA) and at present represents the ITA on the Council of EATA and is an active member of its Professional Training and Standards Committee and Council of Certification. She was one of the first people to practice TA in Britain and has been running training programmes in TA since 1975. Together with Ian Stewart she founded and co-directs the Berne Institute in Nottingham.

Geoff Mothersole is a Clinical Psychologist and Chartered Counselling Psychologist and at present works as a Consultant Psychologist for Worthing Priority Care NHS Trust, where he manages a Short Term Counselling Service. He also works at the Bracton Centre, Bexley Hospital, Kent, a forensic unit, where he specialises in work with violent and sexual offenders. Geoff also has a private practice as a Psychotherapist and Supervisor in Brighton, is past Professional Development Officer for the UKCP and is a Visiting Tutor on the MSc in TA Psychotherapy at Metanoia Institute, London. He has published several book chapters and articles, and has a particular interest in current developments in short-term and cognitive approaches to psychotherapeutic work.

Ulrike Müller was born in 1948 in Freiburg (Black Forest), Germany where she still lives and works. She studied German and English language and literature and has been a Grammar School teacher for 15 years. During the 1980s she also worked as a school Counsellor during which time she came into contact with transactional analysis. She completed her clinical training and has been in private practice since 1991 and a Provisional Teaching and Supervising Member since 1997. Besides other activities she offers special training groups for teachers. As a transactional analyst she has written articles about theoretical issues, one of which was published in the international *Transactional Analysis Journal* (January 2000) and she has recently completed a translation of Eric Berne's *Transactional Analysis in Psychotherapy* into German.

David Rawson is a Certified Transactional Analyst and Provisional Training and Supervising Transactional Analyst. He has many years experience as a Manager and Senior Therapist in a residential therapeutic community for young, seriously disturbed people. Currently he is Co-director of Connect Therapeutic Community in Birmingham which uses transactional analysis as a general theory of personality and a therapeutic methodology and provides a national resource to Health Trusts and local authority Social Services. After several years of intense focus on the development and expansion of the community into its current successful form, his attention and energy is now mainly given to training and supervision of the specialist TA staff team.

Keith Tudor is a qualified Social Worker and Psychotherapist and an experienced Supervisor and Trainer. He is registered with the UK Council for Psychotherapy (UKCP) both as a Clinical Transactional Analyst and as a Group Psychotherapist and Facilitator. He is also a Provisional Training and Supervising Transactional Analyst. He is a Director of Temenos in Sheffield and its Person-centred Psychotherapy and Counselling courses and is interested in the integrity of as well as the dialogue between different theoretical approaches to psychology and therapy. He is widely published in the field of social policy, counselling and psychotherapy including two books *Mental Health Promotion* (Routledge, 1996) and *Group Counselling* (Sage, 1999) and is series editor of *Advancing Theory in Therapy* (to be published by Routledge).

Mark Widdowson is a qualified Counsellor, a Level Two Thought Field Therapy Practitioner, in advanced TA training and has a private practice, based in Sheffield. His background is in complementary health practice (Shiatsu and Oriental Medicine) and, prior to becoming a therapist, was a Community Mental Health Worker working with people with complex problems, for which he won an award. Mark has written about gay affirmative approaches to TA. He has a particular theoretical interest in the integration of TA with object relations and self psychology; and his professional interests include working with disorders of the self and with survivors of abuse in long-term work, although he also enjoys brief contract work with a wide variety of client groups including adolescents.

Introduction

Keith Tudor

After some discussion, a therapist agrees to see her client three times a week for 20 minutes instead of once a week for an hour.

Towards the end of his session A gets upset and cries. His therapist ends the session at the agreed time.

Towards the end of his session B gets upset and cries. His therapist agrees to extend the session by 10 minutes.

Therapist C walks into her consulting room. Her client is already seated and asks for a few minutes alone, to which C agrees.

A client arrives for his regular appointment. The therapist answers the door looking dishevelled; he has forgotten the time.

A client turns up at the right (clock) time but a day early for her initial meeting. The therapist agrees to see her.

Client D consistently arrives five minutes late for her appointment. Her therapist challenges her about this.

Client E consistently arrives five minutes late for her appointment. Her therapist decides not to confront her; instead he empathises with her difficulty in organising herself. It later transpires that the client is dyslexic which, in this case, affects her ability to organise her time.

Having begun therapy in September, a client wishes to take an extended winter break and resume therapy the following March as, emotionally and psychologically, she hibernates. After some discussion, her therapist agrees to this arrangement.

After five years of working together, meeting weekly, a client and therapist agree that as a way of ending they will meet every month for a while. After three meetings they subsequently decide to meet quarterly for three further and final sessions.

A therapist works with a client – a child – for sixteen sessions, spaced out over two and a half years.

These are all familiar scenarios for the therapist (I use the term generically to include counsellors, psychotherapists and counselling psychologists), the last of which represents Winnicott's (1980) work with '*The Piggle*'. Such scenarios, amongst other therapeutic considerations – such as (in transactional terms) assessment and diagnosis, treatment planning or direction, the contract and the nature of the therapeutic relationship – all involve an appreciation of time as a significant parameter in and of therapy. Therapists, therefore, need to have or to develop a consciousness of temporality as well as tempo and an awareness of the meaning of time for clients as well as themselves and all sorts of levels – philosophical, cultural, political, economic, symbolic, practical and clinical.

A brief essay on and about time

The concept of time has preoccupied philosophers since time began – '"time" has, throughout history, been used like a mirror for human nature. It is a blank screen onto which societies have always projected images of themselves' (Griffiths, 2000: 32). Much of Greek philosophy was concerned with the concepts of eternity and transience. St Augustine suggested that time cannot exist in itself but that rather we only know about 'time' from the flight of things or the rest of things. In a discussion considering the nature of and relation between space and time Macmurray suggests that: 'we can only distinguish space from time by saying that in space all the elements are simultaneous; not, as in time, successive; and simultaneity is itself a determination of time. This indicates that time is logically prior to space' (1957: 132). He goes on to assert that 'time is the form of action; while space is the form of reflection' (1957: 132) – and that therefore action is prior to reflection. This particular philosophical logic is especially interesting as it initially appears counterintuitive to the creation of the therapeutic space or *temenos* and yet is consistent with the 'action' necessary to engage in therapy and its reflective process – and with more actionistic therapies such as transactional analysis (TA). Philosophical notions of eternity and transience are deeply personal; as the philosopher and scientist Davies suggests: 'the very concept of selfhood hinges on the preservation of personal identity through time' (1995: 16).

Time is deeply cultural. Time and the reckoning of time is not universal: there are many, many times. There is atomic time, block time, cosmic time, Dream Time, imaginary time, inner time, linear time, quantum time, relativistic time, subjective time, time dilation, time flow, time flux, time reversal, time symmetry and timewarp – for explanations of which see Davies (1995). Much of this book has been written just prior to and after the turn of the twentieth century CE (*Common Era*). However, it is not *the* year 2000; it is *a* year 2000. It is also the (*a*) year 157BE (Bahá'í calendar), 2544 (Buddhist), 2057 (Hindu, Vikrami Samvat), 5102 (Hindu, Yugabda), 2527 (Jain), 5761 (Jewish), 1421AH (Muslim), 531 (Sikh) and 1379 (Zoroastrian, Fasli), according to the world's main religions. Of course, all these calendars describe and define a linear time, measured from a particular moment significant to that religion – the birth of Christ, after the Hijra, the birth/death of a Guru, etc. Griffiths (2000) (CE and thereafter) considers many cultures in which time is embedded in nature and named as such in a variety of calendars according to the *landscape* they inhabit: birch, rowan, ash, alder, etc. (according to the lunar calendar and the associated trees sacred to the Celts); 'wind month' then 'spawning month', etc. (Northern Siberia); 'Guinea-fowls-sleep month' followed by 'Rains-rot-the-ropes month' (Madagascar). The *starscape* and significant *time frames* such as the Mayan 260 day cycle representing the nine moons time between conception and birth are further examples of 'natural' time or different frames of reference on and about time. In this context the traditional '50 minute' hour of Western therapy with its origins in the university timetable of late nineteenth century Vienna – Freud lectured in blocks of 50 minutes and transferred this time frame to his practice of psychoanalysis – must be seen as a particularly monocultural construct of the space–time continuum.

Time is also highly political. The definition, measurement and control of time played a significant part in British imperial domination:

> mastering with chronometers, the mystery of longitude was such a breakthrough for navigation that Britain could 'rule the waves'. Chronometers were the handcuffs of slavery, for, once time was tamed, the seas were tamed, and once the seas were tamed, whole nations could be enslaved. (Griffiths, 2000: 32)

In Britain and other countries the industrial revolution effectively moved working-class people away from the land where days were measured by the seasons and the necessities of an agricultural life cycle to the factories where shifts, days, and whole communities became subject to the clock (clocking on), the whistle and the siren. In this context it is perhaps significant that Rastafarians, for instance, make a distinction between time and clocks as in 'clock time is half past nine'. Interestingly, Berne (1975b) says that 'clock time' combined with 'goal time' (the time it takes for an event or activity to be completed) is called 'Hurryup'. Given that many if not most people are governed by clock time, our own sense of time becomes fractured. One client became aware that he was not only 'clock-watching' but 'minute-watching'. He only felt OK if he was *on* time, and this both supported and was reinforced by certain obsessing behaviours and by beliefs such as 'punctuality is a virtue'. His conditional worth, behaviour and beliefs were challenged in therapy; he realised that he was being punctual in order to please people (in TA terms, a 'Please' driver); he began to experiment with letting himself 'off the hook' of a specific minute. Further analysis revealed that he had no sense of himself in which 'I' and 'around' (as in 'I'll meet you around 8 o'clock') could exist in the same sentence. Following this realisation, further therapeutic work on his life script, and positive reinforcement, he became more relaxed *about* time, whilst still being *on* time as far as important arrangements were concerned.

Especially in the West and in Western-dominated societies, we live in a culture in which time is increasingly viewed as a commodity. Time is money. The quick sell, the quick fix, the instant (re)solution, the demand for immediate communication: are all features of market-led, consumer-driven societies and the world of a global market dominated by capital. As Thorne puts it:

> certainly the Zeitgeist exerts its own pervasive influence. We live in an era of management values where the articles of faith are short-term effectiveness, value for money, performance indicators, return on investment, accountability. It is good to remember that this is a modern and upstart faith with few moral roots, with no power to nourish souls and every capacity to destroy them'. (1999: 8)

From another frame of reference, Western man's [*sic*] dominion over time is as irrelevant as the notion that one can 'own' land – as the indigenous First Nations peoples of North America pointed out to the incoming settlers who 'purchased' the land that is now the 'real estate' called Manhattan. More than irrelevant, our obsession with controlling time appears grandiose, perhaps indicative of a collective narcissistic personality disorder!

In post-industrial, postmodern and multicultural societies, we have opportunities to critique 'instrumental reason' with its ideologies of domination, control and success/failure, and the modernist vision of industrial discipline based on the control of chronological time – and, in doing so, perhaps to reclaim ancient wisdom about the *possibilities*, as distinct from the constraints and determinants, of time. In Greek there are two words for time: *chronos*, hence chronological time, and *kairos* which means appropriate time and it is not insignificant that in the West we have adopted the one and not the other. Whilst therapy is bounded and contextualised by chronological time, the process of therapy reflects kairos moments of transformation – and thus time is inextricably linked with concepts of change (*metanoia*) and therapeutic space (*temenos*) and, I argue, the context of community (*koinonia*) (see Tudor, 2001). Personally I live most of my life in (and governed by) *chronos* time. (It is perhaps significant that, according to Greek mythology, the Titan Chronos ate his children, until Gaia intervened and Zeus overthrew him.) Yet, when I lived for a period of my life in a small village in Southern Italy, I adopted a different sense of *kairos* time in my daily and seasonal rhythm – and, indeed, a different, somewhat more relaxed sense of myself. I was recently reminded of this at a conference workshop which, upon entering, I apologised for being late, to which the workshop leader immediately responded by saying 'Don't be sorry. You came when you could.' I smiled in recognition of the confrontation and my own inner sense and memory (particularly from my time in Italy) of this being true for me. The workshop leader then used this exchange to illustrate the theme and sense of oppression she feels as an African American woman, often experiencing being out of time, rushing, having her pace interrupted, etc. by white colleagues.

Not surprisingly, the question of time has preoccupied therapists. Since Freud's (1937) paper on 'Analysis terminable and interminable', the significance of temporality and time in therapy has been analysed and the issue of limited or limiting time in therapy discussed by a number of writers in a number of forms: brief psychotherapy (Malan, 1963); focal psychotherapy (Balint et al., 1972); short-term dynamic psychotherapy (Sifneos, 1979; Davandaloo, 1980); solution-focused therapy (de Shazer, 1985; O'Connell, 1998); time-conscious therapy (Elton Wilson, 1996); 'two-plus-one sessions' therapy (Barkham and Hobson, 1989); even single session therapy (Talmon, 1990; McCann, 1992) – and there is at least one specialist journal on the subject: the *International Journal of Short-Term Psychotherapy*. The history of attitudes to time in counselling and psychotherapy as well as various models of short-term counselling is well summarised by Feltham, 1997. Significantly, with the exception of Elton Wilson's 'time-conscious approach' which I consider to be an *attitude* to therapy, these are all *forms* of therapy; although many are deeply embedded in particular theories and theoretical orientations, their focus on time and limits crosses 'schools' of therapy – and hence the word 'approaches' in the title of this book (and, indeed, in others in this series). In this sense I agree with Samuels, a transactional analyst, when he asserted that 'there is no such thing as short-term psychotherapy – there is short-term intervention with salutory results' (Samuels et al., 1968: 83); to paraphrase him, I suggest that: 'there's no such thing as short-term or brief transactional analysis – there are TA approaches and interventions in a focused/limited therapeutic context with salutory results'. The *approaches* of this book reflect transactional analysis, the *attitude* is time-conscious. The corollary of this is that 'brief therapy' is synonymous with time-limited therapy, although I think this should more often and more accurately be referred to as *resources*-limited therapy; and, indeed, it is the limitations of resources which often drives material and pragmatic concerns about brief therapy. As Thorne (1999) indicates, there are very real pressures on therapists, for instance, from insurance companies who will underwrite only a limited number of sessions; from employers through Employee Assistance Programmes (EAPs) and from GPs who may only be able to fund time-limited input of counselling or psychotherapy. The demands on therapists, for example, based in General Practice and in university counselling services, to meet client needs, together with an increasing insistence on 'evidence-based practice' (which generally refers to only one kind of 'scientific' 'evidence'), and the discrimination within the British national health service in favour of cognitive-behavioural approaches all add to the pressure on therapists to offer time-limited therapy and, in some cases (and already in some countries) to work using only certain theoretical approaches and methods – a political turn which represents theoretical censorship and professional exclusion. Interestingly, in the light of such pressure, Novey (1999) reports a research study into the effectiveness of TA which, amongst other results, confirms that therapy limits due to insurance limitations significantly decrease effectiveness.

As regards the practice of brief therapy, three discussions – concerning time, client suitability and the therapeutic relationship – deserve albeit brief reference. Once the boundary about time in therapy is set, discussions quickly move to 'How long?' as in 'How long is a piece of string?' (How brief is brief therapy? Six sessions? Twelve sessions? 'Is it possible to extend the number of sessions?') – which is why I prefer to think in terms of and discuss the source of limit or limitation. As this is usually resources, it is often more straightforward to talk in terms of money and context (counselling in a health care setting, an EAP, a university counselling service, etc.) as determinants of time in therapy. As regards the specific number of sessions, Feltham (1997) again usefully summarises the considerations of differential time spans in therapy from one session through to sixteen sessions. The studies, vignettes and examples presented in this volume range between one and sixteen sessions, from one day (a unit of time which Berne regarded as the present as far as the Adult ego state was concerned) to several months.

The second discussion is one of client 'suitability'. This is usually framed in terms of what problems are amenable to brief therapy and, by implication therefore, which are not. Feltham (1997) proposes five 'fallible guidelines' as to *who* will benefit from time-limited counselling:

(a) People who perceive their concerns as quite circumscribed.
(b) People who wish to sample counselling without commitment.
(c) Those whose problems or preoccupations are in the mild to moderate band.
(d) Those who are open to focal work.
(e) People who are well motivated and ready.

Whilst at first glance these may appear sensible and uncontentious, even useful, they (especially the first three) link a range of perceptions to a proscribed time frame in counselling or therapy. They do not allow the possibility that the assumptions by which the client is defined (by themselves or others) or is defining their 'problem' may be challenged in one session or even within the first ten minutes of the therapeutic encounter. Defining by problems or people, either way implies and, indeed, *requires* selection. From Berne (1966) onwards, transactional analysts have been sceptical about selection criteria (originally in the context of selection for group treatment): 'the real issue . . . is not the one commonly debated, "What are the criteria for the selection of patients", but the underlying, usually unstated assumption "Criteria for selection are good"' (1966: 5).

The third discussion centres on the therapeutic relationship. There seems to be an assumption or pre-supposition that 'relationship' is incompatible with brief therapy, as if therapists can somehow work therapeutically and not be in relationship. In fact, as Stewart (1996) argues, one cannot not relate. For however short a time, therapist and client are relating. Given the centrality of the therapeutic relationship to the successful outcome of therapy, we need to apply existing perspectives on the nature of the relationship to time-limited work and to focus on the quality of the working alliance throughout the relationship even in the briefest of encounters with clients. Whilst it is clearly possible to work at relational depth in a short time, there is a danger in brief therapy if 'brief' represents a kind of 'short-termism':

> could it be . . . that short-term therapy is the inevitable dysfunctional response to a sick society and that it seems to work for that very reason. We no longer have time to put down roots, to consolidate our beings, to reflect upon our place in the eternal order of things. (Thorne, 1999: 10)

The focus, expressed especially in person-centred therapy, on being and becoming has echoes in the difference between, respectively, the 'block time' of the physicist and flowing subjective time. If conditionality is the bedrock of a theory of pathology, as Bozarth (1998) asserts in discussing Rogers' person-centred approach, when time is limited the client may well experience the therapist's focus, empathy and positive regard as conditional and, far from freeing the client from external threat (Rogers, 1990), the therapist and the therapy itself may only further exacerbate negative internalised external judgements, frames of reference or Parental introjects ('Hurry up, you've only got six sessions'). At the same time, the other side of such danger is opportunity, as symbolised by the Chinese character for 'crisis' which incorporates both these elements. As Taft (1933) points out:

time represents more vividly than any other category the necessity of accepting limitation as well as the inability to do so, and symbolizes therefore the whole problem of living. The reaction of each individual to limited or unlimited time betrays his deepest and fundamental life pattern, his relation to the growth process itself, to beginnings and endings, to being born and to dying. (1933: 12)

Commenting on this passage, Barrett-Lennard suggests that 'for therapists, accepting limitations in and of time brings a certain transcendence of these limits' (198: 124) – a perspective which has echoes of an existential therapeutic approach to the dimensions and struggles of human existence. Taft's perspective also anticipates key concepts in TA about time-structuring (Berne, 1966, 1973; English, 1992) and on the life script (pattern) (Berne, 1975b).

This existential focus on existence in the present and over time (transience and eternity) highlights the importance of theories about time and their relevance to therapy, especially in freeing us from the short-termism of brief therapy. Quantum mechanics and, more recently, chaos theory, have literally exploded previous concepts of absolute time and the linear arrow of time, which derived from the fact that most physical processes have an inherent directionality. Challenging Newtonian physics, the logic of Einstein's theory of relativity is that not just motion but space and time too are relative (implications which Einstein himself refused to accept). Dylan Thomas in effect summarises the relativity of time and the associated concept of multiple present times in *Under Milk Wood*: "The hands of the clock have stayed still at half past eleven for fifty years. It is always opening time in the Sailors Arms' (1954: 36). Isham, a quantum-gravity expert, explains:

a central feature of the general theory of relativity is that all such decompositions of the space–time are deemed to be admissible and of equal status. In this sense 'time' is a convention; any choice will do provided only that events can be uniquely ordered by the assigned values of time. (1993: 58)

This has specific implications for therapy and the therapeutic encounter. One is that *people collapse or 'decompose' space and time*. One supervisee presented her work with a six-year-old child 'Cara' (in the context of her residence in a children's home). The child, who had disclosed sexual abuse by her father, also disclosed abuse by the staff at the home (all of whom had been supervised during their contact with the girl). One understanding of this was that the girl had collapsed the time frame of her past abuse (by her father) into and with the present. Another implication is *the importance of supporting the client's internal valuing process* specifically in ordering time. It is less important to argue about or to confront a particular linear sequencing of time in relation to a particular story; instead we need to be helping the client make their own (present) sense of the past and the future, what Stern (1985) refers to as the *narrative* (as distinct from the literal) point of origin of a particular problem:

> Time present and time past
> Are both perhaps present in time future,
> And time future contained in time past.
> . . .
> What might have been and what has been
> Point to one end, which is always present. (Eliot, 1944: 13)

Following the 'disclosure' the therapist worked with Cara in a way which conveyed her belief in Cara's story, focusing on attuning to the (present) resonance in Cara of the (past) abuse and on communicating her empathic understanding. This perspective, which at this point prioritises phenomenological over empirical 'reality', connects with a third therapeutic implication of the general theory of relativity which is *the notion of multiple 'realities'* alongside multiple time frames. It is (and was) possible to accept both Cara's past and present reality of abuse alongside the staff's present reality of care and non-abuse.

These perspectives, informed by current research and developments in a number of fields including physics and philosophy, inform and are informed by field theory and the social construction of realities. This is consistent with the postmodern 'narrative turn' in therapy which, in its view that meanings emerge, disappear and change in the context of our interactions, certain understandings of TA script theory predate (see Allen and Allen, 1997). Such narratives, of course, equally apply to 'brief therapy' itself. Thus, in the spirit of critical enquiry, I question the linkage of 'presenting problems' and even 'people who . . .' (Feltham, 1997) to specific time limits, preferring instead to acknowledge the inevitable if not necessary limitations of context and money/resources as defining the therapeutic milieu within which (à la Taft) the client – and therapist – may explore, in however brief an encounter, the meaning of such limitations for their lives. Just as St Augustine proposed that the world was made *with* time and not *in* time, so the time-conscious and constructivist therapist focuses more *with* and *about* time than *in* or *on* time and how such 'time with' that is therapy is constructed and co-created. Time is in itself part of the therapeutic milieu and, of course, what is being presented by the client (and therapist). Just as it has little meaning to talk about *before* creation (as if time existed before creation), it makes little sense to talk about 'before' a particular state, way of being, problem or pathology. The past 'problem' is present as it is being (re)presented, discussed, understood, analysed, etc. This is also consistent with the demolition (thanks to Einstein) of the absolute categories *the* past, *the* present and *the* future (as nominalisations) which are replaced by a more fluid and relative relationship between events and meanings and it is precisely the relationship between persons and persons, and persons and meanings which forms the basis of TA, that is, literally, the analysis of transactions.

Introducing the book, TA, time and brief therapy

This book is one of a series on *Brief Therapies*. As the reader will already be aware from the above, I take the view that TA is *an* approach to brief therapy rather than a brief therapy in itself. That said, TA probably has more claims to being a brief therapy than many other theoretical orientations – and, indeed, a number of brief therapies, including solution-focused therapy, draw upon TA concepts (usually without reference or acknowledgement). TA's claim to brevity is now explored, briefly, in relation to three significant areas of TA theory which focus on time: the ego-state model, time structuring and time framing, and the concept of cure and specifically the one-session cure.

The ego-state model
As Stewart observes: 'the time dimension is a central organising principle in TA theory. It is at the heart of the ego-state model itself' (1996: 27). Berne (1975a) viewed the personality as a complex system organised in structures corresponding to different evolutionary levels

- A system linked to the organisation of instinctual drives, basic needs and primary emotional experiences – the Child ego state or what Berne originally referred to in terms of 'psychic organs' as the *archeopsyche*.
- A system aimed at organising introjected psychic material – the Parent ego state or *exteropsyche*.
- An elaborative system connected to the analysis of the here-and-now – the Adult ego state or *neopsyche* (see Figure I.1).

Clearly, as descriptions of personality structure and phenomenological realities, both Parent (Introjected Parent) and Child (Archaic Child) ego states are echoes of the past, whilst Adult (Integrated or Integrating Adult) is present and present-centred. In the TA literature, whilst much attention has been given to the past (working with the Parent and Child) in terms of structural and developmental models, methodology and techniques, generally there has been less focus on the present in terms of the Adult ego state – for a critique of which see Summers and Tudor (2000).

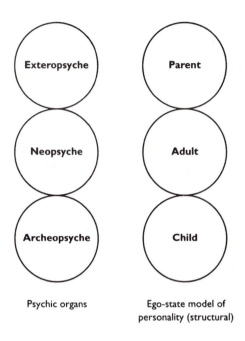

Psychic organs

Ego-state model of
personality (structural)

Figure Intro.:1 *Psychic organs and corresponding ego states (Berne, 1975a)*

From time structuring to time framing
Berne (1966, 1973) identified six ways of structuring time which he viewed as a response to a basic human hunger for structure and structuring. They are (according to Berne, in order of 'safeness'): withdrawal, rituals, pastimes, activity, (psychological) games and intimacy. These are useful especially in the context of relationships (e.g. playing games in order to avoid intimacy), social and cultural life (e.g. the importance of rituals), work (e.g. the importance of pastimes as distinct from gossip) and, perhaps most obviously, in terms of time management. However, in the light of postmodernism, such categorisation appears a particularly modernist attempt to structure a theory of time. More recently, transactional analysts (some, such as Stewart, 1996, influenced by concepts drawn from Neuro Linguistic Programming [NLP]), have been developing ideas about time frames and, indeed, deconstructing time itself. Stewart (1996) develops the notion of a person's roots being in the future (rather than the past); action and change being in the present; with the past for information only – he then links this to TA treatment planning (discussed in this volume in Chapters 6 and 7).

Further postmodernist critiques within TA are represented by a critical review of life script theory (Cornell, 1987), a focus on the transactional creation of realities (Schmid, 1991), work on narrative and postmodernism (Allen and Allen, 1995) and on constructivism (Allen and Allen, 1997) and on co-creative TA (Summers and Tudor, 2000). Allen and Allen summarise this 'narrative turn' in TA about time:

> in traditional transactional analysis we usually accept the idea that the past determines the present and the present the future. However, it is equally possible – and clinically it is often obvious – that the present can color our memories of the past. As our present changes, so may our recollections and understandings of the past. The past is not a fixed, immutable, monolithic structure. (1997: 92)

In a similar logical 'about turn', Mellor and Mellor (2000) discuss ways in which we may predict the past (in the context of remembering the future):

1. Evaluate how we are in the present.
2. Consider what it was that helped us get to today in the states we are in, with the capacities we have and with our current hopes, dreams and aspirations.
3. Think about how we would like our lives to be.
4. Consider the past that we think we need to have had for our lives and ourselves to be the way we would like to be.
5. Imagine vividly, acutely, intensely and fully that we had these pasts.

The one-session cure

The dangers and opportunities of time-limited therapy referred to above are equally reflected in TA (as with other) approaches to 'brief' therapy. In response to interminable psychoanalysis, Berne was concerned to effect cure as quickly as possible and was thus sceptical and challenging of 'making progress' or 'getting better' therapy. His aim was to cure people – and preferably in one session. Similarly, Talmon (1990) who, having discovered that many if not most clients drop out of therapy after one session, systematically developed a way of making the most of clients' ability to 'cure' themselves in one session. Cure is the goal and underlying assumption of TA – a perspective which, traditionally, has lead TA to be viewed from both within and without as a direct(ive), actionistic therapy. The positive aspect of this approach is that it takes and promotes a proactive, contactful, inquiring, attuned and involved relationship in therapy and confronts the somewhat detached and (in TA terms) passive behaviours of some therapists and some forms of therapy. As Stewart (1996) suggests, there are two valuable presuppositions embedded in Berne's recommendation of the one-session cure: the first, that people can be cured;

and the second, that cure can be quick. Equally, the danger of this approach lies in the potential for the therapist to 'Hurry Up' and 'Be Perfect' (two of the identified Parental *driver* messages which encourage conditional OKness in the child/subject). However, the potential grandiosity of the one-session cure is mediated by the fact that cure is 'facilitated by a mutually agreed upon and verifiable contract' (Woollams and Brown, 1978: 206), and that 'failure' to achieve this cure is seen more as a challenge to mutuality, efficiency and excellence – qualities which mark Adrienne Lee's contribution on the one-session cure in this volume (Chapter 7).

Berne's (1975a) four definitions of cure – social control, symptomatic relief, transference cure and script cure – may be taken as describing a continuum of cure and, for some TA therapists (including contributors in this present volume), as thus offering a framework for understanding what may be 'cured' in brief or time-limited therapy – and, equally, what may not (for further discussion of which see Chapter 1). Following Samuels' assertion (referred to above) that 'there is no such thing as short-term psychotherapy – there is short-term intervention with salutory results', he and his colleagues continue:

> The patient's situation may be bettered . . . In the case of short-term disturbance, short-term intervention can restore some stability to the patient, and, ideally, in the process the patient's Adult can be 'hooked' into a working long-term partnership. Therefore, it is important for the therapist to switch at an early stage from a Parent role in order to obtain an Adult-to-Adult contract. (Samuels et al., 1968: 83)

This is a clear statement that 'some stability' is 'cure' in terms of social control or possibly symptomatic relief but not cure in terms of transference or script resolution.

The structure of the book

The book comprises two parts. Chapters in Part I introduce transactional analysis and brief therapy. For those readers unfamiliar with TA, in Chapter 1 Ulrike Müller and I introduce the fundamental elements of TA theory applying them to brief therapy and conclude with a review of ethical considerations as regards brief therapy. Historically, within TA, three 'schools' have developed: the Classical School, the Redecision School and the Cathexis School – and, indeed, it is a requirement for qualification and accreditation that all TA practitioners are familiar with the theory and practice of all three schools.[1] There are a number of differences between the Schools, based on aetiology, diagnosis and treatment methodology (see Woollams and Brown, 1978) including the use of regressive techniques, and on their relationship to transference (see Tudor, 1999). (For further discussion regarding the schools of TA, see Barnes, 1977.) Whilst Wilson and Kalina (1978) divided the Classical School into Bernean and Social Transaction, I consider a more useful distinction in this respect, both historically and topically, as that between Classical psychodynamic TA and the equally Classical cognitive tradition in TA, a distinction reflected in Chapters 2 and 3, respectively. In Chapter 2 Helena Hargaden defines psychoanalytic TA and develops a transferential ego-state model with which she analyses not only transactions between therapist and client but also intrapsychic transactions, linking this to developmental considerations. As Hargaden suggests, Berne himself outlined a psychoanalytic TA (Berne, 1975a) which, generally, he left to others to develop, whilst he himself developed the cognitive and behavioural tradition within TA.

In Chapter 3 Geoff Mothersole explores the use of Classical TA, taking and developing a cognitive constructivist approach. He discusses the similarities between cognitive approaches and TA and the application of these two interlocking traditions to short-term work. Of the schools of TA, redecision therapy is, arguably, the most obvious as an approach to brief therapy and indeed an edited book has been published on redecision therapy as a brief, action-oriented approach (Lennox, 1997).

In Chapter 4, Jim and the late Barbara Allen describe the redecision process and its neurophysiological underpinnings and, importantly, include a section on redecision work with children. If redecision therapy is the most obvious in its application to brief therapy, then the Cathexis School of TA is the least obvious, given its history of long-term reparenting work with disturbed clients including those with psychotic processes. In Chapter 5 David Rawson reviews and renews the theory and practice of the Cathexis School and its application to brief therapy in the context of the work of the Connect Therapeutic Community in Birmingham.

In TA, as in the wider community of counselling and psychotherapy, integration is the *zeitgeist*. In Chapter 6 Mark Widdowson and I reflect on this work with a particular client, drawing out the theoretical – and metatheoretical – implications for an integrating transactional analysis and view this as a metatheoretical process rather than a 'school'. The logic of the school division within TA is, of course, that each has its own view of supervision and training and, to a certain extent, this is the case; however, the supervision of TA approaches to brief therapy is beyond the scope of this present volume. As regards training, there are no specialist training courses in brief TA therapy – a situation I welcome as I am sceptical of the overly pragmatic turn a number of training courses are taking in training therapists for (and almost only for) short-term, resource-limited work.

Part II comprises two specific applications of TA to brief situations. In Chapter 7 Adrienne Lee takes up Berne's challenge of the one-session cure in a unique, unedited transcription and reflection on one complete session of therapy. I am particularly grateful to Adrienne (and to 'Frank') for putting her (and their) therapeutic work in the public domain for general study. Finally, in Chapter 8 Steve Dennis reports on his work, which draws on both TA and NLP, offering short-term (4 session) therapy for post-trauma stress in the context of an Emergency Service. Over the years TA has, as have other therapies, developed a language, originally designed to make psychological and psychotherapeutic concepts more accessible to the client and the lay reader. Indeed, some of these terms, most notably psychological 'games', as in *Games People Play* (Berne, 1968), have become common parlance; others, however, require an explanation perhaps further than the immediate context allows and, to this end, indicative 'definitions' of key TA concepts referred to in the book are offered in a Glossary.

A note on terms and permissions

As an editor I have been particularly concerned to organise a volume which both expresses an integrity of purpose, approach and organisation, and at the same time acknowledges and indeed welcomes difference as is illustrated in the different approaches of the contributors. In taking the 'School' approach to representing TA, especially in Part I, my aim has been to encourage both integrity and diversity. In this spirit, I have edited for consistency *within* rather than *between* chapters and thus the contributors express different views not only about theory, method and practice but also on terms such as client/patient, counselling/psychotherapy/analysis/therapy, brief therapy/time-limited therapy, etc. This extends to British and American spellings, especially given the contribution of American colleagues (Chapter 4). Finally, all case study material, for which clients have given informed consent and written permission, has been anonymised and suitably disguised.

Time has been a significant issue as regards this book. Whilst in many ways it has evolved, grown and been completed in its own appropriate (*kairos*) time, it was late in terms of its initial chronological time deadline and I thank both Steven Palmer and Gladeana McMahon, the series editors, and the publishers for their patience and flexibility in this regard. I am grateful to all the contributors for the quality of their work, their spirit of participation in an evolving project – and their willingness to be edited! I extend a heartfelt thanks to my friends and colleagues Helena Hargaden, Charlotte Sills and

Graeme Summers who have in various ways encouraged my renewed interest in TA and the dialogue between theoretical approaches, and without whom both I and this book would be the poorer, intellectually and personally. Finally, I am also aware of the times that this book has taken me away especially from my immediate family and I acknowledge and thank both Louise and Saul – and, more recently, Esther – for their tolerance in this regard, and for their love and understanding in all regards, of multiple realities, and in many time frames.

Note

1 There is some discussion with the TA community as to what constitutes a 'school'. Barnes' (1977) definition of a 'school' still stands, although Wilson and Kalina (1978) identified the radical psychiatry tradition as a fifth school, and Woollams and Brown (1978) expanded this, adding their own Huron Valley Institute as an example of 'eclectic TA' and Kahler's (1974) miniscript as a representing a 'school' of TA which emphasises script process. More recently (in the last ten years), 'integrative TA' is viewed by some as representing a fourth 'school' within TA.

References

Allen, J.R. and Allen, B.A. (1995) 'Narrative theory, redecision therapy, and postmodernism', *Transactional Analysis Journal*, 25(4): 327–34.

Allen, J.R. and Allen, B.A. (1997) 'A new type of transactional analysis and one version of script work with a constructivist sensibility', *Transactional Analysis Journal*, 27: 89–98.

Balint, M., Orastein, P.H. and Balint, E. (1972) Focal psychotherapy: An example of applied psychoanalysis, London: Tavistock.

Barkham, M. and Hobson, R. (1989) 'Exploratory therapy in two-plus-one sessions', *British Journal of Psychotherapy*, 6(1): 79–86.

Barnes, G. (1977) 'Introduction', in G. Barnes (ed.), *Transactional Analysis after Eric Berne: Teachings and Practices of Three TA Schools.* New York: Harper's College Press. pp. 3–31.

Barrett-Lennard, G.T. (1998) *Carl Rogers' Helping System.* London: Sage.

Berne, E. (1966) *Principles of Group Treatment.* New York: Grove Press.

Berne, E. (1968) *Games People Play.* Harmondsworth: Penguin. (Original work published 1964.)

Berne, E. (1973) *Sex in Human Loving.* Harmondsworth: Penguin. (Original work published 1970.)

Berne, E. (1975a) *Transactional Analysis in Psychotherapy.* London: Souvenir Press. (Original work published 1961.)

Berne, E. (1975b) *What Do You Say After You Say Hello?* Harmondsworth: Penguin. (Original work published 1972.)

Bozarth, G. (1998) *Person-centred Therapy: A Revolutionary Paradigm.* Llangarron: PCCS Books.

Cornell, W.F. (1987) 'Life script theory: A critical review from a developmental perspective', *Transactional Analysis Journal*, 18(4): 270–82.

Davandaloo, H. (ed.) (1980) *Short-term Dynamic Psychotherapy.* New York: Jason Aaronson.

Davies, P. (1995) *About Time: Einstein's Unfinished Revolution*. Harmondsworth: Penguin.

de Shazer, S. (1985) *Keys to Solutions in Brief Therapy*. New York: W.W. Norton.

Eliot, T.S. (1944) 'Burnt Norton', in *Four Quartets*. London: Faber & Faber. pp.13–20.

Elton Wilson, J. (1996) *Time-conscious Psychological Therapy*. London: Routledge.

English, F. (1992) 'My time is more precious than your strokes: New perspectives on time structuring', *Transactional Analysis Journal*, 22: 32–42.

Feltham, C. (1997) *Time-limited Counselling*. London: Sage.

Freud, S. (1937) 'Analysis terminable and interminable', in J. Strachey (ed. and trans), *The Standard Edition of the Complete Psychological Works of Sigmund Freud*, Vol. 23. London: Hogarth Press.

Griffiths, J. (2000) 'Local time', *Resurgence*, 199: 32–4.

Isham, C. (1993) 'God, time and the creation of the universe,' in E. Winder (ed.), *Explorations in Science and Theology*. London: RSA.

Kahler, T. with Capers, H. (1974) 'The miniscript', *Transactional Analysis Journal*, 4: 26–43.

Lennox, C.E. (1997) *Redecision therapy: A Brief, Action-oriented Approach*. New York: Jason Aaronson.

Macmurray, J. (1957) *The Self as Agent*, Vol.1. London: Faber & Faber.

Malan, D.H. (1963) *A Study of Brief Psychotherapy*. London: Tavistock Publications.

McCann, D.L. (1992), 'Post-traumatic stress disorder due to devastating burns overcome by a single session of eye movement desensitization', *Journal of Behavior Therapy and Experiential Psychiatry*, 23(4): 319–23.

Mellor, K. and Mellor, E. (2000) *Predicting the past and remembering the future*. Workshop presentation, The Berne Institute, Nottingham.

Novey, T. (1999) 'The effectiveness of transactional analysis', *Transactional Analysis Journal*, 29(1): 18–30.

O'Connell, B. (1998) *Solution-focused Therapy*. London: Sage.

Rogers, C.R. (1990) 'The characteristics of a helping relationship', in H. Kirschenbaum and V.L. Henderson (eds), *The Carl Rogers Reader*. London: Constable. (Original work published 1958.) pp.108–26.

Samuels, S.D., Teutsch, C.K. and Everts, K. (1968) 'Short-term psychotherapy', *Transactional Analysis Bulletin*, 7(28).

Schmid, B. (1991) 'Intuition of the possible and the transactional creation of realities', *Transactional Analysis Journal*, 21(3): 144–54.

Sifneos, P.E. (1979) *Short-term Dynamic Psychotherapy: Evaluation and Technique*. New York: Plenum Press.

Stern, D. (1985) *The Interpersonal World of the Infant*. New York: Basic Books.

Stewart, I. (1996) *Developing Transactional Analysis Counselling*. London: Sage.

Summers, G. and Tudor, K. (2000) 'Co-creative transactional analysis', *Transactional Analysis Journal*, 30(1): 23–40.

Taft, J. (1933) *The Dynamics of Therapy in a Controlled Relationship*. New York: Macmillan.

Talmon, M. (1990) *Single Session Therapy*. San Francisco, CA: Jossey-Bass.

Thomas, D. (1954) *Under Milk Wood*. London: J.M. Dent .

Thorne, B. (1999) 'The move towards brief therapy: Its dangers and challenges', *Counselling*, 10(1): 7–11.

Tudor, K. (1999) '"I'm OK, You're OK – and They're OK": Therapeutic relationships in transactional analysis', in C. Feltham (ed.) *Understanding the Counselling Relationship*. London: Sage. pp. 90–119.

Tudor, K. (2001) 'Change, time, place and community: An integral approach to ther-
    apy', in P. Lapworth, C. Sills and S. Fish (eds), *Integration in Counselling and
    Psychotherapy: Developing a Personal Approach*. London: Sage. pp. 142–51.
Tudor. K. (in preparation) 'The Adult ego state', in H. Hargaden and C. Sills (eds), *Ego
    States*. London: Worth Reading.
Wilson, J. and Kalina, I. (1978) 'The splinter chart', *Transactional Analysis Journal*, 8(3):
    200–5.
Winnicott, D.W. (1980) *The Piggle*. Harmondsworth: Penguin.
Woollams, S. and Brown, M. (1978) *Transactional Analysis*. Dexter, MI: Huron Valley
    Institute Press.

Part I

TA and Schools of TA

Chapter 1

Transactional Analysis as Brief Therapy

Ulrike Müller and Keith Tudor

In this chapter we trace the theoretical elements of transactional analysis (TA) by which it may be considered as an effective approach to or even form of brief or time-limited therapy. First, the roots of TA as a brief therapy are considered, following which the interrelation between diagnosis, contracting and treatment direction is discussed in the context of what is commonly viewed as the aim and goal of TA, that is, 'cure'. The traditional interventions of TA are illustrated with scenarios from the practice of brief therapy, and the chapter concludes with a review of ethical considerations including the indications for – and contraindications to – brief therapy. In offering an overview across various traditions within TA, the chapter illustrates key theoretical concepts and constructs with reference to brief TA therapy in practice and offers especially the lay reader an introduction to the following chapters (2–5) which then develop these traditions or 'schools' of TA. As with other chapters, some of the more technical TA terms and concepts used are summarised in the Glossary.

The historical roots and theoretical foundations of TA

In his last book *What Do You Say After You Say Hello?* Berne (1975b) cuts through the Gordian knot of what he refers to as 'making progress therapy', arguing instead for 'curing patients therapy', the slogan of which is 'Get well first, and we'll analyse it later if you still want' (1975b: 377). In many ways this illustrates the concern Berne expressed throughout his career and as is evident in his writing: to find the quickest, shortest, most effective and accessible therapeutic intervention and cure. This both reflects and is supported by TA's three basic philosophical tenets: that people are at an existential level 'OK'; that everyone has the capacity to think; and that people can decide their own destiny – and that these (early childhood) decisions can be changed.

TA theory is built on four foundational pillars:

- The structural model of *ego states* – the structure of personality
- *Transactions* – which deal with communications between people
- Psychological *games* – repetitive sequences of transactions
- *Scripts* – life patterns.

Taking an historical view, in each of these may be seen the origins and theoretical foundation of TA as a brief therapy. A review of these is followed by a discussion of concepts of 'cure' in TA therapy which offers a framework for distinguishing brief therapeutic work.

Ego states

Berne originally trained as a psychiatrist and in 1941 began training as a psychoanalyst. Between 1940 and 1943 he was in the US Army Medical Corps, during which, as a part of his work, he examined servicemen returning from the Second World War. Due to the conditions of these examinations, Berne became interested in and adept at quick and accurate psychiatric and psychotherapeutic diagnosis. For this he drew on his studies of the ego psychology of both Federn (1952) and Weiss (1950) (see Berne, 1957). To Federn's notion of ego states, Berne added a significant amendment: that, as well as being experienced internally, each category of ego states was shown in a distinctive set of behaviours (Stewart, 1992). This is the origin of the behavioural diagnosis of ego states.

Berne conducted most of his own therapeutic work in groups and formulated TA theory based on this experience (see Berne, 1966) – indeed, TA has traditionally been viewed as essentially a group therapy. Observing group members, Berne realised that they interacted by repeating certain patterns or *psychological games* (analogous, in psychodynamic terms, to repetition compulsion). If one group member behaved in a parental way, they would get a complementary childlike reaction from another group member and vice versa (the stimulus and response comprising the *transaction*). Mostly, these reactions did not fit or were incongruent with here-and-now 'reality'. In order to explain what he observed, Berne developed a model which allowed the inner differentiation of the ego; this was his structural analysis of the personality which he termed the ego-state model. Depending on the specific stimulus in the group and cathexis of the individual, one ego state becomes active and 'acts out'; either the Child ego state or the Parent ego state dominates the situation and other group members react in a complementary way. In those situations, the person's reality-testing capacity almost completely disappeared. Berne called this reality-testing capacity of the ego the Adult ego state. By contrast, the Child ego state comprises early introjections and fixated traumas which, when activated, create a distorted perception of reality and includes the concomitant feelings associated with that archaic reality. The Parent ego state similarly comprises introjections which, in this case, generally symbolise the identification with normative sentences and social role behaviour as modelled by the subject's original parents/carers and/or parental, caring and authority figures.

Ego state diagnosis is a precise science, 'a matter of acuteness and observation plus intuitive sensitivity' (Berne, 1975a: 69), based on the observation of total behaviour and experience. The complete diagnosis of ego states involves observation of *behaviour* as expressed through a person's demeanour, gestures, voice, vocabulary, etc. This diagnosis is corroborated both by others' responses such as a childlike reaction (the *social* or *operational* diagnosis) and by the client reporting *historical* information i.e. which parental figure was the prototype for their behaviour. Finally, the diagnosis is validated if the person can re-experience the assimilated parental ego state – the *phenomenological* diagnosis. On the basis of this sophisticated yet accessible model it is easy to confirm an ego state diagnosis *with* the client and within a few minutes is a procedure which provides the basis both of a model of health and of psychopathology (including excluding and contaminated ego states).

Transactions
Berne was concerned to develop a theory of social action; indeed, especially in its early years TA was also referred to as a 'social psychiatry' (e.g. Berne, 1975a). Berne defines a transaction 'consisting of a single stimulus and a single response, verbal or non verbal [as] the unit of social action. It is called a transaction because each party gains something from it, and that is why he engages in it' (1975b: 20). It is the analysis of transactions as a basic social unit of communication in terms of ego states (also referred to as 'TA proper') which forms the basis of this theory of social action and interaction. In this we can again see Berne's emphasis on observability. Given that the behavioural clues to ego states are observable (behavioural diagnosis) so too are the changes or shifts in ego states which occur when people communicate. From his observation and analysis of transactions, Berne (1966) developed three rules of communication:

1. If one person overtly acts from Parent ego state and another from Child ego state, both behave in a complementary way which excludes the here-and-now reality-testing capacity (Adult ego state). With such complementary transactions, which may also be Parent–Parent, Adult–Adult, Child–Child, etc., communication can proceed indefinitely (first rule of communication).
2. Complementary transactions come to an end if one participant changes ego state; this often leads to some confusion and a 'crossed transaction' which results in a break in communication (second rule of communication).
3. If on an overt or social level, people are transacting, e.g. Adult–Adult or Child–Parent but their non-verbal, hidden messages come from one of the other ego states via covert ulterior transactions then the outcome of the transactions and indeed the communication is determined at this psychological level (third rule of communication).

Transactions reflect and, indeed, are the relationship between people; thus it is helpful to understand the transactional patterns within relationships – for example, as a couple, between parents and children, as well as at work – as, having understood them, the parties involved have the chance and options to change such patterns. This, of course, is also the case for the therapeutic relationship between client and therapist.

Again, as with the diagnosis of ego states, the analysis of transactions is an accurate, accessible and quick form of analysis and diagnosis. It also provides an accessible and transactional way of analysing transference and countertransference as they are classically conceptualised – or 'co-transferential relating' (see Summers and Tudor, 2000). Thus, if a person is crossing an Adult–Adult transaction with a response from their Child ego state, s/he is relating to that other person as if they were in their childhood and thus projecting some qualities, experience, fantasy or phantasy onto that other person. As Stewart observes: 'Berne's second rule of communication does not simply deal with the rather trivial question of whether communication is comfortable or otherwise. More importantly, it points out that the "break in communication" will always be related to transference or countertransference' (1992: 37).

Games

It follows from this that all transactions which are not clear Adult–Adult (overt or covert) transactions can be understood (in terms of the ego state structure of the personality) as an unconscious repetition of early interactions which have failed to satisfy needs, analogous to Freud's concept of 'repetition compulsion'. When observed in present everyday life, such repetitions do not fit the actual situation and appear as a hiccup in clear communication. The stimulus and/or response are based on script beliefs and feelings. This hidden, unconscious aspect of communication is a paradoxical one: with the hope that unmet needs may finally be fulfilled juxtaposed with disappointment (even expectation) that the discourse ends up as usual without getting the desired result and satisfaction. A game usually follows a series of complementary transactions which is broken by one party, perhaps out of an unconscious resentment, who then crosses the communication, with resulting confusion and 'bad' feelings on both sides. Berne called such a sequence of transactions a game, i.e. 'an ongoing series of complementary ulterior transactions progressing to a well-defined, predictable outcome' (1968: 44). Significantly, he chose an expression which has the association of winning. The gain (or 'pay off') in a transactional game, however, is generally the confirmation of one's script beliefs and feelings rather than the experience of a satisfying solution.

In the therapeutic situation the therapist must not label or discount the client's behaviour as 'gamey' (which in itself could be a game!), but rather understand the (hi)story behind it. Indeed, the client needs to 'play the game' in therapy in order that the therapist may help them:

(a) to be aware of the hidden aspects of the game including its advantages (see Berne, 1968)
(b) to understand their pattern of behaviour as a game.

Transactional and game analysis – naming the game rather than shaming the client – is the basis of developing the client's awareness, understanding and ability to change through having different (behavioural) options and satisfying the unmet psychological need or human hunger which led to the game in the first place. In order to be able to analyse the games a client will offer or attempt to play within the therapeutic situation and relationship, the therapist has to know their own script patterns as well as the hooks by which they are likely to get drawn into a game.

Transactions	Therapist's comments
Client (C): What shall we talk about today?	
Therapist (T): Is there anything you want to talk about?	This is crossing the invitation to be symbiotic, to be active for the client.
C: I'm sorry. Perhaps I'm wasting your time. I don't feel as if I have anything to talk about.	The client appears to be apologising for not having a problem or issue.

T: It seems as if you have to entertain me.

This crossed transaction (identified through the use of the word 'entertain') reveals the way in which the *therapist* used to have to please his mother.

In any case it is important that the therapist considers the level of anxiety which has been shown by the client. Behavioural change is only possible if the level of anxiety is relatively low. Only then will the client be willing to try new patterns to gain the fulfilment they long for such as intimacy when and through playing games. Only then will they be willing to create new patterns which are more appropriate to getting present unmet needs met and to stop the old repetitive patterns by exposing or ignoring the games.

Game analysis is especially helpful in a family context which is often rich in patterned transactions. A nine-year-old daughter invites her parents to get into a game around waiting for her to come to dinner every evening. The parents, for their part, wait, get angry and resentful. The therapist involved with the family exposed this interaction as a 'power play' and offered alternatives: for the parents to inform their daughter early enough about dinner time and to stay with the consequences of their decisions, e.g. to eat dinner without her and not to offer her dinner if she comes after dinner time; and for the daughter to express her views about food, diet and eating times. In offering these options, it was useful to inform the parents that a nine-year-old girl would not starve if she misses a meal, that is, they would not do her harm by being consequent and having consequences. Often knowledge leads to decontamination (see pp. 36–7 below)

Scripts

There are a number of definitions of script in the TA literature; indeed, Berne himself worked on this as a concept and theory for over 12 years. In doing so he drew on a number of post-Freudian and other influences such as Otto Rank; indeed, as he points out in his last book (Berne, 1975b), there is nothing new about the concept of life script and acknowledges the concept in other psychological approaches (Adler's 'life style', Jung's archetypes and persona, Erikson's life cycle, etc.) as well as the influence of Joseph Campbell, who wrote *The Hero with a Thousand Faces* (Campbell, 1968) which Berne describes as 'the best textbook for script analysts' (1975b: 47). However, he distinguishes his script theory from many other observations and statements, asserting that: 'the crux of script theory lies in structural analysis. Without the theory of ego states . . . there can be an infinite number of pertinent observations and statements, but there can be no script theory' (1975b: 400). Originally defining script as a transference drama, viewed operationally as a complex set of transactions, Berne's last definition is of script as 'an ongoing program, developed in early childhood under parental influence, which directs the individual's behavior in the most important aspects of his life' (Berne, 1975b: 418). As Stewart and Joines (1987) point out, this definition has a number of components:

- The script is a *specific* life plan – and it is its specificity which distinguishes TA script theory.
- The script is directed towards a payoff – this is often expressed as a final or closing scene.
- The script is decisional – and, therefore, redecisional.
- The script is reinforced by parents and/or significant carers – these influences may be analysed by means of a script matrix (Steiner, 1966).
- The script is outside of awareness – Berne refers to it as being preconscious.
- 'Reality' is redefined to justify the script – i.e. people interpret reality within their own frame of reference.

Given more recent developments in script theory and especially a constructivist understanding, we add that:

- Script is cultural (see White and White, 1975; Summers and Tudor, 2000).
- Scripts are co-created (see Cornell, 1988).
- An individual has a number of scripts (see Allen and Allen, 1995).

As with most aspects of TA, script theory has been developed with the purpose that it is accessible to practitioners and clients alike. The *script matrix* showing the roles the ego states of the parents play in the formation of the child's script was developed by Steiner (1966). Berne discovered certain patterns in scripts which are generally referred to as *process script types*. The elements of script make up the *script apparatus* (Berne, 1975b); in the same book Berne published *script questionnaires* designed to elicit various components of the script (see Appendix 1). In later developments, Goulding and Goulding (1976, 1978) identified twelve injunctions which influence the script and Kahler and his colleagues identified five second-by-second behaviour sequences or *drivers*. Importantly for the present focus on brief therapy, Kahler (1978) has developed the *miniscript*. Finally (in this brief historical review), Erskine and Zalcman (1979) developed the *racket system* (later *script system*), a model which explains the nature of life script.

The central aspect of the miniscript are the five 'drivers': Be Strong!

Try Hard! Please Me! Hurry Up! and Be Perfect! – drivers which either reinforce the early injunctions or are a conscious *counterscript* given by the parents in later childhood. Essentially, drivers reflect a position of conditional OKness and may be temperamental (inborn 'nature') as well as nurtured as early survival strategies and encouraged at different developmental phases by parents. The miniscript describes four positions beginning with the Driver (I'm OK if . . . I'm perfect, etc.), followed by the Stopper (I'm not OK, You're OK), the Blamer (I'm OK, You're not OK), or the Despairer (I'm not OK, You're not OK). In the therapeutic context we meet the drivers when clients come into contact with the underlying injunctions, for example: 'I try hard and please my wife(/mother), otherwise she wouldn't love me' (i.e. 'I'm OK if I try hard to please'). Given their anxiety, it is often difficult for the client to accept permission not to try hard . . . and to wait to see what will happen in the relationship. In the end this is the task – and purpose – of *deconfusing* the Child. The driver may be part of a first degree *impasse*: 'I know I should try hard, but I don't want to' – a cry often heard from pupils and students. Although, as a general rule, the therapist should not work with the first-degree impasse before the second-degree impasse has been resolved, there may be contexts such as school counselling when the therapist has to override this general advice. In this case a supportive attitude on the part of the counsellor may help the student to find a way out of the dilemma without necessarily contacting the underlying injunction. Similarly with the driver 'Be Perfect', a subtle guide may help a pupil to accept a poor academic result whilst nevertheless feeling OK. 'Be Strong' often means 'Don't need any help, don't become ill, otherwise you'll be a burden (for Mum/Dad)'. The miniscript and the process model are particularly useful tools for brief therapy in identifying underlying personality patterns and adaptations from observing split second driver behaviours (see Stewart, 1996).

Diagnosis, contract, treatment planning – and cure

In many ways TA has a somewhat traditional medical model of healing (*therapia*), involving diagnosis→treatment→cure. This is no doubt influenced by Berne, his father's medical background and his own aspirations to be a 'real doctor'. The traditional and executive power of the doctor is, however, challenged by TA's emphasis on the contractual method which makes the therapeutic enterprise bi-lateral and leaves the power in or with the patient. In this section we examine some of the wealth of TA literature on contracts and contracting and treatment planning or what Stewart (1996) refers to as 'treatment direction' relevant to time-limited work (diagnosis having been largely covered in our examination of foundations of TA in the previous section) and introduce this by way of discussing the goal of TA 'treatment', i.e. cure.

Cure
Based on his critique of psychoanalysis on the one hand (regarding the limited goal of 'gaining insight' and concerning the length of treatment) and 'supportive' therapy on the other hand (with the danger of a Parental paternalism actually strengthening defences), Berne developed specific notions of 'cure'. He identified four goals or stages of cure (Berne, 1975a):

1. Symptomatic or social control – the control of dysfunctional behaviours.
2. Symptomatic relief – relief from the subjective discomfort of the dysfunction such as anxiety, panic, depression, etc., often obtained through structural analysis.
3. Transference cure – when the client stays out of script only by substituting the therapist for the original parent.
4. Script cure – when 'the person's own Adult takes over the intrapsychic role of the therapist' (Stewart, 1996: 18).

There is an argument that brief therapy addresses – and can only address – the first one or two of these goals or cures. There are often situations where immediate remedy is necessary to prevent a bad outcome, from the necessity to remove a splinter (literal or metaphorical) to acute crises involving violent or other damaging behaviour. Such situations need a change as quickly as possible. Berne's challenge to find the 'splinter' and pull it out before analysing why the person got a splinter in the first place lies at the heart of his transactional approach to the practice of psychotherapy and keeps the practitioner focused on the agreed goal with expediency. Social control, therefore, has to be the first aim of therapy: 'that is, control of the individual's own tendency to manipulate other people in destructive or wasteful ways, and of his tendency to respond without insight or option to the manipulations of others' (Berne, 1975a: 23).

Berne was aware that the observable behaviour or presenting problem has its origin in intrapsychic structures (script) and that, generally, the changing of the script requires long-term psychotherapy. Nevertheless, with the insight gained through structural analysis, and the analysis of transactions and games, clients learn to change their own behaviour and gain symptomatic relief. Gaining social control and symptomatic relief includes having more competence in handling and structuring relationships. Berne's differentiation between structural and transactional analysis for achieving social control and symptomatic relief on the one hand, and script analysis for structural rearrangement and deconfusion of the Child ego state on the other hand, provides a framework for viewing TA as a genuine form of brief therapy.

Of course, the logic of Berne's position about healing and goals is the notion of the 'one-session cure' to which he urged his trainees to aspire:

> the goal of transactional analysis is to cure as many patients during the first treatment session as is possible. This means that the aim is 100% success and any failure to achieve this percentage is viewed as a challenge. 'Cure' is not an ambiguous and vague term around which the patient and the therapist play mutually attractive games but is clearly defined in the course of treatment. (Berne et al., 1996)

Stewart (1996) points out the significance of this in terms of the 'pre-suppositions' we as practitioners carry about therapy. He suggests that Berne's advocacy of the one-session cure implies that people can be cured, and that cure can be quick. Stewart goes on to point out that in accepting these pre-suppositions we automatically offer clients – and ourselves – more possibilities. In parallel, the one-session cure often involves the permission to stop or start doing something.

> One client came to therapy in an acute professional and financial crisis which was characterised by his pattern of 'running away' – a 'Get Away From' operation (Ernst, 1971). Near the end of the session and almost as an aside, he mentioned his little daughter for whom he did not care. The therapist confronted him with the fact that this behavioural pattern meant not being responsible. When the client came for the second session, he told the therapist how he had been struck by her confrontation and that he now understood his lifetime pattern and said he was now ready to take responsibility, including for his little daughter. Whilst it cannot be guaranteed that the man has changed his behaviour in ways which will be maintained, he has at least begun to think about his old patterns for the first time in his life.

The one-session cure works when a changed behaviour in a certain circumstance will be sufficient; when, following some brief structural analysis, the client is ready to give room to a certain insight; when certain information about reality is needed to help solving a conflict; and when they are ready to take their own advice. Since Berne, not many transactional analysts have taken up his challenge regarding the one-session cure – or at least not many have published on this, an omission rectified by Adrienne Lee's contribution to this present volume (Chapter 7). In his research into single session therapy, Talmon (1990) found that 78 per cent of his clients considered that they had significantly improved because of it.

Contract, diagnosis and treatment direction
Stewart suggests that there is 'a continual three-way interplay between contract, diagnosis and treatment direction' (1996: 15) with constant reflection and revision in the light of practice and, with acknowledgement to Guichard (1987), represents this as a treatment triangle (see Figure 1.1). Just as in any equilateral triangle the angles are congruent (in the mathematical sense), so it is (and must be) in the relationship between these elements of TA therapy: for instance, the diagnosis of a self-harming script and the treatment direction of escape hatch closure (Holloway, 1973) must be congruent with a contract 'I want to stop smoking'. Not only is such congruence desirable, but an understanding of contracting, assessment, diagnosis and treatment planning now forms part of the core competencies for transactional analysis psychotherapists as defined and accepted by the European Association for Transactional Analysis (1999) and the International Transactional Analysis Association (1999).

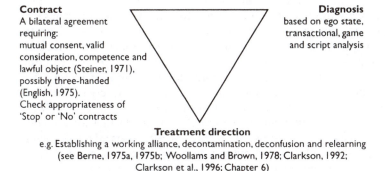

Contract
A bilateral agreement requiring: mutual consent, valid consideration, competence and lawful object (Steiner, 1971), possibly three-handed (English, 1975).
Check appropriateness of 'Stop' or 'No' contracts

Diagnosis
based on ego state, transactional, game and script analysis

Treatment direction
e.g. Establishing a working alliance, decontamination, deconfusion and relearning (see Berne, 1975a, 1975b; Woollams and Brown, 1978; Clarkson, 1992; Clarkson et al., 1996; Chapter 6)

Figure 1.1 *The treatment triangle (based on Stewart, 1996)*

CONTRACTS AND CONTRACTING   One of the philosophical tenets of TA – that everyone has the capacity to think – gives rise to one assumption of TA therapeutic practice that the client is principally able to cathect their Adult ego state. The therapeutic relationship is thus one between adult – and Adult – partners. The contractual method, a mutually agreed statement of change, operationalises this. A contract is mutual, that is to say both parties take responsibility for the procedure; it contains the client's explicit intention for change and formulates the realistic goal/s, for example, 'I want to learn to care for myself', 'I want to behave in an adult way in relation to my mother' are both examples of the client being aware of what they want to change and what their goal is. The therapist's task is first to help the client formulate the contract in an Adult way with a realistic goal and, secondly, to examine regularly whether the client is still moving in the direction they wanted to go. If not, the therapist must address and even confront this and possibly enable the client to work out a new contract. The process of contracting is one way of helping the client to cathect Adult. Given its emphasis on the contractual method, TA has an extensive literature on contracts and the process of contracting (see Steiner, 1971; English, 1975; Sills, 1997).

Sometimes clients need contracts to enable them to *stop* behaving or *not to* behave in a way which harms or endangers themselves or others. This involves self and social control in acute situations such as being violent towards children or a partner. Such 'Stop' or 'No' contracts 'establish controls from within' (Berne, 1975a: 21). 'I'll stop beating my children', 'I won't hurt myself' and 'I won't go crazy' are all stop contracts which close the 'escape hatches' (Drye et al., 1973; Holloway, 1973) through which the client would otherwise 'escape' or flee into violence, self-harm or madness. Such contracts are unconditional decisions which the client makes to themselves (and are not promises to the therapist). Stewart (1996) views the closing of escape hatches as having two advantages: first as a practical protection against tragic outcomes and secondly as facilitating movement out of script. Such undertakings confront the client to activate their Adult problem-solving capacities. In crisis situations, these decisions are helpful because the clients are forced to decide whether they will commit to a non–harming contract for a specific period (24 hours, 1 week, etc.) or to face the consequences such as (preferably) voluntary admission to a psychiatric hospital. The TA approach to 'no suicide' and no harm contracts is reviewed, respectively, by Mothersole (1996, 1997).

TREATMENT DIRECTION   The phrase 'treatment direction' carries two implications: that it relies on the expertise (knowledge, skills, experience) of the therapist in having a plan or sense of direction, and that it unfolds in a particular sequence. Stewart's point about the continual three-way interplay between the treatment direction, contract and diagnosis somewhat modifies the second, sequential (and somewhat outdated) implication; a similar point about a continual two-way interplay between therapist and client regarding the course of therapy may both modify the inherent danger of 'the expert' and the potential for the abuse of power without losing the advantage and potency of expertise, and also more accurately reflects current ideas and values about the nature of the therapeutic relationship (see Tudor, 1999b). TA models of treatment direction are elaborated in Chapters 6 and 7. Here, in the next section, we concentrate on classical techniques of intervention in TA and apply them to brief therapy.

Techniques of intervention in TA brief therapy

Berne (1966) identified eight therapeutic operations which, classically, form the technique of transactional analysis (and which were originally formulated as sequential operations):

INTERROGATION (OR 'MARTIAN QUESTIONING')   asking questions in order to document and elicit information which promises to be decisive. In a typically humorous and iconoclastic way, Berne, developed this notion of being Martian: the Martian therapist behaves as if they come from another planet without any idea of Earthling life or like a very young child that starts to learn what adults really mean when they are speaking or acting. Thus, the Martian therapist always keeps some steps *behind* the client and enables them to come to know what they feel and think about a certain situation, how they understand what is going on. The Martian therapist wants to know what the client is feeling and thinking about a certain event and does not assume that they know something in an omnipotent way. Groder defines Martian as 'the willingness to intuitively see through the images and beliefs that nurtured us during our personal and social struggle to survive' (1976: 365). This is part of an adult (and Adult–Adult) relationship. The therapist trusts in the client's resources of being able to clarify their problems and to find solutions which fit for them, thus taking their share of responsibility. Trusting clients' capacity for self-knowledge and for knowing what they want and need, the therapist has to ask (simply): 'What do you mean by that?', 'What does this situation mean for you?', 'What does this feeling mean for you?', 'How do you understand the situation?', 'What lets you be angry, sad, glad?'. The therapist does not interpret the client's statements from their own frame of reference, but leaves space for the clients to create their own truth. Thus, clients become aware of their inner reality and learn to trust their own perceptions. Their adult capacity is strengthened to decide how to deal with knowledge gained through this process. Nothing else is meant when the Gouldings say 'The power is in the patient' (Goulding and Goulding, 1978). Only the clients themselves can know their inner processes and their solutions. Only then and on this basis should the therapist add an interpretation (see below), because now (then) the client's Adult ego state is strong enough to examine the offered interpretation, to refuse it if it does not fit and otherwise to accept it without being necessarily rebellious. Such questioning forms the basis of brief, even very brief, TA therapy. Sometimes such questioning leads to what might be termed the 'spontaneous one-session cure', that is, when without planning or contracting for (only) one session, the client goes away and, on reflection, feels positively and sufficiently challenged by such questioning that they subsequently decide that they do not need further therapy. One such client wrote to the therapist several years later thanking her for having 'changed my life' (see Chapter 2).

SPECIFICATION   categorising certain relevant information; often used by the therapist as a preparation for a subsequent explanation. Berne suggests that specification may be assertive, e.g. 'So you . . . ' (which, for Berne, corresponds to 'non-directive' therapy), or informative, e.g. 'That's more of the Child in you'.

CONFRONTATION   using 'information previously elicited and specified in order to disconcert the patient's Parent, Child, or contaminated Adult by pointing out an inconsistency' (Berne, 1966: 235). Sometimes clients recount an event (how they behaved, what they thought, how they felt, etc.) in a paradoxical or incongruent way. In response, the therapist may highlight this by saying: 'You told a sad story and you laughed', 'Somebody treated you unjustly, and you weren't angry'. The client may respond to the therapist's intervention or question with a tangential or blocking transaction. For example, at the end of a couple's therapy session the woman was asked how she felt. First, she said what she had realised about her husband ('I now see the hurt boy in you'), then she went back into the past ('We always had difficulties in talking about our feelings'). Only when confronted explicitly that she had not answered the therapist's question, did she answer simply: 'I am painfully moved'. Of course, the client may offer a symbiotic invitation and the transactions may end up in a game. In any event, the task for the therapist is to confront the client's reaction: the purpose is to make it transparent that the client has avoided coming into touch with an important aspect of their Child or Parent ego state. Usually it is a painful experience and hence the client will (attempt to) avoid it. With the therapist's protection and support, the client may work through the pain and so gain insight and self development. Confrontation usually takes place as a crossed transaction; this is because the therapist usually responds from Adult, while the client's stimulus comes from either Child or Parent. Crossed transactions always involve confusion and rearrangement in the addressed ego state. If the therapeutic situation is well prepared, this rearrangement means a step in the direction of development; if the confrontation is too threatening, the client's (or therapist's) energy will be engaged in order to re-establish the old pattern.

EXPLANATION   attempting to strengthen (recathect), decontaminate or reorient the Adult, is an intervention to be used, according to Berne (1966), 'at every opportunity and when the patient has been properly prepared and his Adult is listening' (p.237). After having strengthened the reality-testing capacity, i.e. the Adult ego state, the therapist can take the chance to give some additional explanations about reality in the specific context. This may include simple information and models for problem-solving. It is important to test whether the client is already able to receive such explanations in Adult or whether their other ego states still have the power of definition – and, therefore, redefinition in order to support the script. What this often entails is how far the client is ready to trust the therapist's explanations and to hold them as true.

A 45-year-old woman from rural Sicily living in Germany came into therapy with a psychiatric diagnosis of severe depression. Following this diagnosis, her psychiatrist had prescribed her anti-depressants saying that she would have to take them all her life. The reason why she had gone to the psychiatrist in the first place had been panic attacks. She subsequently sought and found a transactional analyst because she now had two types of panic: the original one, and one induced by the psychiatric diagnosis and the psychiatrist's 'curse'. Although she had a depressed reaction to the medication, it was clear that the client was by no means 'depressed'. She was alert, had vivid eyes and spoke a lot in her own language. For the first session she came with her grown-up daughter who was reluctant when the therapist told her not to come to the next session. After the second session, the client felt able to come the whole way alone without being accompanied by her daughter. The reason for her panic attacks were twofold. First, there was a strong symbiotic family situation. The client's son had been the first who had broken the family culture by preferring to leave the family home and live alone. This decision had been the precipitating cause of the mother's panic attacks. After a few sessions the client was willing and able to accept a loosening of the family bonds and, at the same time, to expand the radius of her own movements. This had to be a balancing act between the needs of the modern (and foreign) urban reality and a particular rural tradition of Southern Europe. Although in this frame of reference, the client at first could not deal with the idea that her two grown-up unmarried daughters should live on their own, by the end of the therapy there was some movement in this direction. Secondly, the client had nourished the disturbance (or this 'reality') of the son's decision with reference to superstition and her belief in the 'bad glance' (*malocchio* or 'evil eye'). Thus, it was easy for the client to believe that evil-thinking relatives had brought this misfortune on her family in this way. Of course, the panic grew as to what would happen next. The therapist's most important intervention, following initial questioning, specification and confrontation, was to reassure the client through explanation that she was not depressive and that she did not need the anti-depressants. The therapist then went on to help her to discover her own resources to deal with the changed situation. The third step she did on her own: to renew contact with the fantasised 'evil relation' and thereby to prove her fantasies as not fitting the reality. After five sessions the client's problem was solved, that is to say, the therapist did not try to change the frame of reference but to help the client adapt it to the changed situation – and, in this, the therapist accepted the superstition as part of the client's frame of reference.

ILLUSTRATION   using an anecdote, simile or comparison to reinforce the confrontation and seen as directly relevant to the preceding successful confrontation, generally humorous and, whilst targeted at all three ego states, intelligible to the Child and therefore couched in age-appropriate language. Fairy tales offer examples of good and often universal illustrations: a client tells a story about 'Trying hard' to which the therapist responds: 'First you must clean the kitchen before you can go to the ball' (Cinderella). Instead of talking about injunctions, it may be enough to mention the curses of the wicked fairy in Sleeping Beauty. The context of group therapy is especially useful in offering illustrations in that the therapist whilst working with one member can address other members of the group at the same time.

CONFIRMATION   using new confrontations to confirm the same issues, used when the therapist's Adult is strong enough to prevent the client's Parent using it against their Child and is therefore sometimes used tentatively. One example of this is the permission transaction. Sometimes knowledge alone will not do. It may happen that the childlike part within the client needs permission to give up damaging behaviour and to practice a healthier one. This mainly occurs when dealing with driver behaviour.

After a group marathon one of the authors (UM) said to a young woman: 'You may still learn; you don't have to know and handle everything'. The client heard that sentence as a permission not to be perfect. Months later she told me how important that sentence had been for her. She could change her attitude in her work and in relation to her employer, that is to say, she could stop exploiting relationships.

The therapist can only give a permission if the ground for it is well-prepared. There must be a high level of confidence and the readiness to take and integrate the permission. Again the level of anxiety should be considered. Giving permissions means reframing normative parental sentences: to replace restrictive parental precepts with the permission to respect the client's own vital desires. If, for instance, loyalty towards the parental figure has not yet been worked through in therapy, such a permission will hardly work. Precepts and drivers are also the client's protection from unbearable emotional hurt and, at worst, if deprived from them prematurely, they could harm themselves or even commit suicide. In the above case example the covert and finally overt permission was: 'You needn't care for your mother any longer; you are a good enough daughter'.

INTERPRETATION   'stating ways of understanding a situation, thereby correcting distortions and regrouping past experiences' (Swede, 1977: 25). In structural ego state terms, interpretation is dealing with the pathology of the Child which is presented in coded form; it follows from the previous interventions and interpositions (the primary object of which is the cathexis and decontamination of the Adult). For example:

> *Therapist:* It seems to me as if you weren't allowed to make noise.
> *Client:* Yes, enjoying life was forbidden.
> *Therapist:* How lonely you were; nobody came when you cried.
> *Client* [*starts crying*].
> *Therapist:* It looks like the little boy had to protect Mother.
> *Client:* I was responsible for her good feelings.

It is important to offer an interpretation as a possibility to understand the situation so that the client can confirm it or deny it when the therapist has misunderstood the client's material. The client's confirmation is an important indicator as to whether the therapist has understood the situation correctly.

CRYSTALLISATION   a statement of the patient's position and, according to Berne (1966) 'the technical aim of transactional analysis . . . where crystallising statements from the therapist will become effective' (1966: 245). In other words, crystallisation is an Adult–Adult transaction which confirms that the contractual therapeutic aim has been reached. It is the therapist speaking, for example: 'Now, you are able to leave the symbiosis with your daughter' or 'Now, you are able to be happy on your own without waiting for your husband to provide you with a happy situation.' At this moment the client often requires ongoing therapy in order to deconfuse the Child. In the first example the client wanted and went on to resolve the inner symbiosis with her (dead) mother.

As we observed at the beginning of this section, these are classical, Bernian interventions and techniques. They do not account for the focus in more recent years on empathy, empathic attunement and empathic transactions (Clark, 1991), the latter which have the specific purpose of deconfusing the Child (see also Hargaden and Sills, forthcoming).

Other TA techniques applicable to TA brief therapy
As evidenced by this book, there are many aspects of TA which are not only applicable to brief therapy but were formulated with efficiency and focused work in mind. Concepts, theories and techniques are explained in subsequent chapters as they are introduced (and are defined in the Glossary). Here we comment briefly on the application of four particular concepts.

STROKES   As confrontation is the intervention to disturb and disconcert old patterns, strokes are the means to reinforce new patterns. To stroke a client for changing is nourishing the Child's need for being recognised in their efforts (indeed the Italian word for strokes *riconoscimenti* translates as recognition – which is consistent with and echoes Berne's (1973, 1975a) notion of recognition hunger). Both confrontation and stroke are means of containing and thus reaching the client's Child ego state, even if the focus of the therapy is the work with the client's Adult. To stroke a client can mean the therapist expressing joy about a client's redecision or praising them for behaving differently. It can include the message of confidence that the client will reach their goal. One important caution is that the therapist has to check carefully whether their stroke encourages adaptation instead of enabling them to amplify their options autonomously. Only if it is completely clear that the new behavioural pattern has been chosen by the client genuinely as their own option are strokes a healthy behavioural reinforcement.

DECONTAMINATION   Various techniques, including Berne's therapeutic operations (see pp. 31–6 above), help to decontaminate the Adult ego state, a key and early aspect of TA 'treatment'. Often this is a process of clarification which enables the client to realise the feelings and thoughts which come from ego states other than the Adult one and which have influenced their reality-testing capacity. Once decontamination has taken place, some information about reality may be helpful, by which the Adult ego state is reassured of its reality-testing capacity. This combination (of clarification and information) is often sufficient to help change behaviour. As an example, during a weekly group session three participants realised that they had been unwanted children. To accept that subjective truth and to realise how that traumatic experience had influenced their everyday behaviour enabled them to make clear individual contracts for change.

Brief TA therapy will result in decontamination and, equally, decontamination marks the success of brief TA therapy. The result of decontamination is to come into contact with repressed feelings. The more that these feelings are accepted as being OK, the more the symptoms which have been a replacement for those feelings can disappear. Clients then experience symptomatic relief. Finally, the therapeutic aim is to enable the client to behave in and from their Adult ego state so that the Adult can maintain control of the personality in stressful situations (see Berne, 1975a). In other words, the Child and Parent ego states need no longer be cathected if this would cause inappropriate, unsuitable or even damaging or dangerous behaviour.

DISCOUNTING AND THE DISCOUNTING MATRIX   'Discounting is an internal mechanism which involves people minimizing or ignoring some aspect of themselves, others or the reality situation' (Schiff et al., 1975: 14). As an internal process discounting itself cannot be observed; its effects, however, are expressed externally through passive behaviours. This theory and the practice of confronting passivity was developed particularly by the Cathexis School within TA (see Chapter 5). With the help of the discount matrix (Mellor and Sigmund, 1975; Schiff et al., 1975) the therapist easily can see whether a quick solution will be possible or not.

Table 1.1   *The discount matrix (Mellor and Sigmund, 1975; Schiff et al., 1975)*[1]

Mode	Type of discounting		
Existence	T_1 Existence of stimuli	T_2 Existence of problems	T_3 Existence of options
Significance	T_2 Significance of stimuli	T_3 Significance of problems	T_4 Significance of options
Change possibilities	T_3 Changeability of stimuli	T_4 Solvability of problems	T_5 Viability of options
Personal abilities	T_4 Person's ability to react differently	T_5 Person's ability to solve problems	T_6 Person's ability to act on options

1   According to Schiff et al. (1975), discounting occurring at any point on the table also involves discounting in the row below it in the type to the left (and vice versa), thus if a parent discounts the significance of a baby's crying (T_2) by shutting the door to the baby's room, they are also discounting the existence of the problem for the baby (also T_2).

The less insight and awareness of reality the client has, the more difficult the therapeutic situation will be: disputing the existence of a stimulus ('What cough? I didn't cough' $[T_1]$) is more serious than arguing about the possibilities for change ('Oh, I've always had it, I've learned to live with it' $[T_3]$). Discounting operates at individual and organisational levels. Pavlou (1998), for instance, discusses racism in the TA community in terms of the discount matrix.

SELF REPARENTING   One variety of permission is self reparenting (James, 1974; James and Goulding, 1998). If a client is well organised, it is easy to support them activating their parental competence in which case they can satisfy special needs of early childhood for themselves without getting sad or angry and without rescuing.

> Speaking about her panic attacks during the night, a client could conflate them with her anxiety and emotional loneliness when she was a little girl in a German town burning during the Second World War. As she acknowledged the association, she at once developed ideas about how to comfort that lonely anxious child which she still experienced being during the night.

Self reparenting enables the client to come into contact with certain unmet needs of childhood and to activate their own parental competence and resources in order to satisfy those needs. There are many situations in which we wish regressive desires to be fulfilled and there is nobody there but ourselves to provide this. Structurally, self reparenting is an Adult ego-state transaction in internal dialogue.

In these two sections we have aimed to introduce key TA concepts and constructs, some of which reflect a brief therapy approach in themselves (based on Berne's concern for speed and efficiency) and others which are applicable although not exclusive to brief or time-limited therapy, TA or otherwise. In the remaining sections of this chapter we briefly turn our attention to ethical considerations as well as indications for and contraindications to brief TA therapy.

Ethical considerations

All clinical transactional analysts must be members of the appropriate national organisation which, in turn, in Europe is affiliated to the European Association for Transactional Analysis (EATA) which has ethics guidelines and guidelines for professional practice (EATA, 1998) to which members subscribe. (In addition, individuals may also be members of the International Transactional Analysis Association.) The EATA guidelines are helpful in framing ethical and professional practice and in highlighting certain ethical considerations in brief therapy.

Primum non nocere – Above all do no harm (Guideline C)
This principle, which derives from moral philosophy and the ethics of non-maleficence, was cited by Berne (1966) as one of three 'therapeutic slogans' and is reflected in the EATA ethics guidelines: 'it is the primary protective responsibility of EATA members to provide their best possible services to the client and to act in such a way as to cause no harm intentionally or by negligence' (1998: 2–1). In relation to brief therapy, this requires the therapist to be aware of the limitations of the time-limited context. Thus, given TA's concern to protect the client from the negative or even destructive internal Parent, following a crisis intervention, for instance, the therapist must ensure the client's safety including, where necessary, referral to specialist help or institutions.

Informed contractual relationship (Guideline E)
Again, on the basis of contractual method, TA practitioners are required to enter into a contract only if they have the competence and intent to fulfil it. Thus practitioners need to be aware of their role, skills and training. Psychiatrists, nurses, teachers, social workers, etc. are not, by virtue of their original professional training, counsellors or psychotherapists. This is particularly poignant when, say, a teacher sees a need, perhaps recognising that a pupil needs therapy which the teacher cannot provide and which the pupil and even the parents may not be willing to accept from anyone else. In these circumstances it is easy to allow oneself to be seduced by the need to attempt the necessary therapeutic work or even a 'one off' session even though not trained to do so.

No exploitation (Guideline F)
Whilst this guideline makes explicit reference to financial and sexual matters, exploitation is not limited to these two areas. Practitioners also need to be mindful of possible clinical exploitation of clients, perhaps based on the narcissistic needs of the therapist. A classic example of this is when the client feels under pressure to be 'cured' which may occur if script analysis is done hurriedly or prematurely – see Hewitt (1995) for a model which clarifies the consequences of this (and also Chapter 6). Anti-therapeutic consequences of this include resistance which, significantly (and subversively), may be described as 'an error of empathy on the therapist's part' (Speierer, 1990: 343) or unhealthy adaptation.

Suitable environment (Guideline J)
This encompasses the specification of confidentiality, physical safety, etc. and also, literally, the suitability of the environment for procedures

such as brief therapy. This is an issue in the context of some institutions which run short-term therapy groups of about six to twelve weeks. Usually, as institutions and hospitals have limited availability of time, they only can provide brief therapy, even if their clients are diagnosed as having disorders which contraindicate brief interventions.

In these circumstances, it is especially important for the therapist to be aware of this contextual limitation alongside any contractual requirements and to accept social control as an important progress if not cure. Although some (even most) group therapists select clients for their groups, Berne (1966) was very clear about questioning the pre-supposition of this approach, arguing that 'the real issue . . . is not the one commonly debated, "What are the criteria for the selection of patients?", but the underlying, usually unstated assumption "Criteria for selection are good"' (1966: 5). The only exceptions to this policy of non-selection for Berne were essentially irreversible conditions such as Alzheimer's and those in special conditions such as a pending divorce or other legal suit. However, other writers on groups (e.g. Yalom, 1995; MacKenzie, 1996) favour selection and individual preparation for time-limited groups (also see Tudor, 1999a).

The group 'marathon', originating in the encounter group movement of the 1960s, is, by definition, a time-limited therapy. Given a suitable environment and a qualified and experienced therapist, these can be very effective. Participants of such group marathons usually want to deal with one particular problem and thus come with clear contracts for change. Sometimes it is one special script theme they want to work through

> 'I want to understand why I always behave aggressively and dependently or get depressed in certain situations', 'I want to understand why I always choose men with whom I can't live intimately'. After a number of years of individual therapy where she had dealt with her poor capacity for intimacy, the group marathon enabled this client to reach the underlying anxiety of the splendid isolation she created in relationships.

Another advantage of the group setting as suitable environment is to enable participants to do bodywork. The group setting provides protection for both client and therapist.

Indications for and against TA brief therapy

With the first contact, an initial diagnosis is made in order to identify whether brief or time limited therapy is appropriate. The best indications for brief TA therapy are:

For the client	*For the therapist*
To have a clear problem or issue, to be aware of it and to be able to concentrate on it.	To have an ability to diagnose, contract and formulate a treatment plan quickly and efficiently.
To be well-functioning.	
To have an ability to cathect Adult.	To be able to distinguish between different types of cure and their implications for therapeutic practice.

The following are some examples of common presenting issues where brief therapy may be indicated:

- A client who wants help to make a decision about whether to apply for a job.
- A couple who want help in resolving conflict or in coming to a decision whether to separate.
- An employee who is experiencing stress at work.
- A student who is anxious about his exams and wants help through his preparation.
- A former client who returns in order to resolve a new problem which has arisen.

Some clients present in a crisis in which they are acting out of their confused Child ego state. They often need permission to cathect their Adult capacities and can then decide how to behave and what resources they can activate. It is of little help only to comfort the student's panicked Child ego state when the exam is in four weeks; rather the therapist must help them to activate their Adult capacity in order to pass the examination. During an acute crisis, firm 'Stop' or 'No' contracts are often necessary for the client to gain social control in the specific situation and prevent damaging or violent behaviour. Once the crisis is over, therapist and client have to decide whether long-term therapy is necessary, for example with clients with personality disorders, and whether they can and are willing to provide and engage in it.

If the client's capacity for reality-testing is seriously disturbed or distorted, brief therapy is contraindicated. If the goals of TA brief therapy are defined as social control and symptomatic relief, then the same decision must be made if the therapy requires:

1. The unfolding and working through of transference processes, or
2. Regressive therapy, as such work has to be embedded in script analysis which, by this definition, involves longer term therapy, possibly in the context of a residential (therapeutic community) or institutional (psychiatric hospital) setting.

Having offered this overview of TA brief therapy, the next four chapters consider the particular contribution of each of the three 'schools' within TA to the practice and development of TA as a brief therapy.

References

Allen, J.R. and Allen, B.A. (1995) 'Narrative theory, redecision therapy, and postmodernism', *Transactional Analysis Journal*, 25(4): 327–34.

Berne, E. (1957) 'Ego states in psychotherapy'. *American Journal of Psychotherapy*, 11: 293–309.

Berne, E. (1966) *Principles of Group Treatment*. New York: Grove Press.

Berne, E. (1968) *Games People Play*. Harmondsworth: Penguin. (Original work published 1964.)

Berne, E. (1973) *Sex in Human Loving*. Harmondsworth: Penguin. (Original work published 1970.)

Berne, E. (1975a) *Transactional Analysis in Psychotherapy*. London: Souvenir Press. (Original work published 1961.)

Berne, E. (1975b) *What Do You Say After You Say Hello?* London: Corgi. (Original work published 1972.)

Berne, E., Steiner, C. and Dusay, J. (1996) Transactional Analysis. (Original work published 1973.)

Campbell, J. (1968) *The Hero with a Thousand Faces*. New York: Pantheon.

Clark, B.D. (1991) 'Empathic transactions in the deconfusion of ego states', *Transactional Analysis Journal*, 21(2): 92–8.

Clarkson, P. (1992) *Transactional Analysis Psychotherapy: An Integrated Approach*. London: Routledge.

Clarkson, P., Gilbert, M. and Tudor, K. (1996) 'Transactional analysis', in W. Dryden (ed.), *Handbook of Individual Therapy*. London: Sage. pp. 219–53.

Cornell, W.F. (1988) 'Life script theory: A critical review from a developmental perspective', *Transactional Analysis Journal*, 18(4): 270–82.

Drye, R., Goulding, R. and Goulding, M. (1973) 'No-suicide decisions: Patient monitoring of suicidal risk', *American Journal of Psychiatry*, 130(2): 118–21.

English, F. (1975) 'The three-cornered contract', *Transactional Analysis Journal*, 5: 383–4.

Ernst, F. (1971) 'The OK corral: The grid for get on with', Transactional Analysis Journal, 1(4): 231–40.

Erskine, R. and Zalcman, M. (1979) The racket system: A model for racket analysis. *Transactional Analysis Journal*, 9(1): 51–9.

European Association for Transactional Analysis (1998) 'Ethics guidelines', in *Training and Examination Handbook*. Nottingham: EATA.

European Association for Transactional Analysis (1999) *Core Comptence for Transactional Analysis Psychotherapists*. Document available from EATA, Les Toits del'Aune, Bat. E, 3 rue Hugo Ely, F-13090, Aix-en-Provence.

Federn, P. (1952) *Ego Psychology and the Psychoses*. New York: Basic Books.

Goulding, R. and Goulding, M. (1976) 'Injunctions, decisions and redecisions', *Transactional Analysis Journal*, 6 (1): 41–8.

Goulding, R. and Goulding, M. (1978) *The Power Is in the Patient*. San Francisco: TA Press.

Groder, M (1976) 'Guest editorial', *Transactional Analysis Journal*, 6(4): 365.

Guichard, M. (1987) *Writing the Long Case Study*. Workshop presentation at the European Association for Transactional Analysis Conference, Chamonix.

Hargaden, H. and Sills, C. (forthcoming) *Transactional Analysis – A Relational Perspective*. London: Routledge.

Hewitt, G. (1995) 'Cycles of psychotherapy', *Transactional Analysis Journal*, 25(3): 200–7.

Holloway, W. (1973) 'Shut the escape hatch', Monograph IV in *The Monograph Series I-X*. Medina, OH: Midwest Institute of Human Understanding. pp. 15–18.

International Transactional Analysis Association (1999) *Core Competence for Transactional Analysis Psychotherapists*. Document available from ITAA, 450 Pacific Avenue, Suite 250, San Francisco, California 94133–4640, USA.

James, M. (1974) 'Self-reparenting: Theory and process', *Transactional Analysis Journal*, 4(3): 32–9.

James, M. and Goulding. M. (1988) 'Self-reparenting and redecision', *Transactional Analysis Journal*, 28(1): 16–19.

Kahler, T. (1978) *Transactional Analysis Revisited*. Little Rock, AR: Human Development Publications.

MacKenzie, K.R. (1996) 'Time-limited group psychotherapy', *International Journal of Group Psychotherapy*, 46(1): 41–60.

Mellor, K. and Sigmund, E. (1975) 'Redefining', *Transactional Analysis Journal*, 5(3): 303–11.

Mothersole, G. (1996) 'Existential realities and no-suicide contracts', *Transactional Analysis Journal*, 26(2): 151–60.

Mothersole, G. (1997) 'Contracts and harmful behaviour', in C. Sills (ed.): *Contracts in Counselling*. London: Sage. pp. 113–24.

Pavlou, A.M. (1998) 'Racism in the TA community', *ITA News*, 52: 14–17.

Schiff, J.L., Schiff, A.W., Mellor, K., Schiff, E., Schiff, S., Richman, D., Fishman, J., Wolz, L., Fishman, C. and Momb, D. (1975). *Cathexis Reader: Transactional Analysis Treatment of Psychosis*. New York: Harper & Row.

Sills, C. (ed.) (1997) *Contracts in Counselling*. London: Sage.

Speierer, G.W. (1990) 'Toward a specific illness concept of client-centered therapy', in G. Lietaer, J. Rombauts and R. Van Balen (eds), *Client-centered and Experiential Psychotherapy in the Nineties*. Leuven: Leuven University Press. pp. 337–59.

Steiner, C. (1966) 'Script and counterscript', *Transactional Analysis Bulletin*, 5(18): 133–5.

Steiner, C. (1971) *Games Alcoholics Play*. New York: Grove Press.

Stewart, I. (1992) *Eric Berne*. London: Sage.

Stewart, I. (1996) *Developing Transactional Analysis Counselling*. London: Sage.

Stewart, I. and Joines, V. (1987) *TA Today*. Nottingham: Lifespace.

Summers, G. and Tudor, K. (2000) 'Co-creative transactional analysis', *Transactional Analysis Journal*, 30: 23–40.

Swede, S. (1977) *How To Cure: How Eric Berne Practiced Transactional Analysis*. Corte Madera, CA: Boyce Productions.

Talmon, M. (1990) *Single Session Therapy*. San Francisco, CA: Jossey-Bass.

Tudor, K. (1999a) *Group Counselling*. London: Sage.

Tudor, K. (1999b) '"I'm OK, You're OK – and They're OK": Therapeutic relationships in transactional analysis', in C. Feltham (ed.), *Understanding the Counselling Relationship* London: Sage. pp. 90–119.

Weiss, E. (1950) *Principles of Psychodynamics*. New York: Grune & Stratton.

White, J.D. and White, T. (1975) 'Cultural scripting', *Transactional Analysis Journal*, 5(1): 12–23.

Woollams, S. and Brown, M. (1978) *Transactional Analysis*. Dexter, MI: Huron Valley Institute Press.

Yalom, I.D. (1995) *The Theory and Practice of Group Psychotherapy* (4th edn). New York: Basic Books.

Chapter 2

Brief Psychotherapy Using Psychoanalytic TA

Helena Hargaden

In writing about brief therapy I find that my starting point is the question: What is brief therapy? Is it one day? one month? one year? one decade? When questioning the nature of short-term therapy it occurred to me that Berne was one of the forefathers of brief therapy. In the context of expensive and time-consuming psychoanalysis he introduced the idea of the one-session cure which continues to be a challenge to us all! In Britain the idea of brief therapy has been taken up particularly by the National Health Service culture which demands short-term treatment because of economic restraints. Curiously the same culture seems not to apply the same strictures to drug therapy which can often be costly and long-term. But surely all therapy is a type of brief therapy? Maybe there is no such thing as a therapy which is complete or ended. One of the most interesting cases of brief therapy I have ever heard of involved a patient attending an established and experienced psychotherapist for one session only. In that first session, after some preliminary exchanges, the patient seemed lost in thought. The psychotherapist pondered whether to intervene or not. She spent most of the session deliberating and eventually when the session was up the therapist had not intervened. They said goodbye and the man never returned. The psychotherapist wondered if she should have intervened after all but was still not sure. Five years later she received a letter from the man thanking her for changing his life. It seemed that he had used the therapeutic hour most effectively, made decisions and gone away to put them into action. For this he thanked the psychotherapist whom he deemed to have greatly helped him. So, what happened? How did the therapist help the patient and could it have happened with a less experienced therapist? If the therapist had intervened, or not struggled and deliberated, would the outcome have been different? Using the relational model of transactional analysis (TA) psychotherapy (Hargaden and Sills, 1999) described below, I think the fact that the therapist was able and willing to struggle in the session, able to contain her own anxiety, go into her own internal world and reflect upon the feelings that she was picking up were crucial to the outcome of what we could call a 'one-session cure'. This story and analysis raises another important question for me which is: Why is brief therapy so readily linked to focused, outcome- and solution-based therapy? I will attempt to answer this in one word: anxiety. I think many psychotherapists feel very anxious to get results, to tie things up, to be seen to be effective. It is understandable that she may want to feel in control of feelings and experiences that can seem very threatening to the patient who has never learned how to deal with them; feelings which are easily communicated to a sensitive therapist who picks them up. Solution-focused therapy seems so attractive because it offers this structure and control. In this chapter I want to make a case for non-focused brief therapy in the form of psychoanalytic transactional analysis.

In this chapter I define psychoanalytic TA as initially described by Berne. I then trace further developments of psychoanalytic TA particularly looking at the transferential model of ego states (Moiso, 1985) and countertransference (Novellino, 1985). In particular I draw upon the most recent development of psychoanalytic TA as represented by my work with Sills in our forthcoming book *Transactional Analysis: A Relational Perspective* (Hargaden and Sills, in preparation). In this book we propose a way of working with the Child ego in the deconfusion stage of psychotherapy. Our map consists of two specific areas:

i – a theory of self-utilising the structural model of ego states.
ii – a transferential paradigm drawing upon Moiso's (1985) transference model, in which we distinguish between three different types of transference:
Introjective Transferences – the Co longings
Projective Transferences – the defensive transferences P_1+/P_1-
Transformational Transferences projective identification, i.e. Cô/Pô projections

The transferential domains overlap and although all transference is potentially transformational we make a special case for projective identification. For the purpose of this chapter I briefly elaborate and illustrate this relational model with some case vignettes. I then draw upon the relational model to discuss brief psychoanalytic transactional analysis with specific reference to my work with a particular patient in brief psychotherapy.

The relational model of transactional analysis differs primarily from most other forms of TA in two specific ways:

i – it is a move away from symptom modification towards an attempt to understand internal psychic structures
ii – the use of the therapist's 'self' in the therapeutic relationship to bring about change.

The History of Psychoanalytic Transactional Analysis

Berne placed psychoanalysis 'methodologically as a highly specialised aspect of structural analysis' (Berne, 1975: 12). When referring to psychoanalysis he suggests that we use structural analysis of personality in order to decontaminate the Adult ego state, thus strengthening this ego, as a preparation for psychoanalytic treatment: 'it is apparent how transactional analysis, game analysis, and script analysis were a good foundation for subsequent psychoanalytic work . . .' (Berne, 1975: 163, 164). Berne described psychoanalysis, in structural terms, as deconfusing the 'Child and resolving the conflicts between the Child and the Parent' 1975: 90). It seems that Berne viewed the therapeutic process in a highly structured way in which he described phases of psychotherapy beginning with decontamination of the Adult and leading eventually to deconfusion of the Child ego state. He suggests that this stage, otherwise known as 'the psychoanalytic phase' is a 'luxury rather than a necessity' (1975: 90). When referring to deconfusion Berne says that:

> psychoanalytic cure in structural terms means deconfusion of the Child with a largely decontaminated Adult as a therapeutic ally. The therapy may be regarded as a kind of battle involving four personalities: the Parent, Adult, and Child of the patient, with the therapist functioning as an auxiliary Adult. (1975: 162)

Berne therefore sees deconfusion of the Child ego state as analogous with psychoanalytic treatment. He observed psychoanalytic treatment to be based upon free association with a suspension of censorship, meaning that: 'the Child will speak freely without interference from either the Parent or the Adult' (1975: 163). In Berne's view, psychoanalysis involves a dynamic in which: 'the Child speaks in their [Parent and Adult] presence and they hear it first hand' (1975: 163).

Berne set out his view of psychoanalytic TA in *Transactional Analysis in Psychotherapy* (Berne, 1975). However, psychoanalysis has changed significantly since Berne's day and in common with other theoretical models, the use of empathy and the complex potential inherent in an analysis of the transferential relationship has been more widely acknowledged. Whilst Berne recognised the existence of the transferential relationship which he described as a clinical relationship based upon crossed transactions (Type 1) which involve 'Adult–Adult stimulus crossed by Child–Parent response' (Berne, 1966: 299), he did not consider the transferential relationship to be a central feature of transactional analysis psychotherapy. Some transactional analysts since, in keeping with the change taking place in psychoanalysis, have delved more into the significance of such a relationship. In particular we are indebted to Moiso (1985) for his award winning article entitled 'Ego states and transference' in which he uses structural analysis to describe two types of transference. One is a more conscious type of transference which he refers to as P_2 transference. In this type of transference Moiso demonstrates how rackets and games are re-enacted and accessible to analytic treatment approaches which are cognitive and behavioural. In the second type of transference, the one which primarily concerns us here, he identifies a more unconscious type of transference in which the patient seeks to transfer aspects of his emotional experiencing to the psychotherapist. Moiso describes this as P_1 transference, in which the patient projects good and/or bad objects onto the therapist. He describes this as immature P_1 functioning which mainly involves borderline and pathological narcissistic features. For those patients presenting with these disorders of the self he suggests we need to use a TA psychodynamic approach since these early experiences are not accessible to redecision or reparenting techniques. I think of patients' experiencing in such situations as the 'inarticulate speech of the injured heart' (Hargaden and Sills, 1999: 8) and hold this as a metaphor when considering the Child ego state.

According to Berne, then, psychoanalytic TA is a highly specialised branch of structural transactional analysis. However, he reveals a paradoxical view of psychoanalytic TA as, on the one hand, he seems to deem it a luxury, whilst, on the other hand, he refers to it as a 'superior' process of deconfusion because 'the Adult functions throughout', as opposed to the decathecting of Adult involved in regressive therapy (Berne, 1975: 165). Berne left it to his successors to develop their interest in this branch of transactional analysis preferring instead to concentrate upon cognitive-behavioural TA (see Chapter 3). However, many transactional analysts have found it necessary to seek more in-depth understanding of the Child ego state and deconfusion processes because of the type of features they have noticed in their patients. For instance Clark (1991) reports on the increasing proportion of patients presenting with symptoms which suggest a disorder of the self, displaying narcissistic and borderline features. Haykin (1980), Woods and Woods (1982), Novellino (1985), Moiso (1985), Erskine (1987), Blackstone (1993) and others have also developed our understanding of the deconfusion process of Child ego states and the propensity of narcissistic and borderline symptoms which demand an understanding of the self.

The Relational Model (Hargaden and Sills)

One of the theoretical problems which emerged in developing psychoanalytic TA was that TA lacked a theory of self. In our original article, Hargaden and Sills (1999), we propose a theory of self using the structural model of ego states (see Figure 2.1). This theory provides transactional analysts with a lexicon in which to discuss the aetiology of disorders of the self as in the 'cohesive self' (Figure 2.2.) and the 'underdeveloped self' (Figure 2.3). Our theory of self is influenced by object relational theory, drawing on the work of Klein (Mitchell, 1986), Fairbairn (1940/52), Balint (1968) and others; and the self object matrix (Kohut, 1977; Stolorow et al., 1987). In addition we further develop Moiso's transferential model to include diverse transferential phenomena (Figure 2.4). Whilst Berne (1966) recognised that the countertransferential relationship was becoming a significant feature in psychoanalysis, we go further and view the transferential relationship as a *central* feature in psychoanalytic transactional analysis: it is the vehicle by which the patient attempts 'to communicate unarticulated experience of which she is unaware' (Hargaden and Sills, 1999: 8). I therefore view the transferential relationship as synonymous with the therapeutic relationship. Furthermore, the concept of 'transference' seems to me to evoke the possibility for multiple realities to co-exist within the relational domain. It is in this domain that the speech of the injured heart is communicated to the therapist non-verbally through behaviour, coded language, symbolically and so on. The creativity of desperate patients often seems infinite in their need and attempts to be heard and understood about experiences and feelings that they simply cannot verbalise directly. When Tricia arrived for her session she pressed a photograph into my hand. I looked at the photograph of a woman, dressed in a trench coat, looking rather severe. I felt angry, even enraged; I almost wanted to jump up and down on the photograph and tear it to pieces. I restrained myself! When I looked up at Tricia – she was smiling. I asked her why she had given me the photograph and she said it was to show how 'nice' her mother was. I thought, 'I don't think so', but it was too early to say this. I knew from Tricia's history that she has been very controlled and emotionally hurt by her mother and at the same time she has had to deny her emotional experience in order to keep the attachment (A_{1+}). It is my hypothesis that Tricia responded from an adapted part of her self, which we refer to as A_{1+} in the model of self (Figure 2.3). It is the 'I'm okay if . . .' part of the personality and consists of the child's successful adaptations to the counterscript messages of the parents. The foundation of self, which we refer to as A_0, emerges, in part, from the relationship between infant (C_0) and mother/other (P_0) (Figure 2.1).

It is in the intersubjective domain of mutual interaction with a self-regulating other (Stern, 1985) that we suggest the cohesive sense of self develops (A_0). When the infant experiences cumulative misattunement

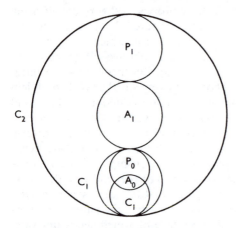

Figure 2.1 *The self – the child ego state*

and/or non-attunement from her environment then she has no way of dealing with this except by splitting off what Klein refers to as the 'undigested experiences' (Mitchell, 1986). In Tricia's sense of self (A_0), as I came to understand her, she had experienced aspects of her emotional responses as unmanageable. In order to keep the attachment with her environment (P_0), she had split off elements of her emotional experiencing (Figure 2.3). In our theory of self we locate split off aspects of self as part of C_0 and in P_1 (Figure 2.3). Up until the time Tricia pressed the photograph into my hand I had had an intellectual grasp of her hurts and injuries from childhood and, although sorry for what had happened to her, I had felt detached from the significance of her experience. In the moment of looking at the photograph I knew in my heart the extent of the hurt and rage suffered by Tricia. It was, however, too early to make this interpretation. When I commented that her mother looked severe in the photograph, Tricia's smile wavered but it was some time later in the therapy that she eventually connected with her internal rage. Generally speaking, transference caould be understood as the promptings by the unconcious to 'organise experience and construct meanings' (Stolorow et al., 1987: 146). In this instance Tricia went on to express her frustrations, disappointments and rage as they became more conscious for her, within the intersubjective realm of an attuned relationship (Stern, 1985).

The transferential ego state model (Figure 2.4) distinguishes between different types of transference. Moiso (1985) linked P_1 to object relations, differentiating between good and bad introjected experiencing (in our model P_{1+} and P_{1-}). We show another level of transference in our relational model (Figure 2.4) which involves the patient directing

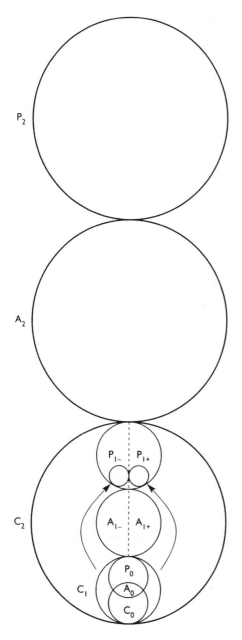

Figure 2.2 *The cohesive self* (A_0 indicates adequately cohesive self.
------ permeable division in A and P, indicates possibility of integration.)

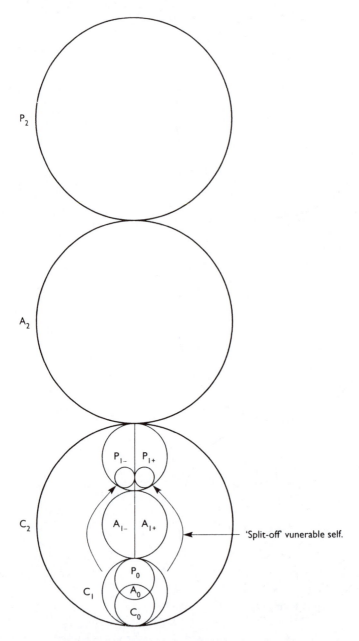

Figure 2.3 *The underdeveloped self* ('Split-off' vunerable self.
—— impermeable division in A and P, implies more fragmented self.)

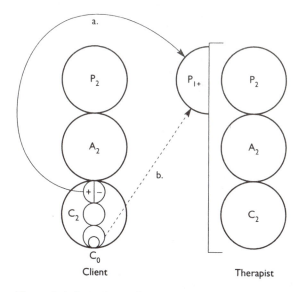

Figure 2.4 *Projective and introjective transferences (based on Moiso, 1985)*
a. Projective Transferences
b. Introjected Transferences (Idealising, mirroring or twinning transferences)
c. Transformational Transference (Projective Identification)

towards the therapist yearnings which represent the early unmet needs of the infant. These have been identified by Kohut (1971) as the narcissistic transferences which he describes as mirroring, idealising and twinning transferences. We refer to these as the introjective transferences and understand them as developmental needs. The self-object needs which, in his view, never go away but can be best understood by Erskine's (1996) extrapolation of the self object needs into relational needs. The relational model includes a third category of transference (Figure 2.5) which is identified as a C_0 transference (which includes the 'split-off' vulnerable self). This suggests that the patient's core or split-off self is 'felt' by the therapist who finds herself containing and feeling something which is hard to identify as 'other' than the patient. This is best understood as a process of projective identification (Ogden, 1991) where the psychotherapist begins to feel almost as though the patient has take a type of residence within her. In the above vignette, when I experienced my irrational fury, I had indeed seemed to find Tricia in myself: 'in order to find the patient we must look for him within ourselves' (Bollas, 1987: .202). Her cut-off, split-off parts (C_0) transmitted themselves to me through the symbolism of the photograph and the way in which she pressed it into my hand.

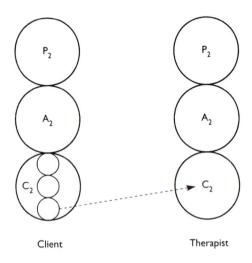

Figure 2.5 *Transformational transference (projective identification)*
P_0 and C_0 material projected into therapist

Novellino (1985) shows how an accurate analysis of countertransference can contribute to an understanding of the most profound
intrapsychic dynamics of the patient. He outlines several types of
countertransference. In our work (Hargaden and Sills, 1999) we draw
upon Novellino's use of countertransference and extend it to include
projective identification (Ogden, 1991). We suggest empathic
techniques based upon Berne's (1975) therapeutic operations for
working with the deconfusion of the Child ego state, which involves, in
particular, the use of the therapist's 'self' and the provision of a hold-
ing/containing presence for the patient. Our relational model is based
upon the view that deconfusion of the Child ego state is not so much a
stage but *an inherent aspect* of psychotherapy which is present from the
beginning of the therapeutic relationship. In this model the therapist is
used as a transformational object.

It is our clinical observation that many patients present themselves for
therapy feeling internally quite regressed whilst presenting with a functioning Adult which can disguise their fragility of self. This is
particularly marked in patients who have an overemphasis upon performance and a well developed adaptation to the environment (A_{1+}).
The relational model concurs with the traditional psychoanalytic view
of transference as regression: 'transference may be said to be an attempt
of the patient to revive and reenact, in the analytic situation and in
relation to the analyst, situations and phantasies of his childhood.
Hence, transference is a regressive process' (Waelder, 1956: 367–8).

Whilst we locate the transferential relationship as central to the thera-peutic work we do not accept that it is necessary or desirable to engage in regressive techniques of therapy. Indeed, a distinguishing feature of psychoanalytic transactional analysis, and, in particular, our relational model, is its differentiation from the specific use of regresive tech-niques. Instead, we are of the view that the presence and engagement of the emotionally available therapist is what is most effective in the process of therapy. It is the therapist's emotional involvement which makes possible the recovery of aspects of self. Such integration allows for the patient to develop the capacity to enjoy life in the here-and-now even with all the disappointments, betrayals and capriciousness of life.

Heimann (1950) regarded countertransference as the analyst's emo-tional response towards the patient and believed that such a response provided the analyst with her most useful tool for understanding the patient's unconscious. In the TA relational model of self, the use of the therapist's 'self' is central to psychotherapy: 'the therapist's recep-tivity to her subjective responses to the client and her willingness to engage with her experience is a central feature in relational psy-chotherapy' (Hargaden and Sills, 1999: 11). The relational history of the psychotherapist, therefore, is a significant factor in the therapeu-tic situation. The therapist's ongoing sensitivity and her way of organising her experience will shape and impact the therapeutic relationship.

Mostly I work with long-term patients, but sometimes patients need to come along and use a therapist to do something which seems often very profound and effective and is accomplished within a short space of time. In my work as a psychotherapist (although not a psychoanalyst), I recognise my propensity to follow one of Freud's dictums (also cited by Bollas) in which he said that the analyst 'must turn his own uncon-scious like a receptive organ towards the transmitting unconscious of the patient' (Freud, 1912: 115). Similarly, Bollas (1987) talks about 'cultivating a freely-roused emotional sensibility, the analyst welcomes news from within himself that is reported through his own intuitions, feelings, passing images, phantasies . . . [concluding that] in order to find the patient we must look for him within ourselves' (1987: 201–2). He refers to the presence of two patients in the analytic encounter, a concept with which I resonate (as demonstrated in the theory of self outlined above). It seems to me that those aspects of both the patient and psychotherapist are present in the therapeutic encounter and that it is up to the psychotherapist to acknowledge, recognise and hear the drum beat of her own inarticulate heart longings in the service of understanding the communication from her patient. Bollas (1987) refers to the countertransferential readiness in which an internal space is created 'which allows for a more complete and articulate expression

of the patient's transference speech than if I were to close down this
internal space and replace it with some ideal notion of absolute mental
neutrality or scientific detachment' (Bollas, 1987: 202). The relational
model therefore requires that the therapist pick up the feelings since we
believe that feelings are the raw material which will inform her as to
what was lacking in the early self-object failures (Figure 2.6). For
instance, emotional experiencing that was disallowed in the original
infant/other dyad will be cut off from the sense of self as in the underdeveloped self (Figure 2.3). Defences against such affect emerge within
the transferential relationship and need to be picked up by the therapist
through the countertransference:

> when remnants of early self object failure have become prominent in struc-
> turing the analytic relationship, a central curative element may be found in
> the self object transference bond itself and its pivotal role in the articulation,
> integration, and developmental transformation of the patient's affectivity.
> (Stolorow et al., 1987: 74)

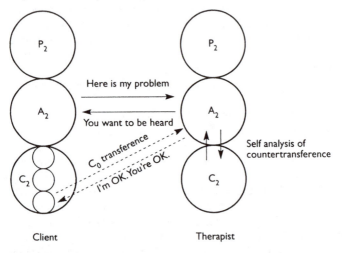

Figure 2.6 *The therapeutic transaction*

A case of brief therapy

In the following vignette I intersperse the narrative (plain text) with my
subjective experiencing and use of that within the relationship (itali-
cised text). The discussion revolves around my use of 'self' and an
imaginative analysis of the countertransference:

A middle-aged woman called 'Marie' described herself as carrying a
'basketful of pain'. She said that she wanted to understand its meaning
and to leave with optimism. She had never been in therapy and had led

a very purposeful life as a political activist from a South American country, and later as a university lecturer. She had been married for many years and had several children. Recently she had left her husband and embarked upon a disastrous love affair which was ending as she entered the therapy and, in fact, was her professed reason for entering the therapy. *In a short space of time I found myself admiring of her guts, intelligence, verve, sensitivity and compassion, particularly in relation to her political activities. After the first session I thought that this would be a lengthy therapy and that it would entail an in-depth exploration of her Child ego state. I wondered if the disappointing 'love affair' was perhaps evidence of erotic needs that maybe spoke of unresolved pre-Oedipal or post-Oedipal experience (Mann, 1997). Upon communicating elements of my tentative assessment to Marie in the second session she looked doubtful but seemed to consider the possibility.*

My countertransferential responses began from the minute I answered the door. From the start of the therapy I picked up an incongruence in her presentation. She seemed very humble, smiling and almost subservient, yet something in her manner invoked a sense of respect and a feeling of equality between us. As I heard her story I felt admiring of and excited by her political past. I was propelled into my past by her accounts of her revolutionary activity. In times between sessions I found myself thinking of her quite a lot, particularly when I walked the dog. My mind travelled back over the landscape of my own youth and my political involvements. I knew of the history of her country and had myself demonstrated, gone on vigils and been emotionally and intensely involved in the politics of that time and of her country. I pondered upon my political past, my involvement in feminist causes and political involvement against 'apartheid, internment, partition, conscription and silence' (Warshaw, 1984). I had paid a kind of price for my political engagement but had never been imprisoned or tortured for my involvements. Through the process of my own therapy I had become less romantic about my political engagement, understood my Victim position and yet could still hold onto the integrity of my political feelings in my search for a more just society. As I reflected upon all this I swung back and forth in my feelings about Marie. In touch with my youthful revolutionary fervour, I felt a passionate admiration for her. The Victim in me identified with her suffering revolutionary Victim position. Then I would swing to a more considered view and ponder upon how, why and what had lead her to such experiences. I then moved to a view of us as women of integrity, intent upon justice and with the guts to fight for what we believed in. I understood my temptation to romanticise and admire her on the one hand or conversely be tempted to reduce her involvement to merely that of a Victim when in fact she had defended against horrendous capitalist crimes against her people.

As the story of the love affair emerged she expressed her disappointment and we looked at the meaning of the affair for her. It had coincided with the end of her marriage and seemed to offer potential, but instead she was left to deal with feelings of betrayal and bewilderment, a sense of helplessness, loss of confidence and direction. She was a highly intelligent woman in the rather advanced stages of, what appeared to me, an overwhelming and unnecessary humility. *I had a sense, from the beginning, that she did not really buy into her own humility but was running it past me to see if I was susceptible to such a view. I understood this as a presentation of her adapted self (A_{1+}).* Although she was asking me for advice, help and wisdom *I simultaneously sensed a type of pride in herself and a strength of will and character which she was unable to hide, even under all the smiles. She clearly had a fairly robust sense of self (A_0). This was helpful to me now in understanding Marie. I knew her to have a strong mind and a strong heart and yet there was something problematic which I was struggling to identify.*

Stolorow et al. (1987) talk about how transference may be understood as an expression of the 'continuing influence of organising principles and imagery that crystallised out of the patient's early formative experience' (1987: 36). It was in the third session when she spoke of her anxiety and guilt about leaving her abusive husband *that I began to feel irritable with her and started to recognise that masochism was a strong feature in her presentation. Her suffering became less admirable to me and, without wanting to diminish her sense of integrity, I began to wonder if she had inherited a feeling for martyrdom from a combination of her ailing and ageing mother, her Catholic upbringing and socialist aspirations.* As she told the story of the love affair *I became indignant about the way she was being treated by her 'so called' lover. When walking the dog and reflecting between sessions I thought about how much guilt she carried, how she struggled with her needs which were so pitted against a sense of obligation and morality. I found myself ruminating, almost bitterly, that her Catholic background had enabled her to acquire much of what is necessary for a guilty personality! Why so bitter? I had long since shrugged off the shackles of my own Catholic upbringing but what if I had not? I might feel really fed up to the teeth with all the suffering, the socialism, the Catholicism, the martyrdom, the abusive husband, the . . . (I almost found myself cursing in the park with the dog!)*

By the fourth session I decided to challenge her seeming commitment to suffering with my understanding of her masochism. I hoped that I was not too insensitive when I did this because I also recognised that her whole life had been built upon selfless ideals. She gave due consideration to this as to all my other interventions with intelligent thought and reflection. We talked about the concept of selfishness and I teased her a little with some self disclosures about my own commitment to selfishness. *I knew this to be particularly powerful in the context of her felt sense of being so understood by me in her political and religious experiencing. In some ways I used my subjectivity to play with her at this point: 'the aim of releasing the subjective state of mind into play is to reach the patient and provide him with a scrap of material that facilitates the cumulative elaboration of his own internal states of being' (Bollas, 1987: 206).* She left and there was a break of a fortnight before we next met because of a brief holiday. When she returned she said she had done a lot of work, grieving for the loss of the love affair and how it had triggered other losses she had experienced, but more than that she had decided that she would suffer no more. She had thought very carefully about my words and realised that yes, she had spent her life suffering and giving for others, and that was now over. She said this solemnly and I sat waiting with bated breath to hear what excesses of selfishness she may have lined up for herself. She told me that she had turned down the offer of a lucrative job and had decided to return to her own country where she could now live in peace (because of political changes); she would work at the university, and although with nowhere near the same remuneration that she could expect here, she would be in the hills, valleys and familiar terrain of her homeland with her own people with whom she shared a political history and culture, and that this was what she wanted most in the world. *I felt very moved by this. In that moment I felt changed by her as I allowed myself to be impacted by her impeccable sense of integrity about what was right for her.* When she arrived for her last session I wondered if she would waver but she did not. She was not overly grateful to me but appropriately appreciative of our work together, as indeed I was myself. I did not try to dissuade her as it seemed to me that the therapy was complete. We had looked at her expectations, her needs, her past experiences, her mothering, her time in prison, her children and her marriage to another political prisoner which had backfired so badly over time and ended so recently. *When reflecting upon this brief therapy I realised that I had felt very connected with Marie. I had thought about her quite frequently outside of the therapy. The more 'gritty' my response became, the more she seemed clear about her real feeling, thoughts and desires. Initially she presented herself as failing, maybe almost helpless, in the world of love and romance, and unsure as to her direction. Some of my irritation was that I did not feel particularly contacted or persuaded by her false self presentation. I think my emotional availability to pick up on what lay underneath enabled her to experience herself as the person she was and maybe even for the first time in her life to be able to decide and act upon what she truly wanted for her self. My availability* *for her to use me as a transformational object meant that she experienced aspects (C_0) of herself that had previously been denied and relegated to the 'selfish bin' by her mother, her church and her socialist comrades. Her mother had endorsed suffering as a way of being in the world with messages about 'Suffer for me' and 'Suffer like me'. That I was not impressed by her suffering (although clearly supposed to be), whilst understanding it, was an essential component in her process of redeciding to live for her 'self': 'it is on the plane of the daydream and not on that of facts that childhood remains alive and poetically useful within us' (Bachelard, 1958: 16). My daydreaming about her on my walks, when I allowed the 'phenomenology of [my] imagination' (1958: 17) some expression, opened up my understanding of her predicament and experiencing of the world. Would it be too fanciful to imagine that my walking and musing were reflected in her eventual decision to return to her homeland?*

Contraindications for brief therapy?

For patients who have a fragile sense of self or are fragmented and empty, however, such overt use of the therapist's subjectivity is often counterproductive. For those patients who experience the need for prolonged self-involvement, the therapist's subjectivity can feel irrelevant and rupturing of the therapeutic need to be fully and completely heard without much interruption. When working specifically in the introjective transference for instance, I have sometimes felt like a lamppost or a bin, wondering what on earth use I am for the patient as he leans against me or throws information into me. It can feel difficult to contain the sense of feeling useless and used and maybe bored, while the patient 'rattles on' and yet this may well be the first time they have ever had the opportunity to work things out for themselves with an involved other who was willing to listen patiently and attentively, just as a parent will do with the maturing child. Sometimes I have insisted upon making a comment, and it has felt like insistence, only for the person to politely wait for me to finish and then continue as though I had not spoken. The client's narcissistic issues can press heavily on the therapist and trigger her own narcissistic needs, in response to which she needs to hold and contain this tension. For patients who reveal borderline features requiring the therapist to work in the projective or transformational domain, the therapist's subjectivity can be experienced as an attack upon them, or an attempt to overwhelm them. At the same time they require an emotional responsiveness from the therapist who needs to be able to contain the tension between her own subjective responses and the need to offer an emotionally non-intrusive contact. The psychotherapist's capacity both to reflect upon and contain her own subjectivity (Slochower, 1996) will be a defining feature in such a therapy. I recall a particular patient who needed me to fight with him. It seemed that only when he felt I truly engaged in a negative encounter could he trust my genuineness. Of course I was sometimes drawn into expressing my understanding and learned to my cost that he experienced this as annihilating and therapeutically ineffective. I had to learn, with him, to bracket my subjectivity whilst staying emotionally available until he was ready to feel safe enough to internalise the 'good' aspects of the therapy.

These observations seem to me to beg the question of how adequate and/or effective brief therapy can be for patients with a more fragile sense of self. Whilst in one sense I view brief therapy as inadequate to their needs, my observation is that some very good and effective therapy can happen even with those who has a fragile sense of self. I think this is because they are able to meet some of their self-object needs and experience themselves, maybe for the first time ever, as being valuable enough to be heard and attended to in a respectful and thoughtful manner. For those patients with borderline features, if the ending is adequately managed, I think that brief therapy can offer the opportunity for connection and separation in an attuned intersubjective relationship which can often spur them on to seek further help.

One danger of brief therapy is that some may re-experience the abandonment without therapeutic gain. In part this relies upon the skills of the therapist in facilitating the ending of the relationship, but can unconscious forces be so easily mastered? In the above case study, I was able to do an effective piece of brief therapy for several reasons. One is that Marie had a strong sense of self, although in my view her sense of self was implicated in a type of martyring of her self (A_0). At the same time she had a robust sense of identity. Our brief work together enabled her to experience her sense of self (A_0) with less ambivalence. She was able to make changes in her personality structure (A_{1+}). Through the process of our relating I think something changed both in her sense of self and in her external adaptation to the world. Marie had an opportunity to re-experience aspects of her 'self' in ways which altered her experience of 'self' and enabled her to make different life choices. In my view changes which take place for a patient are by-products of the therapy and not the focus of it. Recently, a patient, upon leaving therapy after four years and in attempting to describe the meaning of it all for her, said that she felt she had introjected a sense of unstructured space. There had been many moments in that therapy where I had found myself daydreaming and coming to with a start and wondering what on earth I was doing. I do not think it too fanciful to consider that this patient 'made' me dream. That I was then able to accept this aspect within myself without censoring myself as an unworthy, unfocused good-for-nothing psychotherapist maybe offered her the possibility that she too could let go of some of the obsessively compulsive internalised structures which had so clogged up her creativity. We had of course discussed these unconscious, co-created experiences once I had analysed my countertransference and explored the meaning with her.

In summary, I would like to crystallise the following points about psychoanalytic TA and brief therapy. Brief therapy does not have to be solution-focused or controlled by an over concern about outcome in order to be effective. The theory of self and relational model offer the possibility for theoretical consistency when working with an indepth consideration of the Child ego state, otherwise known as deconfusion of the Child. Whereas some models in TA often seem concerned to control, master and tame the forces inherent in the Child ego state, this relational map offers the opportunity to chart the terrain for understanding experiences without trying to control them. As stated, an understanding of the transferential relationship is central to this model, for how else can the patient communicate the inarticulate speech from their injured heart. It is through an exploration of the transferential relationship that we can bypass the notion that there is such a thing as an 'objective' reality and, instead, train ourselves to attune to several different realities within the therapeutic relationship. Implicit in this model is an understanding that the patient is not always capable of collaborative analytic work, and that not all patients can tolerate or make use of the intersubjective process. Intuitive understanding of our patients then becomes more urgent when working in the context of brief therapy and treatment directions clearly need to vary depending upon the patient's sense of self (A_0).

References

Bachelard, G. (1958) *The Poetics of Space*. Boston, MA: Orion Press.

Balint, M. (1968) *The Basic Fault*. London: Tavistock.

Berne, E. (1966) *Principles of Group Treatment*. New York: Grove Press.

Berne, E. (1975) *Transactional Analysis Psychotherapy*. New York: Grove Press. (Original work published 1961.)

Blackstone, P. (1993). 'The dynamic Child', *Transactional Analysis Journal*, 23(4): 216–34.

Bollas, C. (1987) *The Shadow of the Object*. London: Free Association Books.

Clark, B.D. (1991) 'Empathic transactions in the deconfusion of the Child ego states', *Transactional Analysis Journal*, 21(2): 92–8.

Erskine, R.G. (1987) *Theories and Methods of an Integrative Transactional Analysis – A Volume of Selected Articles*. San Francisco, CA: TA Press.

Erskine, R.G. and Trautmann, R.L. (1996) 'Methods of integrative psychotherapy', *Transactional Analysis Journal*, 26: 316–28.

Fairbairn, W.R.D. (1940/1952) 'Schizoid factors in the personality', in R. Fairbairn, *Psychoanalytic Studies of the Personality*. London: Routledge & Kegan Paul. pp. 3–27.

Freud, S. (1912) Recommendations to Physicians Practising Psychoanalysis. *The Standard Edition of the Complete Psychological Works of Sigmund Freud*. London: Hogarth Press.

Hargaden, H. and Sills, C. (1999) 'The Child ego state – An integrative view: An exploration of the deconfusion process', *ITA News*, 54: 19–23.

Hargaden, H. and Sills, C. (in preparation) *Transactional Analysis – A Relational Perspective*. London: Routledge.

Haykin, M. (1980) 'Type casting: The influence of early childhood experience upon the structure of the Child ego state', *Transactional Analysis Journal*, 10(4): 354–64.

Heimann, P. (1950) 'On counter-transference', *International Journal of Psycho-Analysis*, 31: 81–84.

Kohut, H. (1971) *The Analysis of the Self*. New York: International Universities Press.

Kohut, H. (1977) *The Restoration of the Self*. New York: International Universities Press.

Mann, D. (1997) *Psychotherapy – An Erotic Relationship*. London: Routledge.

Mitchell, J. (ed.), (1986) *The Selected Melanie Klein*. London: Peregrine Books.

Moiso, C. (1985) 'Ego states and transference', *Transactional Analysis Journal*, 15(3): 194–201.

Novellino, M. (1985) 'Self-analysis of countertransference in integrative transactional analysis', *Transactional Analysis Journal*, 14, 63–7.

Ogden, T. (1991) *Projective Identification and Psychotherapeutic Technique*. New York: Jason Aronson.

Slochower, J. (1996) *Holding and Psychoanalysis*. Hillsdale, NJ: Analytic Press.

Stern, D.N. (1985) *The Interpersonal World of the Infant*. New York: Basic Books.

Stolorow, R.D., Brandchaft, B., & Atwood, G.E. (1987) *Psychoanalytic Treatment – An Intersubjective Approach*. Hillsdale, NJ: The Analytic Press.

Waelder, R. (1956) 'Introduction to the discussion on problems of transference', *International Journal of Psycho-Analysis*, 37: 367–8.

Warshaw, J. (1984) 'No time for love', in C. Moore, *The Christy Moore Song Book*. London: Brandon Books. (Original work published 1977.)

Woods, S.K. and Woods, M (1982) 'Treatment of borderline conditions', *Transactional Analysis Journal*, 12(4).

Chapter 3

TA as a Short-term Cognitive Therapy

Geoff Mothersole

In this chapter I explore the use of classical transactional analysis in short-term work and examine its value as a cognitive constructivist approach. I discuss some of the ways that cognitive thinking can inform the practice of short-term work, as well as some of the connections with and challenges to TA. The final part of the chapter concentrates on practical issues in short-term psychotherapy.

Broadly speaking, taking a cognitive constructivist view means taking a view of people that emphasises the role of our internal maps of reality, in which human beings are seen as acting on and organising stimuli from the environment according to our own idiosyncratic strategies. Such a view emphasises the constructions that we place on the world, rather than seeing human beings as subject to either the vagaries of internal processes or external conditioning as emphasised historically by the psychoanalytic and classical behavioural approaches respectively. Thus our perception of events, the interpretation that we place on them and the meaning ascribed, is an active process based on a personal world view. This perspective is central to both TA and the cognitive approach (Alford and Beck, 1997) and is in accord with Piaget's (1953) cognitive developmental model. The view is perhaps best summed up by Jones: 'we are not passive observers of our respective social worlds, but active forces in the shaping of those worlds. To an important extent, we create our own social reality by influencing the behaviour we observe in others' (1986: 41). As with most ideas, there seems to be a continuum of views from those who take a view that there is no verifiable empirical reality to those who take a more balanced approach. These positions have been referred to as, respectively, radical constructivism and critical constructivism (Mahoney, 1989). The former disputes the existence of a verifiable external reality, emphasising the role of personal and idiosyncratic constructions of the world. The latter, on the other hand, accepts the existence of empirically verifiable, objective truths as well as subjective reality, seeking to avoid what Mahoney (1989) referred to as the dualism of an either/or position. This is a position very much in line with

the cognitive approach and is, in my view, the only rational and practical stance to take if we are to avoid a solipsistic and narcissistic
overemphasis on the subjective, which would be as damaging as psychology's past underemphasis of it.

TA and cognitive approaches

Central to this way of explaining the complexities of human functioning is the notion of a 'frame of reference' (Sherif, 1936). He was
the first to argue, drawing on gestalt psychology, that stimuli are never
reacted to in isolation. Rather, we experience everything in relation to
other stimuli, both past and present, and that this network of related
factors influences both what we perceive and how we ascribe meaning
to it. As a social psychologist, Sherif was especially interested in the
external frame. Coffin (1941) enlarged on this, emphasising that where
we have a clear internal or external structure in a situation, we are
likely to accept material only where it fits with the frame of reference.
The term was also used within TA by Schiff et al. (1975) in what is in
effect a cognitive model, emphasising as it does the role of discounting
of stimuli in order to maintain the pre-existing frame of reference
(see Chapter 5). Their definition of the frame of reference as 'an overall perceptual, conceptual, affective and action set, which is used to
define the self, other people and the world' (Schiff et al., 1975: 50)
remains useful. Frames of reference can usefully be considered in
terms of the concept of locus of control (Rotter, 1966). He suggested
that individuals vary in the extent to which we experience control over
our life (internal locus), or experience events as occurring beyond our
control and due to external factors such as fate or chance (external
locus). Fixed positions at either end of the continuum tend to be associated with clinical problems. The former may be present in certain
psychotic and narcissistic presentations. The latter is associated with a
number of problems, including depression, anxiety and hostility (see
Yalom, 1980) as well as suggestibility (see Gudjonnson, 1992). Yalom
also links locus of control with Witkin's (1962) concepts of field
dependence and field independence. The former involves experiencing
events as embedded in their environmental context. The individual
finds it difficult to keep foreground separate from context, whilst at the
latter end of the continuum, individuals have no difficulty in separat-
ing parts of the field from their background. At the dependent end of
the spectrum there is a tendency for experience to be global and dif-
fuse, whilst at the independent end it is delineated and structured
(referred to as 'global' and 'articulated' cognitive styles respectively by
Witkin). One can immediately see links with the overgeneralising style
of the histrionic and the overdetailing style of the obsessive

compulsive. For further and fascinating connections with clinical problems, the reader is referred to Yalom (1980).

The other central concept is that of the 'schema'. The term has a long pedigree in psychology, and can be traced back to Head and Holmes (1911). Bartlett (1932) first used the term in its current sense of an active organisation of past experiences that helps order the perception and understanding of current events. Piaget (1953) used the term to refer to the organising principle by which actions and learning are generalised from one situation to future similar situations. He saw them as central to the cognitive organisation of the individual and to the way in which we structure our responses to the world into repetitive patterns. Schema then can be thought of as relatively stable cognitive patterns which form the basis of our interpretation of situations and constituting 'the basis for screening out, differentiating and coding the stimuli that confront the individual' (Beck et al., 1979: 12). Bricker and Young (1993) define them as 'important beliefs and feelings about oneself and the environment which the individual accepts without question. They are self perpetuating, and are very resistant to change' (1993: 2). This definition is especially useful as it emphasises that schema have affective components and are not to be viewed as some purely rational mechanism. They can be seen as the building blocks of the frame of reference, and the connections with the TA concepts of early decisions, the stroke filter, discounting and the core beliefs of the racket system are clear. The latter can be viewed as a superb working model of any particular schema in action.

In the practice of short-term psychotherapy, several of the concepts of the classical school of TA are essential. The model of energy postulated by Berne (1975) which he labelled 'cathexis', after the analytic term (Freud, 1955), provides a useful organising framework. In this model, we are viewed as having three states of psychological energy. The first is free cathexis, which is a state of conscious wilful control. Contrasted with this are unbound and bound cathexs. The former describes the experience of thoughts, feelings, experiences and behaviours that are felt to be ego-dystonic by the individual and occurring despite their attempts at control. The compulsion to check experienced by someone with an obsessive compulsive disorder is one example. Here, the individual 'knows' that the compulsions are illogical and unhelpful, but still 'feels' a need to act compulsively. An even starker example is the re-experiencing, avoidance and extreme arousal experienced by individuals with post-traumatic stress disorder (PTSD), where states wash over the current adult experience of the individual in a way that is unbidden and beyond their control (see Chapter 8). Bound cathexis on the other hand is the portion of the self that is unavailable. It is akin to the analytic concept of repression.

Space and the focus of this chapter preclude a discussion of the problems and pitfalls of this concept, linked as it is with the debate about recovered memory. Suffice it to say that I am personally extremely sceptical about the evidence for the existence of completely repressed memories. In my experience what happens is that painful events, especially those that are too much to integrate because of an individual's age or emotional state, may be avoided because there is no way that they can be brought into the frame of reference by the twin processes of accommodation and assimilation (Piaget, 1953).

Looked at together, bound and unbound cathexs can be seen as describing the sense of being drawn to some internal state against one's current wishes (unbound) as opposed to finding certain aspects of one's internal world hard to access (bound). Metaphorically, unbound cathexis can be described as being like the waves of experiences that wash over the deck of current reality, whilst bound cathexis is like the parts of the underdeck that are hard to access. Coupled with the above are the concepts of deconfusion and decontamination. The latter can be thought of as the process whereby we come to accept the evidence for a position that is at odds with our subjective and affectively charged reality, whilst still subscribing at some level to that subjective reality. It is akin to what Wachtel (1977) referred to as 'intellectual insight', and is often characterised by statements such as 'I know it's not rational, but I still feel it . . .', as in the above example of obsessive compulsive symptoms. A person who has achieved a level of decontamination in a particular area will be able to hold on to a particular perspective. For example, 'When I have a panic attack I will not die and it will pass'. They may however still experience an internal pull towards a different experience, for instance, still feeling the anxiety in the above example. There is a sense of having cleared a rational space which may sometimes come under internal attack. Cognitive therapy (Beck et al., 1979) provides an extremely well researched explanation of the nature of contamination in depressed and anxious individuals. It also gives some excellent therapeutic guidelines for achieving decontamination, a point acknowledged elsewhere, notably by Schlegel (1998). Deconfusion on the other hand implies a fundamental shift in the subjective reality towards a congruence of intellect and emotion. It can be seen as akin to Wachtel's (1977) concept of emotional insight, and in terms of Berne's cathexis model involves a fundamental shift of energy from a bound or unbound state to a free state.

The TA concepts of decontamination and deconfusion may be linked to Piaget's (1953) concepts of assimilation and accommodation. Assimilation is the filtering or modification of incoming stimuli to fit with our pre-existing schema, whilst accommodation refers to the changes we make in those schema to fit with external reality.

Decontamination, altering our self talk in ways prescribed in both TA and cognitive therapy, and working towards simple behavioural and thinking shifts, can all be seen as working at the level of assimilation in that we are seeking to help the client allow in new information without too much distortion. Often this is sufficient, an individual's schema being sufficiently flexible to deal with the new material, use it and shift accordingly in their desired direction. In Berne's (1975) terms, we achieve symptom relief and social control. An example is Mrs B, a well-functioning woman who, following a period of unacknowledged stress, had developed acute anxiety at the prospect of driving on larger roads. This anxiety led, in classic fashion, to her avoiding the situation, thereby becoming more anxious than ever about it. She was encouraged to understand her reaction in the context of her prior stressors, and over five sessions worked on a series of graded tasks to achieve her goal of being able to drive on certain local major roads whilst experiencing only minor anxiety. The latter fact was crucial, as she had got herself to the position in which any anxiety was bad and to be avoided at all costs. It was only when she realised that she could manage perfectly well with a moderate level of anxiety that she got herself out of her perfectionist trap and made overcoming her problem much easier for herself.

Of course the situation is often much more complex than this, and it rapidly becomes clear that the individual's current problems are significantly supported by their core views of themselves and others. In classical Berneian terms we need to help the client address their past in order to make an impact on the present and future by fundamental internal readjustments. This is the level of schema change, where our task is to assist in the process of accommodation, or the readjustment of schema in the light of conflicting information. Here we are drawing the sting from past experience or introjected concepts, in order to reduce the internal pressure towards homeostasis. It is this fundamental 'structural readjustment and re-integration' (Berne 1975: 246) as we make adjustments to central schemas which marks the qualitative shift that is deconfusion.

Perhaps TA's greatest strength is its ability to provide models for both intrapsychic and interpersonal behaviour, a fact largely attributable to its roots in object relations thinking. Central to this is the idea of life positions (Berne, 1962), a concept central to both intrapsychic conceptualisation of self and other and to interpersonal processes. The idea of core enduring representations of the relationship between ourselves and others has a long and growing tradition outside of TA theory. Bowlby (1969) described what he referred to as working models, which are based on whether the child expects others to generally respond with support and protection, and whether they see themselves as the sort of person to whom others respond in a helpful way. These are seen as central to the individual's style of attachment with others. More recently, Bartholomew and Horowitz (1991) concluded that by conceptualising the individual's image of self and other as either positive or negative, four combinations could be produced. These are self positive/other positive, self negative/other positive, self negative/other negative and self positive/other negative, exactly akin to Berne's classification of almost 30 years earlier, although he is not referenced by them. Through empirical research on non-clinical participants, Bartholomew and Horowitz produced evidence that goes some considerable way to validating their (and Berne's) model. It is fascinating that just as Berne's idea is not acknowledged by others, so the validation of one of the core facets of its theory seems to have gone unrecognised within TA. This seems especially unhelpful, as the concept of attachment is increasingly used in the psychotherapeutic literature. It is certainly central to the development of the idea of interpersonal schema (Safran, 1986; Safran and Segal, 1990; Liotti, 1991) which are seen as generalised representations of self–other interactions based on previous experiences. Interpersonal schemas are affective and cognitive maps based on the sense that we make out of childhood experiences. They are derived in the context of relationship. As Leventhal (1982) pointed out, we establish them both in terms of our perception of the external events and in terms of our internal reactions to those events. Looked at in this way, interpersonal schemas act as a conceptual bridge between archaic ego states and introjected ego states. Both are our encoding of different aspects of the same interaction or set of interactions. In any significant interaction with parental figures as a child, we are experiencing our own reactions and simultaneously constructing an image of the parental figure. Thus in any representation of a situation, we will have a map of how it was for us and a map of how we perceived the other with whom we were interacting. More than this, each is experienced in relation to the other. Perhaps in view of this, it would be helpful to conceptualise archaic and introjected ego states as merely two sides of the same coin, rather than as separate entities. They are both manifestations of, and change points in, the interpersonal schema. Such core interpersonal schemas comprise the frame of reference, by which the narrative of an individual's life is both experienced and created in a continuous feedback loop. They are the mechanisms by which the story is created.

There is another challenge in this concept for mainstream TA theory, which has usually emphasised such ego states as historical truths. I believe that such a view is increasingly untenable, for a brief synopsis of which see Brandon et al. (1998). As will be clear by now, our core schemas are generalised representations abstracted from previous experiences. This is in line with Stern's (1985) concept of 'representations of events that are generalised' (RIGs), which are abstractions of experiences distilled into an average prototype. Such generalised abstractions do not describe an event that ever happened exactly that way (Stern, 1985) but contain a representation of the meaning and the expectations that the individual has aggregated from clusters of similar experiences. Thus in therapy, our task is to work with what Stern (1985) refers to as the narrative point of origin of a particular problem, using this as a metaphor. It is often more of a narrative than a literal historic truth (Spence, 1982). Simplistic notions of humans as storing all memories in sequential and literal form are no longer tenable, and should be consigned to history. TA concepts of decisions need to be seen as narrative events, constructed to encapsulate some key aspects of the individual's perception of the world, as opposed to necessarily verifiable historical truths. Going back to the 'original scene' may have therapeutic value on some occasions, but let us not fool ourselves that this scene is anything more than a current version of how the story went. For more on narrative approaches the reader is referred to McLeod's (1997) excellent text.

Another of Berne's key concepts, 'script', has gained a central place in cognitive and integrative conceptualisations of psychotherapy. It was introduced into the mainstream literature by Abelson (1976), again without reference to Berne. Beitman (1994) comments that, while 'schema may be construed as a still photograph, the script is the movie based on the theme of the core schema' (1994: 206). He goes on to comment that examining the script associated with schema is a crucial aspect of change, and that the playing out of the script in the here-and-now relationship with the therapist can offer a method by which it can be analysed. Others such as Landau and Goldfried (1981), Mahoney and Freeman (1985), Persons (1989) and Novaco and Walsh (1989) also use the term, often in a way that overlaps with the concept of 'games', to describe patterns that are shorter, more specific and less determined than is usually the case in TA. Within family therapy, Byng-Hall (1985) uses the term in a way that is more akin to the standard TA usage, a connection that he acknowledges. Various theorists have identified the clinical importance of these repetitive patterns, naming them 'cyclical maladaptive patterns' (Schact, Binder and Strupp, 1984), 'cyclical psychodynamics' (Wachtel, 1977) and the 'reciprocal role procedures of cognitive analytic therapy' (Ryle, 1990), the latter of whom again draws from TA and other concepts without acknowledgement.

Stripped of surface differences, the common theme of all these ideas is that we create stories or myths by which we structure and understand our lives. Scripts act as the template that shape the next chapters or episodes, making it likely that certain themes or patterns will emerge to colour the next parts of the story. To the extent that these themes are pervasive and limiting or damaging, they become the subject of clinical attention, as we seek to help individuals create a greater flexibility within their key schema and the associated patterns of role responses.

Why short-term psychotherapy?

For a thorough review of the literature on short-term psychotherapy the reader is referred to Hoyt's (1995) excellent chapter. Since Alexander and French (1946), there has been a steady questioning of what they referred to as the 'almost superstitious belief that quick therapeutic results cannot be genuine' (p.v., cited in Elton-Wilson, 1996). Such questioning seems especially appropriate when one considers the considerable amount of evidence to indicate that the vast majority of therapy is brief, with the average length of contact being between three and eight sessions (Garfield, 1986; Koss and Butcher, 1986; Budman and Gurman, 1988; Bloom, 1992). Even in a specifically 'long term' setting, Howard et al. (1989) found that over half of patients seen had below 13 sessions, and only one-third had over 26 sessions. Thus, whilst short-term therapy is often dismissed as being something that is associated with budgetary and service constraints, there is clear evidence that suggests that the vast majority of therapeutic contact is short term.

There also seems to be some evidence that the greatest portion of change occurring in psychotherapy happens within the earlier sessions. Howard and his colleagues (1986) estimated that 75 per cent of those who benefited from therapy did so in the first six months. Recent research within TA (Novey, 1999) which compared results from 248 clients with the data from Seligman's consumer research study (Seligman, 1995) indicates that longer term treatment seems to lead to greater improvement and satisfaction as assessed by the client. However, a simple re-analysis of the data indicates that the percentage of 'added value' experienced for those who attended therapy for over six months was relatively small. For those who attend psychotherapy for up to six months, the overall improvement figure, derived from client's responses to three questions, was just over 77 per cent. This figure rises to just short of 82 per cent for those who attended therapy for between six months and two years plus. Thus again, whilst there is clearly a 'dose related effect', it seems that the greatest improvement takes place in the early sessions, with diminishing returns for the time and effort invested after six months or so.

Despite this, there still seems to be a pervasive 'clinician's illusion'

(Cohen and Cohen, 1984) extant in many quarters that the typical psychotherapy client is long term. The reasons for this are, in my view, connected with issues to do with clinician's satisfaction, financial and training needs, and an undervaluing of extra therapeutic change, i.e. change due to events outside of the therapeutic milieu.

Overall, therefore, it seems that a short-term approach fits with the very pragmatic choices that the bulk of individuals make regarding the pursuit of therapeutic change. Perhaps most important for me is the fact that a short-term approach makes psychotherapy available to individuals who for financial, cultural or other personal reasons would not be in a position to engage in longer term work.

The focused attitude

There have been all sorts of efforts to define short-term psychotherapy in terms of the number of sessions involved. Personally, I consider this rather akin to the nineteenth century theological debates about how many angels could dance on the head of a pin. Better by far to define it by the attitude of the psychotherapist and by the fact that in short-term work the number of sessions or the time period over which work will occur are agreed in advance. All therapy is time limited, if only because eventually one participant will eventually die if the therapy is not ended before that. What is different about short-term work is that the date of that redundancy is agreed in advance. What I think of as the focused attitude requires a willingness to 'Get in, get on and get out'. It is, as Hoyt (1995) points out, about getting from the problem that brings someone to therapy to the resolution that ends therapy by the most direct and parsimonious route, with no beating about the bush. Our task as psychotherapists should always be to make ourselves redundant, and we forget this at our peril. Berne (1966) describes such an attitude, noting core questions for the psychotherapist to reflect on regarding the client's presence in therapy. The ability of the clinician to maintain a focus relies on a capacity to exercise selective attention and, of course, conversely not to be drawn into certain other areas not directly related to the sought after goal, a point widely made (e.g. Pumpan-Mindlin, 1953; Malan, 1963).

Central to the whole endeavour, however, are the core beliefs of the psychotherapist. If we take a view that short-term work is, by definition, somehow second rate and bound to be superficial, then it is highly likely that this attitude will be sensed by the client. Unless they rebel against it and use it paradoxically as a spur to change, then the outcome is likely to be in line with the expectation. This is of course in line with the TA concept of ulterior transactions and Berne's (1966) third rule of communication. It is also concordant with Merton's

(1948) concept of the self-fulfilling prophecy, which basically refers to situations in which one's initially false expectations create behaviour that leads to those false assumptions becoming true. For a full review of this concept the reader is referred to Wachtel (1994) and Frank and Frank (1991), both of whom explore its value in understanding psychotherapeutic processes. The connections with the TA concept of games are, rather surprisingly, not explored. However, it seems clear that there is considerable overlap between the two concepts in terms of how we create what we expect, and the processes involved in a self-fulfilling prophecy would seem to underlie the repetitive patterns people perpetuate.

Short-term therapy in practice

At the point of seeking help, it is axiomatic that an individual will be experiencing some threat to their frame of reference. Such threats may come because of internal tensions caused by dissonances of various kinds, or because the individual experiences a confrontation of their frame of reference by aspects of the environment. The task of the therapist is to assist them in developing an understanding of how this is happening, and how the current set of problems fits into the narrative of life to date, in order to effect the desired change. The process may be relatively straightforward, involving the assimilation of new cognitive or behavioural methods. In more complex cases, it may involve understanding and changing the ways in which they pre-dispose themselves to experiencing events in certain ways, or induce certain responses from others, because of core schema. Overall, our task is to help the client see that in Korzybski's (1958) terms 'the map is not the territory', that their unhelpful thoughts, feelings and patterns of behaviour reflect a perspective on reality, and as such are amenable to change. In practical terms, it seems that effective and safe short-term psychotherapy relies on three areas, a sound assessment, the development and maintenance of a good working alliance and a clear, agreed focus to the work.

Assessment

Assessment can be seen as having two broad functions. First of all, it seems quite clear that we need to screen out those whose current state makes them highly unlikely to work successfully, at least in the short-term. This is largely a common sense matter of identifying those with a current or latent severe mental health problem. Thus those with psychotic disorders, severe mood disorders and uncontrolled substance use disorders are highly unlikely to be assisted by short-term psychotherapy. There are of course exceptions to this rule of thumb, where a viable focus with a reasonable degree of probability of a successful outcome might be negotiated. Similarly, people with personality disorders characterised by problems with attachment and separation, intense and variable affect and a difficulty in containing self-destructive behaviours are unlikely to be safely assisted by short-term work. Again, there are exceptions to this. Thus with Ms A, a woman with a long history of abuse and a poorly integrated sense of self, short-term work seemed initially a poor bet, especially as she had had previous contact with professionals in which she had become quite dependent and felt very let down when therapeutic contact ended. After a thorough discussion with her about the risks and benefits, it was agreed to work for a limited number of sessions over a period of some months in order that she could experience a separation without losing the value of the previous attachment and without feeling completely destroyed. The focus of the work was upon how she could maintain a good enough sense of herself and the other when that relationship ended without believing that she was being punished and abandoned yet again as she had been by her mother.

It has been clearly demonstrated that both depression and anxiety disorders without complicating factors are highly amenable to a structured short-term approach aimed at gaining control over the symptoms and over the processes that may lead to future problems. For a summary of work on this see Roth and Fonagy (1996).

The second function of assessment is to gain a qualitative feel for the current state of the individual in terms of their ability to develop a focus and maintain it in a short-term relationship. In doing this it is crucial that we gain some sense of their prevailing style of relating to self and other and of the core schema that are likely to be evoked in the therapeutic process. From out of the dialogue of the assessment process begin to emerge core issues or themes. Indeed the entire assessment can be seen as an attempt to elucidate such a dialogue. They may be clear and relatively discreet, for example problematic anxiety in a specific set of circumstances. On the other hand they may be more embedded in the story, such as a tendency to always feel let down by others. Either way, it is essential for short-term work that the psychotherapist and client are able to articulate jointly a focus for the work that is of sufficient clarity and boundedness to be successfully negotiated in the given time frame. Where such a focus cannot be described and agreed upon, then short-term work is by definition contraindicated, unless the focus becomes to achieve greater clarity, which may be a perfectly respectable therapeutic task. For example Ms C presented at the behest of her family and GP with a moderately severe eating disorder. Throughout the course of the initial consultation she was very ambivalent about whether she had a problem that she wished to change. In the end, short-term work was agreed, with the focus on her ambivalence and with the goal of her deciding what the pluses and minuses were for her about dealing with her problem. Once a focus has been negotiated, then of course it must be maintained during the course of psychotherapy. Failure to do so has been shown to have a deleterious effect on outcome (Budman and Gurman, 1983).

The working alliance
Embedded in the assessment and negotiation of a focus is the question as to how motivated the person is to engage, and more specifically how they engage with the individual clinician. Such questions are central to the development of a solid working alliance. Short-term therapy relies on the ability of the client and psychotherapist to engage rapidly in such an alliance. A judgement on this is crucial to the assessment, since if for some reason it seems clear that the client is not in a position to enter into a collaborative relationship with the psychotherapist, then short-term work is contraindicated. An example here is Mr B, a man with a long history of anxiety related problems for which he had physical explanation, believing that they were due to some underlying and undiscovered illness. After a period of exploration in the assessment it became clear that he did not accept the possibility of a psychological explanation for his problems and thus was referred back to his GP.

A working alliance does not of course exist in a vacuum. The alliance exists not as an end in itself, but as a vehicle that is essential in the service of understanding and rewriting agreed on aspects of the individual's life story. In this sense, one cannot consider the alliance without also considering the focus of the work.

The therapeutic focus
Most people entering psychotherapy will have a multiplicity of areas on which to focus. The task of the therapist is to elucidate in the discussion with the client the problematic areas and themes in their story. From this we seek to agree on specific reasons for the therapeutic activity, defined in terms of goals and contract.

It is central to TA theory and practice that the method is contractual. The classic definition being 'an explicit bilateral commitment to a well-defined course of action' (Berne, 1966: 362). TA has built a solid base of pragmatically oriented theory and techniques aimed at the fulfilment of hard contracts and, as such, shares much in common with the cognitive behaviourally oriented approaches (Ellis, 1962; Beck et al., 1979), a point recognised elsewhere (e.g. Bergmann, 1981; Schlegel, 1998).

In my experience, as trainee, trainer and supervisor, there is often some confusion in regard to contracts. This is generated at least in part by the use of the term contract to refer to both the desired end point of psychotherapy and the means by which an individual will use psychotherapy. This confusion is between the aims of the work and the methods that will be used to achieve the desired outcome. It is akin to confusing wanting to go in to town, with getting a bus in order to get there. The classic way in which we invite such confusion is by talking in terms such as 'What is the contract?'. This shorthand conflates aims and methods, and can, at worst, lead to a serious lack of clarity. Such confusion is easily alleviated if we highlight the term 'goal', used by both Woollams and Brown (1978) and Goulding and Goulding (1979) but sometimes missing from other work on contracts. Defined in the *Concise Oxford English Dictionary* as a 'the object of effort or ambition', we can best think of a goal as the desired end state. It is in my view much clearer if we use the term to refer to the sought after outcome of psychotherapy. We can then use the term contract in its strict sense to refer to the agreements between psychotherapist and client as to: (a) the *structure* of the therapeutic relationship (time, fees cancellation, confidentiality, etc.) – the administrative contract in Berne's terms; and (b) the *methods* to be used to achieve the desired outcome – Berne's professional contract.

Woollams and Brown (1978) offer a very helpful categorisation, defining three types of contract: the business contract; the treatment contract which is the 'agreement between the client and the therapist to accomplish a clearly stated goal' (1978: 223); and working agreements. These are statements of intended behaviour, and can be thought of as stepping stones on the road to achieving the overall aim of the psychotherapeutic work. For the purposes of both teaching and conceptualising the contracting process, I find it helpful to use the term 'therapeutic goals' to describe where the client wishes to be, leaving 'treatment contract' to describe how they will get there using psychotherapy. Any such goal can be assessed against criteria for effective goals identified by, for example, Egan (1994) and, from a TA perspective, Stewart (1996). Egan offers a particularly useful framework, indicating that goals should be:

- Specific enough to be verifiable
- Challenging and substantive
- Realistic and sustainable
- In keeping with the client's values
- Set in a realistic time frame.

The separation of goals and contract helps create a clear differentiation between aims and methods; between where we wish to go and how we intend to get there. Such clarity can be helpful in assisting us in steering our way through what can be difficult (and crucial) territory.

The contracting process

The contracting process in short-term psychotherapy involves the elucidation and clarification of the client's goals, and the checking of them against the frame of short-term therapy. The overarching question is 'Can this client safely complete this piece of work in this setting with this therapist?'. The question that I am always reflecting on is whether the work is containable, given the client's current state, history and desired goals. The task of the therapist is, simultaneously, to be elucidating an area of focus in discussion with the client, and to be metaphorically 'shaking the tree' to see whether things fall off. For example, conflict may occur at the level of theory and empirical knowledge. A bereaved person may wish not to feel the loss of their loved one, an aim conflicting with the need to accept the loss and allow the grieving process to occur at an affective level, if the grief process is to proceed to some form of completion. A further area to be considered in the process of goal specification and contract negotiation is the effect on both parties of cultural factors. There is, for example, some evidence (Marsella et al., 1979; Sue, 1981; Grant 1994) that different ethnic groups tend to have differing expectations of psychotherapists in terms of how they will be treated. (The same is true in my experience of clients from different class backgrounds.) Where such expectations are not met, Grant maintains that they may begin to doubt the credibility of the psychotherapist. This may lead to tensions between the culture of psychotherapy being offered and modelled by the psychotherapist, and the culturally derived expectations of the client. For example, the psychotherapist expects to encourage self-direction and autonomy whilst the client expects direction from a high status figure. Any goal/contract negotiation will be fraught with difficulty until such tension has at least been named and explored. Even when we get past this, it is important, especially when working cross-culturally (i.e. where psychotherapist and client have different cultural backgrounds) to check the potential effects of any goal within the individual's cultural frame of reference. This is vital, since actions that have a particular set of consequences in one cultural frame, may have additional or different consequences in another. For example, someone seeking to divorce or leave a violent partner may in some cultures have to face extreme pressure and even ostracism from some members of that culture. This may affect whether the individual chooses to take a particular action, and if they do, what needs to be dealt with in order for the change to be healthy and not self-destructive.

Taken as a whole, the process will thus involve the psychotherapist and client seeking to specify the nature of the client's desired goals. Such goals can be checked for internal applicability to the client by addressing such questions as 'Will achieving this deal with the problems that I am experiencing?', and 'Does it fit for me (the client) in terms of what is important to me?'. Again, Egan (1994) offers some useful questions that we may ask of ourselves in respect of our goals:

- Why should I pursue this goal?
- Is it worth it?
- Is this where I want to invest my limited resources?
- What competes for my attention?
- How strong are the competing agendas?

For the psychotherapist, the goal is checked for a lack of fit with ethical and professional values, as well as with the psychotherapist's personal ability to work with the client towards such a goal at this time in this particular setting. Once all this has been scanned, the question then becomes 'What will the client need to change in order to get there?'. This is where the contract proper comes in, as the client and psychotherapist explore the possible paths that the client could take to achieve their goal. This will often lead to re-specification of the administrative or business contract as the overall structure of the therapy is shaped to provide a proper medium for the achievement of the goal to be realistic. Thus for example a client who came with a simple behavioural goal will need to reconsider if it becomes clear that achievement of it will be undermined by a lifelong pattern of self-sabotage, requiring a different focus in therapy to deal with it. This is where our theories come in, acting as guides to this process. We draw upon our expertise to identify what areas will need to be addressed in the successful pursuit of the goal. The explicit agreement by both parties to work towards a particular goal, with at least a beginning answer to the above question marks the treatment contract. Thought of in these terms, the goal/contract setting process can be viewed as more of a circular than a linear process. In the context of a therapeutic relationship this becomes a co-creation or narrative, with therapist and client identifying client dissatisfactions and desires to move away from or towards particular emotional, cognitive, behavioural, symbolic or physiological experiences and shaping these up to formal goal/contract units in order to facilitate therapeutic movement.

Conclusion

In this chapter, I have explored some of the overlaps between TA and cognitive approaches. I have also outlined some of the ways in which

I conceptualise short-term work using an integration of TA and cognitive concepts, and looked at some of the challenges that current cognitive thinking poses TA.

The use of a short-term approach where the task is one of assimilation/decontamination is relatively straightforward, as in the case of Mrs C above. We can assume a solid working alliance and a lack of substantial hindrances to achievement of the goal. As we move into work at the accommodation/deconfusion level, however, we are by definition seeking to have an effect on more fundamental cognitive/affective structures. This necessitates an increasing focus on the process as well as the content of the psychotherapy, as the therapeutic relationship becomes a vehicle for the playing out, understanding and changing of core ways of experiencing self and other. This point is increasingly recognised in the cognitive approach (Persons, 1989; Beck and Freeman, 1990; Young, 1990).

Practising effective short-term psychotherapy requires an ability to distil the stories that we hear and to extract the essence. We need to be able to develop a quick focus, conceptualise a goal or goals and provide the structure and direction required to help the client achieve them. Simultaneously, we are required to manage the relationship, both in terms of attachment and separation. Looked at in this way it can be seen that, far from being a second-rate therapy, good short-term work is the highest test of a clinician's skills.

References

Abelson, R.P. (1976) 'Script processing in attitude formation and decision making', in J. Carroll and J. Payne (eds), *Cognitive and Social Behaviour*. Hillsdale, NJ: Lawrence Erlbaum.

Alexander, F. and French,T.M. (1946) *Psychoanalytic Therapy: Principles and Applications*. New York: Ronald Press.

Alford, B.A. and Beck, A.T. (1997) *The Integrative Power of Cognitive Therapy*. New York: Guilford Press.

Bartholomew, K. and Horowitz, L.M. (1991) 'Attachment style among young adults: A test of a four category model', *Journal of Personality and Social Psychology*, 61(2): 226–44.

Bartlett, F.C. (1932) *Remembering*. Columbia University Press. London.

Beck, A. and Freeman, A. (1990) *Cognitive Therapy of Personality Disorders*. New York: Guilford Press.

Beck, A., Rush, J.A., Shaw, B.F. and Emery, G. (1979) *Cognitive Therapy of Depression*. New York: Guilford Press.

Beitman, B.D. (1994) 'Integration through fundamental similarities and useful differences among the schools', in J.C. Norcross and M.R. Goldfried (eds), *Handbook of Psychotherapy Integration* New York: Basic Books. pp. 202–30.

Bergmann, L.H. (1981) 'A cognitive behavioural approach to transactional analysis', *Transactional Analysis Journal*, 11(2): 147–9.

Berne, E. (1962) 'Classification of positions', *Transactional Analysis Bulletin*, 1(3): 33.

Berne, E. (1966) *Principles of Group Treatment*. Oxford: Oxford University Press.

Berne, E. (1975) *Transactional Analysis in Psychotherapy*. London: Souvenir Press. (Original work published 1961.)

Bloom, B.L. (1992) *Planned Short-term Psychotherapy*. Boston: Allyn & Bacon.

Bowlby, J. (1969) *Attachment and Loss. Vol I. Attachment*. New York: Basic Books.

Brandon, S., Boakes, J., Glaser, D. and Green, R. (1998) 'Recovered memories of child-hood sexual abuse. Implications for clinical practice', *British Journal of Psychiatry*, 172: 296–307.

Bricker, D.C. and Young, J.E. (1993) *A Client's Guide to Schema Focused Cognitive Therapy*. New York: Cognitive Therapy Center.

Budman, S.H. and Gurman, A.S. (1983) 'The practice of brief therapy', *Professional Psychology: Research and Practice*, 14: 277–92.

Budman, S.H. and Gurman, A.S. (1988) *Theory and Practice of Brief Therapy*. New York: Guilford Press.

Byng-Hall, J. (1985) 'The family script: A useful bridge between theory and practice', *Journal of Family Therapy*, 7: 301–5.

Coffin, T.E. (1941) 'Some conditions of suggestion and suggestibility: A study of certain attitudinal and situational factors influencing the process of suggestion', *Psychological Monographs*, 53, 1–121.

Cohen, P. and Cohen, J. (1984) 'The clinician's illusion', *Archives of General Psychiatry*, 41: 1178–82.

Egan, G. (1994) *The Skilled Helper* (5th edn). Pacific Grove, CA: Brooks/Cole.

Ellis, A. (1962) *Reason and Emotion in Psychotherapy*. New York: Citadel Press.

Elton Wilson, J. (1996) *Time-conscious Psychological Therapy: A Life Stage To Go Through*. London: Routledge.

Frank, J.D. and Frank, J.B. (1991) *Persuasion and Healing* (3rd edn.). Baltimore, MD: Johns Hopkins University Press.

Freud, S. with Breuer, J. (1955) 'Studies on hysteria', in *The Standard Edition of the Complete Psychological Works of Sigmund Freud. Vol II* (J. and A. Strachey, trans and eds). London: Hogarth Press. (Original work published 1895.)

Garfield, S.L. (1986) 'Research on client variables in psychotherapy', in S.L Garfield and A.E. Bergin (eds), *Handbook of Psychotherapy and Behavior Change* (3rd edn.). New York: Wiley. pp. 213–56.

Goulding, R. and Goulding, M. (1979) *Changing Lives through Redecision Therapy*. New York: Brunner/Mazel.

Grant P. (1994) 'Psychotherapy and race', in P. Clarkson and M. Pokorny (eds), *The Handbook of Psychotherapy*. London. Routledge. pp. 75–85.

Gudjonnson, G. (1992) *The Psychology of Interrogations, Confessions and Testimony*. Chichester: Wiley.

Head, H. and Holmes, G. (1911) 'Sensory disturbances from cerebral lesions', *Brain*, 34: 102–254.

Howard, K.I., Davidson, C.V., O'Mahoney, M.T. and Orlinsky, D.E. (1989) 'Patterns of psychotherapy utilization', *American Journal of Psychiatry*, 146: 775–8.

Howard, K.I., Kopta, S.M., Kraus, M.S. and Orlinsky, D.E. (1986) 'The dose-effect relationship in psychotherapy', *American Psychologist*, 41: 159–64.

Hoyt, M. (1995) 'Brief psychotherapies', in A.S. Gurman and S.B. Neisser (eds), *Essential Psychotherapies: Theory and Practice*. New York: Guilford Press.

Jones, E.E. (1986) 'Interpreting interpersonal behaviour: The effects of expectancies', *Science*, 234: 41–6.

Korzybski, A. (1958) *Science and Sanity* (4th edn). Lakeville, CT: International Non-Aristotelian Library.

Koss, M.P. and Butcher, J.N. (1986) 'Research on brief therapies', in S.L Garfield and A.E. Bergin (eds), *Handbook of Psychotherapy and Behavior Change* (3rd edn.). New York: Wiley. pp. 213–56.

Landau, P. and Goldfried, M.R. (1981) 'The assessment of schemata: A unifying framework for cognitive, behavioral and traditional assessment', in P.C. Kendall and S.D. Hooln (eds), *Assessment Strategies for Cognitive Behavioral Interventions*. New York: Academic Press. pp. 363–399.

Leventhal, H. (1982) 'The integration of emotion and cognition: A view from the perceptual-motor theory of emotion', in M.S. Clarke and S.T. Fiske (eds), *Affect and Cognition*. Hillsdale, NJ: Erlbaum.

Liotti, G. (1991) 'Patterns of attachment and the assessment of interpersonal schemata: Understanding and changing difficult patient–therapist relationships in cognitive psychotherapy', *Journal of Cognitive Psychotherapy: An International Quarterly*, 5(2): 105–14.

Mahoney, M.J. (1989) 'Holy epistemology! Construing the constructions of the constructivists', *Canadian Psychology*, 30(2): 187–8.

Mahoney, M.J. and Freeman, A. (eds) (1985). *Cognition and psychotherapy*. New York. Plenum.

Malan, D.H. (1963) *A Study of Brief Psychotherapy*. London: Tavistock.

Marsella, A., Tharp, R. and Ciborowski T. (1979) *Perspectives in Cross Cultural Psychology*. New York: Academic Press.

McLeod, J. (1997) *Narrative and Psychotherapy*. London. Sage.

Merton, R.K. (1948) 'The self fulfilling prophecy', *Antioch Review*, 8: 193–210.

Novaco, R. and Walsh, W.N. (1989) 'Anger disturbance: Cognitive mediation and clinical prescription', in K. Howells and C. Hollins (eds), *Clinical Approaches to Violence*. Chichester: Wiley. pp. 39–60.

Novey, T. (1999) 'The effectiveness of transactional analysis', *Transactional Analysis Journal*, 29(1): 18–30.

Persons, J.B. (1989) *Cognitive Therapy in Practice: A Case Formulation Approach*. New York: Norton.

Piaget, J. (1953) *The Origins of Intelligence in Children*. London: Routledge & Kegan Paul.

Pumpan-Mindlin, E. (1953) Consideration in the selection of patients for short-term psychotherapy', *American Journal of Psychiatry*, 7: 641–652.

Roth, A. and Fonagy, P. (1996) *What Works for Whom? A Critical Review of Psychotherapy Research*. London: Guilford Press.

Rotter, J. (1966) 'Generalised expectancies for internal versus external control of reinforcement', *Psychological Monographs*, 80(1).

Ryle, A. (1990) *Cognitive-analytic Therapy: Active Participation in Change. A New Integration in Brief Psychotherapy*. Chichester: Wiley.

Safran, J.D. (1986) *A Critical Evaluation of the Schema Construct in Psychotherapy Research*. Paper presented at the Society for Psychotherapy Research Conference, Boston, June.

Safran, J.D. and Segal, J.S. (1990) *Interpersonal Process in Cognitive Therapy*. New York: Basic Books.

Schact, T.E., Binder, J.L. and Strupp, H.H. (1984) 'The dynamic focus', in H.H. Strupp and J.L. Binder (eds), *Psychotherapy in a New Key*. New York: Basic Books. pp. 65–109.

Schiff, J.L., Schiff, A.W., Mellor, K., Schiff, E., Schiff, S., Richman, D., Fishman, J., Wolz, L., Fishman, C. and Momb, D. (1975) *Cathexis Reader: Transactional Analysis Treatment of Psychosis*. New York: Harper & Row.

Schlegel, L. (1998) 'What is transactional analysis?', *Transactional Analysis Journal,* 28(4): 269–87.

Seligman, M. (1995) 'The effectiveness of psychotherapy: The consumer reports study', *American Psychologist,* 50: 965–74.

Sherif, M. (1936) *The Psychology of Social Norms.* New York: Harper & Brothers.

Spence, D. (1982) 'Narrative truth and historical truth', *Psychoanalytic Quarterly,* 51: 43–59.

Stern, D. (1985) *The Interpersonal World of the Infant: A View from Psychoanalysis and Developmental Psychology.* New York: Basic Books.

Stewart, I. (1996) *Developing Transactional Analysis Counselling.* London: Sage.

Sue, D.W. (1981) Evaluating process variables in cross cultural counselling and psychotherapy', in A. Marsella and P. Pederson (eds), *Cross Cultural Counselling and Psychotherapy.* New York: Pergamon. pp. 181–4.

Wachtel, P. (1977) *Psychoanalysis and Behavior Therapy: Toward an Integration.* New York: Basic Books.

Wachtel, P. (1994) 'Cyclical psychodynamics and integrative psychodynamic therapy', in J.C. Norcross and M.R. Goldfried (eds), *Handbook of Psychotherapy Integration.* New York: Basic Books. pp. 335–72.

Witkin, W. (1962) *Psychological Differentiation.* New York: Wiley.

Woollams, S. and Brown, M. (1978) *Transactional Analysis: A Total Handbook.* Englewood Cliffs, N.J: Prentice-Hall.

Yalom, I.D. (1980) *Existential Psychotherapy.* New York: Basic Books.

Young, J.E. (1990) *Cognitive Therapy of Personality Disorders: A Schema Focused Approach.* New York: Professional Resource Exchange.

Chapter 4

Redecision Therapy as Brief Therapy

James R. Allen and Barbara Ann Allen

Aged 25, Joe came to treatment because he felt isolated and depressed. Whenever he attempted to make friends, they always seemed to end up taking advantage of him. This pattern had just reoccurred: his fiancée had run off with his best friend and most of his money.

> *Joe:* There is no point in trusting anyone. They just take advantage of you.
> *Therapist:* That sounds like an old decision.
> *Joe:* Well, that's what always happens to me.
> *Therapist:* Joe, shut your eyes and go back to the time when you first decided not to trust people.
> *Joe:* [*after a few seconds*] I've got it.
> *Therapist:* Where are you?
> *Joe:* I am in the garage, crying.
> *Therapist:* How old are you?
> *Joe:* About eight.
> *Therapist:* Go back to that garage and be that eight-year-old boy. What are you feeling? What are you saying to yourself?
> *Joe:* I am angry. Angry and hurt. It's September. I worked all summer doing yards – and I've just discovered that my mother took all my money. I'm saying 'You can't trust anyone, even your own mother'.
> *Therapist:* [*pulling up an empty chair*] Imagine your mother is in this chair. What do you wish to say to her?
> *Joe:* [*as little Joe*] You damn bitch! Why did you take my money? I worked all summer for it, not you. I was going to get a bike. You used it for drugs and booze.
> *Therapist:* [*pointing to mother's chair*] Now sit in that chair. Be your mother and respond to little Joe.
> *Joe:* [*as mother*] I'm sorry, honey. I just needed to relax.
> *Joe:* [*switching chairs and as little Joe*] You and Dad did that to me all the time, even when I was a teenager.

This dialogue continued for about five minutes with Joe playing both himself and his mother.

Therapist: Joe, as a little boy you didn't have many options. But are you going to permit this to continue now?

Joe: Hell, no!

Therapist: Tell her.

Joe: Mother, I'm not going to put up with this. You will never do this to me again – and I'm not going to keep looking for people as exploitative as you and Dad.

Therapist: Say that again.

Joe: I'm not going to keep looking for people like you and Dad. I'm going to start looking – and expecting – people who do not take advantage of me. And if they try, I'll stop them.

Therapist: What are you aware of feeling now?

Joe: I feel settled. And excited. Powerful.

Bob and Mary Goulding developed Redecision Therapy (Goulding and Goulding, 1978, 1979) during the 1960s and 1970s, largely at their Western Institute for Group and Family Therapy near Watsonville, California. At that time, the Esalen Institute in nearby Big Sur was a Mecca for growth and humanistic therapies. Fritz Perls, Virginia Satir and Eric Berne were local celebrities, colleagues and friends. Combining the script theory of Berne with some of the gestalt techniques of Perls (Perls, 1969), the Gouldings developed a brief narrative therapy which can be employed either in groups or with individuals alone. Developing a brief narrative therapy does not seem to have been their intention at the time. Their goal, it seems, was more immediate and concrete: to help people change their lives. However, this approach is brief and it was one of the first therapies to deal directly, specifically and primarily with people's life stories.

The redecision process

Redecision therapy proceeds through the following five stages:

1. Negotiation of a therapeutic contract.
2. Development and expansion of a key scene related to the contract. Such scenes are conceptualized as a rapid route to early decisions about oneself, others and life.
3. Introduction of some new information, experience or emotion into this early scene. The redecision therapist generally utilizes enactment, and experiencing and experimenting in the 'here and now'.
4. Redecision proper.
5. Maintenance planning and reintegration back into family, work groups and community. This includes setting up positive reinforcers to support the new decision.

Stages of the redecision process

Negotiation of a therapeutic contract

A contract for therapeutic change sets the stage for and is the focus of later therapeutic interventions. It is also often the most difficult part of treatment. In redecision therapy, it is the therapist's task to make certain that the contract is for change, and that the goal is measurable, achievable and meaningful. The contract should be phrased in such a way that both the therapist and the patient will know when it has been met. 'I want to feel better' is very different from 'I want to stop beating myself up in my head, and saying I'm no good'. For example, Joe made and completed several successive contracts in regard to his depression: to stop berating himself internally with a barrage of 'Why didn't you?' and 'You should have'; to stop refusing positive strokes; to stop comparing himself unfavorably with others; and finally to stop setting himself up to be treated badly ('kicked') and then feeling victimized and alone. The work described in the initial vignette developed in this later context. The contract should be legal. Finally, it should be acceptable to all ego states of both the patient and the therapist. On the part of the therapist, it is important to make sure no one will be hurt and the social context is taken into account. 'I should stop smoking' is a New Year's resolution type contract (Parent ego state). By itself, it is unlikely to last long. The transactional analyst would try to expand it to include reasons to stop smoking based on current Adult ego state facts (for example health), and something positive the patient's Child ego state might gain (such as having more disposable income) or something negative s/he might lose (such as reeking of smoke). During this process the therapist acts as a kind of travel guide, but one who offers protection to assure that patients do not choose goals that are not in their best interest. No-suicide and no-homicide contracts take precedence over all others. Some therapists would include 'not going crazy' in this list. However, we think that potential lethality needs to be addressed first: once someone is dead therapeutic change is no longer possible.

Therapeutic contracts need to be distinguished from administrative ones. A patient can contract to come in for treatment once a week, pay her/his bill and still not have made a therapeutic contract. A therapeutic contract in redecision therapy needs to be for change, not for explanation, exploration, companionship or self-harassment. A good therapeutic contract allows redecision therapy to be brief and action-oriented, for it circumscribes the patient's problem and limits exploration of the past to those experiences that are directly relevant to it.

Prochaska and DiClemente (Prochaska et al., 1994) have delineated a useful paradigm of change, ranging from *precontemplation*, when people do not see any reason to change, through *contemplation*, when they are aware they have a problem and are thinking about changing but are not yet committed to it and are exploring potential negative aspects of change, and on to *preparation*, when they intend to take specific action in the near future. This is the stage that can end with a good therapeutic contract and lead to the further steps of *action*, *maintenance* and *termination*. That is, redecision therapy fits for people who have decided to change something specific about themselves. If they are contemplating change sometime, but not just yet, or if they see no reason at all to change, then this approach is not for them. They may still find participation in a group useful, however, for the work of other patients may stir up issues that they have not resolved. Alternatively, they might wish to make a contract for exploration or education. This, however, is not the province of redecision therapy proper, although it may well be a precursor to it.

Entranced by redecision therapy, some beginning therapists try to use it in the treatment of all types of psychopathology. However, the approach is intended to deal only with distress resulting from past decisions, not for other sources of psychopathology such as distress arising primarily from a current poor fit with the environment, organic processes or lack of important experiences (Allen and Allen, 1997), although the patient might well make new decisions as to how to deal with these problems differently. Redecision therapy is based on the idea that children make decisions early in life about what they are like, what others are like, and what happens to people like them. Since these early decisions are *made* (and in this sense people decide their own destiny), such decisions can equally be remade or rede-cided.

Development and expansion of a key scene
In redecision work, patients are asked to develop a key scene wherein they made a decision related to their current contract. This may be elicited in several ways: through tracking a phrase or feeling; through utilization of a current or recent incident, early scene, fantasy or dream; through externalizing a problem; or through exaggerating a gesture, movement or inappropriate laugh. The following are typical approaches:

TRACKING A PHRASE OR FEELING   To help a patient recall an early scene, we might say 'Be a little boy and hear the words . . .' or 'Who told you . . .?' while repeating the words the patient has just uttered. We might suggest, 'Shut your eyes and go back to the first time you were feeling this same way or having these same thoughts', 'What is going on?', 'What are you feeling?', 'What are you saying to yourself?'.

Marie (aged 42) came to treatment because of chronic depression. She had made some improvement, but as she was describing this change, she suddenly looked down and looked more depressed.

Therapist: Are you saying something to yourself in your head?
Marie: Yes. I am thinking of my grandmother. She used to say: 'But we are not in this "vale of tears" to have a good time'.
Therapist: Sit in that chair and be your grandmother.
Marie: [*settling in*] Okay.
Therapist: [*to Marie as grandmother*] Grandmother, would you explain to Marie what happened in your life that you thought it good advice to tell Marie that she was not in this 'vale of tears' to have a good time?

As her grandmother, Marie explained the numerous difficulties of her life and how tragedy always ruined her happiness. In order to protect herself from disappointment, she had decided, 'Don't expect anything, and you'll never be disappointed'. As Marie dialogued with her fantasised grandmother, it became clear that her grandmother's motto really summed up the historical experience of her family in Eastern Europe. Her advice was meant to be helpful, and to keep Marie safe in the dangerous world of Eastern European Jewry of the last century.

UTILIZATION OF A BODY MOVEMENT   Key scenes can be developed out of a patient's body movement or gesture. The patient is asked to exaggerate them or to give them a voice. For example, in talking of his parents, Peter began to wipe his nose.

Peter: [*wiping his nose as he talks of his mother and father*]
Therapist: Give a voice to your hand. What is it saying?
Peter: Nothing. It just itches.
Therapist: Give it a voice.
Peter: I'm stopping you from smelling ... from smelling what's going on [*with obvious delight*] ... Oh, that's just what my parents always tried to do to me, to keep me from knowing that their relationship stank.

UTILIZATION OF A DREAM   Every person or thing in a dream can be treated as a projection of a part of the dreamer. Having the patient identify with each person and object in the dream, and then develop dialogues between them, as in traditional gestalt therapy (Perls, 1969), usually leads to elucidation of internal conflicts and pathogenic decisions.

EXTERNALIZATION   Bodily symptoms as well as abstractions such as hope or sorrow can be externalized, and a dialogue developed with them. Often such externalizations turn into a dialogue with a real person from the patient's past. Barbara (aged 24) had trouble talking about her family. She felt that her throat was closing up and that she was being strangled.

> *Therapist:* Imagine the strangler there in the chair. What do you say to it?
> *Barbara:* I hate you! Why don't you leave me alone? Why don't you let me talk?
> *Therapist:* Now, sit in that chair. Be the strangler.
> *Barbara: [as the strangler]* If you talk, you'll give me away.

This interchange led to a dialogue of several minutes between Barbara and the strangler.

> *Therapist:* Who else said that to you besides the strangler?
> *Barbara: [weeping, and replying very slowly]* My uncle. He threatened to kill me and my family if I told that he had sexually molested me.

This led to a fantasised dialogue with her uncle.

It is important to note that major life decisions typically are made when children are quite young, at a time when they believe in magic. Given the world as they knew it, these decisions were believed to have survival value and, as adults, patients still experience them as having this quality. After all, they are still alive!

Introduction of new information, experience or emotion into
the key scene: experiencing and experimenting in 'the Now'
Many key scenes are most easily dealt with through the use of a two-chair conversation between the patient and some important figure from the past. At times, we may interview the patient as if she or he were their own mother or father (or, as in the case of Marie, a grandparent), and explore how it happened they gave the patient the messages they did. This usually creates a new way for patients to see the original situation when they made their early decisions. They experience something new and/or gain some new information. All this is done in the present. Having the patient experience and experiment in the here-and-now and avoid talking about the past are key techniques in intensifying emotion so that it can become a motivating force for change.

An alternative therapeutic technique is to be found in the use of supplementation (Allen and Allen, 1991a). In this process, the therapist facilitates the emergence of 'the rest of the story' or explores important exceptions to the patient's basic life story. We use the stories we tell of our lives to consolidate our memories, and to construct and maintain our identities. We base our expectations on them. However, our stories can be modified or changed, for no one story can convey everything that happened and, in the retelling, we edit them, adding and subtracting, highlighting and minimizing. One of therapists' sources of potency (and danger) lies in our ability to help patients co-construct and modify their stories. We do this by the very questions we ask and what we emphasize, as well as by our non-verbal behaviors. Sometimes redecision work can follow a patient's becoming aware of the 'rest of the story', the parts previously left out. By asking for more details or for exceptions to what the patient believes usually happens – 'aporias' (ramifying contradictions) and 'hyperglossia' (a plurality of voices) in the language of the deconstructionists – the therapist can often facilitate patients changing their view of their lives. This approach generally mobilizes less emotion than the gestalt techniques previously outlined, but it still is useful. A danger, however, is that it can degenerate into an obsessive detailing of the past.

> When our son Michael was in first grade, it was clear that he could read – and clear that he was insisting too much that he could not. It turned out that he feared that we could die and leave him because we were older parents. To reduce this threat, he had decided that if he didn't learn how to read (grow up) we would not grow old. With more information, he was able to decide it really was safe to let others know he could read.

Redecision proper

By re-enacting a key scene and then introducing something new into it, as was done by the Gouldings (Goulding and Goulding, 1978, 1979), or through supplementation and understanding a key scene more fully, or through exploration of exceptions to their basic life story, patients can be freed up to conceptualize the situation anew and to feel differently about it (Allen and Allen, 1991a). As a result, it becomes possible for them to make a different decision from the one they originally made. The therapist guides the process, but it is the patient who makes the new decision and puts it into action.

Most patients find a redecision is made most easily if it involves a scene from early in their lives, because they are children in such scenes, and so easily energize a Child ego state. The redecision is experienced most fully when the featured protagonists in their fantasy dialogues are the people who gave the original messages.

Early in their work, the Gouldings teased out several important injunctions – pathogenic early messages that children use in deciding their life story or script. These may be pre-verbal or non-verbal, and may come from a parenting person (especially from the person on whom the child is most dependent) or from the milieu itself. Some injunctions seem to be elicited by certain characteristics of the child.

The most common injunctions are: 'Don't be', 'Don't be close', 'Don't be you', 'Don't belong', 'Don't feel', 'Don't be a child', 'Don't think', 'Don't make it', 'Don't grow up', 'Don't be important', and 'Don't be okay'. It is of interest that avoidant or dismissing parental behaviors, for example, seem to organize the child's mind so as to reduce access to emotional experience and memory. This may be a basis for the injunctions 'Don't feel', 'Don't be close', and 'Don't know what is going on interpersonally'. Disorganized/disoriented attachment often seems to result in 'Don't be OK', and 'Don't think clearly' in certain areas (Main, 1996). Redecisions are a decision to follow these old messages no longer. We have found it useful also to explore the flip-side of these injunctions, i.e. the permissions that the patient needed and still needs to give her or himself (Allen and Allen, 1997). A large body of current research confirms that these permissions can be conceptualized as forming the basis of childhood and adult resilience (Allen, 1999b).

Some redecision therapists conceptualize injunctions and all the patient's memories as 'real'. However, it is quite possible to do redecision work without assuming privileged access to what 'really' happened many years ago. Rather, it is the clinician's task to help patients move to a narrative that is less restricting than their current one and one that leaves them more options. Whatever the chosen scene or the therapist's belief system about injunctions and 'what really happened', the purpose of redecision work is to help the patient reject pathogenic messages that were previously accepted and to decide something new. In transactional analysis terms, the patient has an emotional experience (Child ego state), makes a new decision from the Free Child ego state, and then gains a cognitive framework for understanding the experience (Adult ego state). Current ideas from uncertainty and chaos theory would explain how, at the point of redecision, even a small amount of new information can have major consequences (Devoney, 1992; Holland, 1995; Boldrini et al., 1998). It is at such interstices of time and space that minimal input may lead to rapid, non-linear change.

Maintenance-planning and reintegration into family and society
Life is not synonymous with a life story or script, however it is the *enactment* of that story. After patients have made a redecision, the therapist's next task is to help them translate it into concrete action in daily life. We generally ask them to close their eyes and to pretend they are back at home or at work: 'Notice the changes you are making and the way you feel, the way you behave, the way you think. How do others respond? Do they notice the changes in you? Who is pleased? Is anyone displeased?'. Patients' replies to these questions may lead to a

new contract and to solving the problem of how best to get future support for their redecisions. This process helps them integrate their new life plans into their actual lives, and makes it clear exactly what they will need to maintain their redecision (see Tudor, 1997).

Redecision therapy is a beginning rather than an end. Although a redecision can be made quite rapidly – usually in a session or two – many patients need reinforcement over a longer time. Such support needs to be planned in, whether it is to come from the therapist, a social support group, or from elsewhere. We prefer that patients practice their redecision without additional immediate therapy, then return later if they encounter difficulties or have something new they wish to change. Many patients will experiment with playing their old games and re-experiencing familiar emotions, but at a reduced level of intensity. They then can either engage in self-harassing internal dialogue that they are 'failing' or congratulate themselves for recognizing what they are doing – and then do something else.

Neurophysiological underpinnings of redecision therapy

Recent neurophysiological research on memory suggests that memory is multimodal, i.e. it includes several different components: *factual* (what happened), *autobiographical* (a sense of self at that time and over time), *somatic* (body experience) *emotional* and *behavioral*. These different components are processed in different neural networks (Squire et al., 1992). The first two components – factual and autobiographical – have been called 'explicit'. They require that a person be paying attention to the event as it occurs. They are accessible to consciousness and are accompanied by a sense of self, time and that something is being retrieved. The others, exemplified by a person's repeating past trauma in behavior or having 'flashbacks' but being unable to relate this to the original trauma are termed 'implicit'. In implicit memory, there is an absence of a sense of self, time and that something is being retrieved.

Factual and autobiographical memory are necessary for script formation. They require good hippocampal and prefrontal cortical functioning. However, the hippocampus is easily affected and, in young children, may actually be destroyed by adrenal corticosteroids which are released in response to stressors. This makes it difficult to integrate traumas into one script.

There are several important implications of these findings for redecision therapy (Allen, 1999b). First, a coherent script is a manifestation of a blending of several neurological subsystems. The left hemisphere weaves a story from what it knows, but, without access to the right hemisphere, the story is incoherent. When the autobiographical, somatosensory and emotional processes of the right brain are drawn on, however, the left brain can make 'sense' of what happened and integrate these disparate kinds of memories into a coherent life narrative. This is a biological justification for using both verbal and experiential techniques in working with scripts, and therefore in doing redecision therapy. Secondly, it seems that the brain functions as an integrated and interconnected system of subsystems which, in turn, are distributed in a parallel fashion. It is self-organizing in the sense of developing firm simpler to more complex states and it is characterized by the fact that small changes in one of its microcomponents (e.g. perception) can lead to large changes in the total system (behavior). This seems to be what happens when a redecision is made. These characteristics beg for explanation in terms of non-linear dynamics of complex systems (Devoney, 1992; Holland, 1995; Boldrini et al., 1998).

Redecision work with children

Work with children differs from work with adults in a number of important ways. First, it is usually not the child who seeks treatment; rather, some adult who wants the child to change, and thus, in Prochaska et al.'s (1994) terms, the child is in the pre-contemplation stage. Secondly, other than for children born with some organic problem, children's psychological suffering is generally due to a lack of fit between the specific child and the people who parent her or him. The poor fit becomes the matrix in which the child receives the negative messages and expectations that interfere with the normal unfolding of development, and unfortunate decisions about self, others and life. Therefore, much work with children – and especially with younger ones – needs to be aimed at environmental changes that prevent pathogenic decisions. Thirdly, children may not yet have made a decision relevant to the issues that brought them to treatment, so can hardly be said to need (or be in a position) to make a redecision. Consequently, the therapist may need to help the child make a *decision*, not a redecision. Fourthly, most of the literature on redecision therapy has focused on work with adults and on decisions made between ages five and eight, during those stages of cognitive development described by Piaget as intuitive and concrete. However, it is during the first few years of life that children develop a sense of security, basic trust, hope, containment and effectiveness. At this stage, the child does not make verbal decisions as such, for the child does not yet have a command of language, but seems to form internal neural network 'models' of self and others. These serve anticipation and expectation (Allen, 1999a). It is on such non-verbal foundations, however, that later verbal decisions seem to be elaborated, as illustrated by the following example.

By the time she was 4 years old, Marie had suffered years of neglect and abuse. She raged, destroyed property, and was unable to attach to people. 'They don't really mean it' she would frequently say as she rejected anything good people tried to give her. She drew a picture of her mother as made of ice and holding a cup of poison that would 'make little children die forever'. Because of her uncontrolled behavior – biting, kicking, spitting, and urinating on people – she required frequent therapeutic holding. Over time, this seemed to provide some sort of non-verbal reassurance that we were safe, would not hurt her, would not let her hurt either us or herself, and would try, however awkwardly, to comfort her and meet her needs. A specific 'redecision' was never verbalized, but she did settle down and begin to trust and relate to others.

For traumatized young people, the combination of problems in auto-biographical memory (the kind of memory processing requiring well-functioning right hippocampal and prefrontal cortex of the brain) and the use of dissociation may make it difficult to reconstruct a clear account of their past. Alternatively, their memory schemata of victimization, betrayal, worthlessness and helplessness make them vulnerable to negative misinterpretations of present situations, to repeat the past with a new set of people, and prone to make decisions such as to be invulnerable robots, super achievers, extremely self-sufficient, emotionally unavailable or always in control.

Close attention to a patient's early internal models of self and others is also important in the treatment of adults. Although rarely discussed, they form a basic aspect of the Child–Parent transference and, for the fortunate, underlie the sense of containment, holding and hope that seem essential for successful psychotherapy (Allen and Allen, 1991b). A further (fifth) difference between therapeutic work with adults and children is that, after about three years of age, children have an ability to play out themes. Consequently, the therapist can then use toys, drawings, puppets, and stories in their treatment, as illustrated by a four-year-old girl who had been severely neglected by her drug-abusing mother.

Louise played out the story of a poor baby dinosaur who called again and again for her mother, but the mother dinosaur never came because she was always too busy and didn't like little girl dinosaurs anyway. As this play continued, it would become progressively more disorganized. However, the therapist introduced a kindly old lion who taught the baby dinosaur how to find other dinosaurs who liked baby girl dinosaurs and could nurture them. Finally, the baby dinosaur decided she could be comforted by a new dinosaur mother.

Similar work can be done through storytelling. The therapist can take a story the child produces and suggest alternative versions of it, versions containing alternative understandings and decisions. Sometimes the therapist can tell a relevant story, perhaps beginning with, 'I once knew a little boy who . . .' or 'When I was young, I had a friend who . . .' – and there are now a number of therapeutic story books on the market. In a similar manner, it is possible to help children introduce into their drawings or puppet play something new but relevant to their distress and pathogenic decision making.

Four therapeutic imperatives

Whether the therapist is doing actual redecision therapy or trying to prevent pathogenic decisions (or doing other types of therapy, for that matter), we identify four major therapeutic imperatives – Crossman's (1966) '3Ps' of permission, protection and potency, with the addition of a health or strength orientation.

Permission

Both children and adults need several different permissions to function well. While all these permissions seem important at all ages, the need for some becomes more important during certain periods and then recedes, to arise again later. In addition, the same permission needs to take different forms at different ages. For example, a very young child needs to feel close in the sense of feeling comfortable and secure with parenting figures. This involves frequent resonance between the child's and the parent's behavioral and emotional mental state. The school-age child needs permission to feel close to and that he belongs to a peer group, while the older adolescent needs to feel comfortable with peers in a way that has growing intimate and sexual overtones. Ultimately, each person needs to give her or himself the permissions s/he needs. The therapist, however, can foster a nurturing environment that will facilitate the process. The following is a list of permissions we (Allen and Allen, 1999) currently find useful:

> To be: to exist and to occupy space
> To be one's self (as regards age, class, color, gender, personality, race and sexuality, etc.)
> To live with zest
> To be appropriately close, to trust and to feel secure
> To allow oneself to be soothed and nurtured and to soothe and take care of oneself
> To be empathetically and mutually responsive with others
> To influence one's environment (to be important)

To experience one's own feelings across a wide range of emotions

To feel that one belongs (in and with family, friends, community, and culture)

To feel okay about one's self, others and the world (and not to make one's self OK by making others not OK or by discounting the contexts in which one lives)

To experiment and to change (and also to fail safely and to use that failure productively)

To think clearly and to solve problems across a wide variety of domains (to be sane)

To experience one's own experiences

To 'make it' in love and work

To make/find meaning

Protection

People often fear change because of what might have happened in the past had they made decisions different from the ones they did make. They may fear that a parenting figure might die or abandon them, that they might die themselves, or that the family (world) might disintegrate. Unfortunately, such possible catastrophes may not be entirely fanciful. Family members are sometimes very threatened, for example, when a member tells of sex abuse or some other secret. They may indeed reject the whistle-blower. The therapist, however, helps the patient explore possible negative consequences of change prior to entering the contract and then endeavors to create a nurturing environment where it is safe for the patient to be spontaneous, in order, in the terminology of transactional analysis, to facilitate the patient's energizing Free Child and Nurturant Parent ego states. To accomplish this, the redecision therapist frequently uses fun and humor and typically gives many strokes for being and for growth. In addition, the therapist helps patients plan ways to continue to keep themselves safe after they return to their homes and their work and to make sure that the redecision is not likely to harm others or harmfully violate the patient's social context.

Potency

Therapists have several types of power – power to help the patient give herself or himself needed permissions, power to offer protection during times of redecision and change, power to emphasize the patient's healthy responses, and power to assist the patient in defining or redefining reality. Despite the literature within TA on aspects of potency and power, this last aspect of therapeutic potency has, until recently, been relatively neglected (see Allen and Allen, 1991a, 1998b).

A strength orientation

Therapeutic theory and practice have been saturated with an emphasis on abnormalities, problems, deficits and disorders. Indeed, some therapists seem on a witch-hunt for abuse, bad parents and psychopathology. Unfortunately, such an approach limits the questions they can ask, the interpretations they make and the interventions they attempt. It is also possible to practice from a perspective that validates strengths and resources. Children make the best decisions they can, given the world as they know it. Then, as adults, the very fact that they are still alive seems to prove that their decisions, however dysfunctional, did have survival value. The redecision therapist needs to validate the helpful aspects of their early decisions, while stroking them for more healthy redecisions and for growth, and needs to draw on their strengths and resources.

In redecision therapy, patients are treated as competent to resolve their own problems, albeit with some therapeutic facilitation. When a patient says, 'I can't' the therapist typically suggests this be changed to 'I haven't' or 'I don't want to'. When a patient says 'Someone made me feel . . .' this is questioned in a way that highlights the fact that s/he had and have other options. When a patient tries to make a contract for someone else to change, this is changed to a goal that the patient can actually achieve her/himself.

Conclusion: Redecision therapy as a treatment modality

The redecision therapist takes charge of the therapeutic process by negotiating a clear contract and establishing a clear, measurable goal. This goal circumscribes exploration of the past and keeps the therapy focused. It should be noted, however, that although the collaboratively negotiated goal is influenced by the therapist, the *power* to make the decision is the patient's alone. Emotional re-experiencing in the present during gestalt work with key scenes provides a motivating force for the redecision, but this heightened emotion is then tempered by a cognitive framework (transactional analysis theory) and maintenance planning. Through the use of transactional analysis terminology, the patient has a way of understanding the experience and of restorying her or his life.

The basic process of redecision therapy is consonant with key tenets of bioethics. Emphasis on a therapeutic contract, patient strengths and the power of the patient to make a redecision all fit with the principle of patient autonomy. Permission and protection are bases for beneficence and non-maleficence, that is, for doing good and doing no harm (Bond, 1993; Allen and Allen, 1998a).

Redecision therapy shares with other constructivist therapies the belief that our stories determine the experiences to which we give attention, the meanings we give them, and thereby the ultimate direction of our lives. Unlike some social constructionists, however, the redecision therapist does not wait for a story to emerge in the therapeutic dialogue, or limit her/himself to suggesting a new story by highlighting exceptions and times when the patient did not follow accustomed patterns, nor does s/he depend primarily on the use of directives. Rather, the redecision therapist guides the therapeutic process but allows the patient to determine the content. Therefore, patients have a sense that they, not the therapist, have made the discovery and that they themselves have chosen their new life narratives. This gives them a heightened sense of power, direction and control over their lives. Then, patients are coached in setting up those contingencies that will support and reward their new behaviors and attitudes. Like problem-solving and solution-oriented therapies, redecision therapy emphasizes new behavior, but it does not put the emphasis on either the problem-solving or the solutions per se, but rather on the redecision patients make, and on their consequent real-life changes and action.

In summary, redecision therapy provides: expectations of and permission for change; a process framework for formulating a clear contracted goal, a redecision related to it, and later support for it in real life; protection during this process; a motivating emotional experience controlled by a cognitive framework; and a clear 'marker-event' that can later serve as an explanation for changes. It is brief because it utilizes an explicit contract that circumscribes the areas of the past to be explored; empowers the patient by utilizing language of self-responsibility and change; mobilizes and directs controlled emotion into action; and then helps the patient establish contingencies that will support her/his changes. Above all, it sets up a process wherein minimum input may leverage maximum non-linear change.

References

Allen, J.R. (1999a) 'Biology and transactional analysis: Integration of a neglected area', *Transactional Analysis Journal*, 29(4): 250–9.

Allen, J.R. (1999b) 'Of resilience, vulnerability – and a woman who never lived', *Child-Adolescent Psychiatric Clinics of North America*, 7(1): 53–71.

Allen, J.R. and Allen, B.A. (1991a) 'Towards a constructivist TA', in B. Loria (ed.). *The Stamford Papers: Selections from the 29th Annual ITAA Conference*. Madison, WI: Omnipress. pp. 1–22.

Allen, J.R. and Allen, B.A. (1991b) 'Transference: A critique, a typology, an alternative hypothesis and some proposals', *Transactional Analysis Journal*, 21(2): 77–91.

Allen, J.R. and Allen, B.A. (1997) 'Redecision therapy with children and adolescents', in C. Lennox (ed.), *Redecision Therapy: A Brief Action-oriented Method*. New York: Guilford. pp. 227–55.

Allen, J.R. and Allen, B.A. (1998a) 'Redecision therapy in the 21st century: Is it relevant?', *International Journal of Redecision Therapy*, 1(1): 7–21.

Allen, J.R. and Allen, B.A. (1998b) 'Redecision therapy: Through a narrative lens', in M. Hoyt (ed.), *The Handbook of Constructive Therapies*. San Francisco, CA: Jossey-Bass. pp. 31–46.

Allen J.R. and Allen, B.A. (1999) 'On receiving the 1998 Eric Berne memorial award for theory', *Transactional Analysis Journal*, 29(1): 11–13.

Boldrini, M., Placidi, G.P.A. and Marazziti, D. (1998) 'Application of chaos theories to psychiatry', *International Journal of Neuropsychiatric Medicine*, 3: 22–9.

Bond, T. (1993) *Standards and Ethics for Counselling in Action*. London: Sage.

Crossman, P. (1966) 'Permission and protection', *Transactional Analysis Bulletin*, 5(19): 152–4.

Devoney, R.L. (1992) *A First Course in Chaotic Dynamical Systems*. Reading, MA: Wesley Addison.

Goulding, R. and Goulding, M.M. (1978) *Power Is in the Patient*. San Francisco, CA: TA Press.

Goulding, M.M. and Goulding, R. (1979) *Changing Lives through Redecision Therapy*. New York: Brunner/Mazel.

Holland, J. (1995) *Hidden Order: How Adaptation Builds Complexity*. Reading, MA: Addison-Wesley.

Main, M. (1996) 'Introduction to special section on attachment and psychotherapy 2: Overview of the field of attachment', *Journal of Consulting and Clinical Psychology*, 64: 237–43.

Perls, F. (1969) *Gestalt Therapy Verbatim*. Lafayette, CA: Real People Press.

Prochaska, J.O., Norcross, J.C. and DiClemente, C.C. (1994) *Changing for Good*. New York: Morrow.

Squire, L.R., Knowlton, R. and Musen, G. (1992) 'The structure and organization of memory', *Journal of Cognitive Neurosciences*, 4: 232–43.

Tudor, K. (1997) 'Social contracts: Contracting for social change', in C. Sills (ed.), *Contracts in Counselling*. London: Sage. pp. 207–15.

Chapter 5

Cathexis: Brief Therapy in a Residential Setting

David Rawson

The genesis of transactional analysis (TA) was in Eric Berne's early work with severely disturbed patients in psychiatric hospitals. TA as an operational model for understanding and working with disordered thinking (contamination) and regressiveness (exclusion), both describes and sets out to cure some of the most basic and commonly encountered symptoms of serious mental illness. Part of Berne's legacy to TA was his demand for effectiveness and his assertion that we, as practitioners should be continually awake to the possibilities for a single-session cure (see Chapter 6), and that anything less would be a failure of professionalism. The theoretical and ethical implications that flow from these grounding principles suggest that TA has something special to offer to a professional – and financial – environment which more and more demands brief therapy with demonstrable effectiveness and value for money.

Whilst these demands are more widely known and appreciated in 'outpatient' therapeutic settings, they are no less – and perhaps even more – present in the context of the more expensive provision of residential therapy. It is brief therapy in the context of a residential therapeutic community, and one which draws on TA and its Cathexis School, which forms the focus of this chapter. Following a brief introduction to the work of Connect Therapeutic Community (formerly Trident Housing Association Therapeutic Community), the principles of Cathexis are introduced and discussed with reference to practice within Connect. In describing the theory of Cathexis and specifically its practice in Connect, the chapter also examines the extent to which this tradition within TA is useful as an approach to brief therapy.

Connect Therapeutic Community

The Cathexis school of TA was – and is – a specialist development of theory and practice for use primarily within a safe, managed, reactive environment or therapeutic community (TC). At Connect, TA provides the community with a direct and concise vocabulary with which to communicate to each other about psychological and emotional experiences in day to day living.

The community has been in existence since December 1987 and was the outcome of several years of discussion and planning by a small group of TA enthusiasts during the 1980s. In its first incarnation Jacqui Schiff (Schiff, 1969; Schiff et al., 1975; Schiff with Day, 1970) was involved in the early planning as a consultant. However, the community as it is now was the consequence of an important and fundamental disagreement and consequent parting of the ways between Schiff and its manager, Jenny Robinson. Although Jenny had (and still has) a wholehearted commitment to the original theory of discounting, passivity and symbiosis developed by Schiff and the early Cathexis group (Schiff and Schiff, 1971; Schiff et al., 1975), she found herself unable to subscribe to the working method then being used by Jacqui Schiff. Briefly this was as follows. Given that discounted, intense feelings, particularly fear, are usually at the core of psychotic problems, Schiff believed it necessary to replicate in here-and-now situations a corresponding intensity before useful communication could take place. While it is true that resolution of psychosis is often achieved by a cathartic reliving of early intensity, Jenny Robinson could not subscribe to methods which resulted in the *creation* of fear in the everyday context of community living. It was on this point that Jenny parted company from Jacqui Schiff. This was a methodology which other members of the TA community also found objectionable and unethical. The ethical, theoretical and political controversy of Cathexis reparenting is summarised by Jacobs (1994). Jacobs, I think wrongly, suggests that this theory is an ideology that supports and promotes totalism, thought reform and the misuse and abuse of power. He is, I believe, creating a conceptual confusion by mixing 'theory' and 'ideology' as interchangeable concepts and does not acknowledge our development in the past 12 years of a therapeutic community methodology within the agreed TA code of ethics. In the community we have developed the intrinsic elegance and ongoing usefulness of the core Cathexis theory on frame of reference, discounting, passivity and symbiosis (a lasting legacy for which we are still grateful to Jacqui Schiff and her colleagues) and have developed our own methodology and practice (see Rawson et al., 1994; Robinson, 1998, 1999).

The community client group is made up of people with severe disturbances most of whom have experience of psychiatric hospitals and about half of whom are to some degree institutionalised by their experiences. By 'institutionalised', I mean that in traditional psychiatric institutions, if a patient begins to behave in ways that are seen as socially appropriate rather than bizarre they are deemed to be doing well and consequently discharged. This does not, however, take account of the possibility that the patient is confused and vulnerable 'inside' and still in need of hospital care and protection. The only way for this person to maintain a place on the ward is to continue acting out. Here at Connect in the TC, residents change their behaviour significantly when they hear and believe that they will not be sent away if they take the risk of acting 'normally'. We find regularly that residents will cathect an Adult ego state at this point and engage responsibly in their own therapy process. Hence institutionalised, low expectations create a cycle of dependency and become a self-fulfilling prophecy.

We also work with an identifiable group of young people who have been raised to a greater or lesser degree in the statutory child-care system. This group presents us with particular problems, in that they have absorbed the care system itself as a Parent ego state, so that social services as an institution becomes a source of a confused set of values, reflecting the input of a sometimes large and disparate group of professionals. For example, a child of 12 was taken into care and reassured that she was safe in a particular home and began to settle down and make good progress on the basis that she trusted the care home manager. A case review was then held and a more senior manager decided that the placement was no longer appropriate, thus negating the assurances given by the manager and resulting in a move to a new and different home and foster care. In the course of eight years in local authority 'care' this process happened six times. Consequently, the incorporated Parent defined itself as a giver of double messages and one that would speak with authority but never actually be 'in charge'.

The community is structured in such a way that behavioural indicators of potentially serious and life-threatening discounts can be detected at a low level of energy and confronted. A rule-bound and time-structured environment can seem petty to the uninitiated. Nevertheless, residents contract in to keep the rules and protocols so that the community is able to react at an early stage to discounts of rules, and thus maintain a safe environment. For example, residents contract to be up, breakfasted and at their first meeting by a specific time. If they are consistently late they will be confronted by their peers. It is likely that the resident will feel sufficiently recognised (stroked) by this to move back down the potentially rising scale of passive behaviours (see below). If this is not immediately successful, a more formal community meeting is called so that recognition is at a higher level of energy than the acting out. Out of the high priority given to safety and security, the community as a whole is attuned to make a meeting such as this override any other considerations at the time. The expectation is that the group will stay together until such time as the resident in question feels calm and recognised.

Cathexis – theory and practice

In this section a number of key theoretical constructs are identified, defined and discussed and illustrated with examples drawn from the therapeutic work of Connect TC. More broadly, they are shown to be developed into a working methodology in the particular context of a therapeutic community. The concepts 'frame of reference', 'symbiosis', 'discounting' and 'passivity' are invaluable additions to the general canon of TA and are not only useful in residential settings with more disturbed clients but are also useful to any therapists using a brief therapy model and wanting to incorporate TA concepts and interventions into their work. For a more detailed account readers are recommended and referred to the seminal work in this tradition *The Cathexis Reader* (Schiff et al., 1975) as well as to Schiff with Day (1970) and Childs-Gowell (1979).

Contracting

The Cathexis school pays close attention to contracting. In our TC we work with people who are sometimes rational and sometimes not. Both clients and therapists make a contract knowing this to be the case. In their part of the contract the client knowingly and responsibly asks for care and protection during those times when they are likely in the future to be irrational or, in terms of structural ego state analysis, in an Excluding Child or Parent or Contaminated Adult. For their part, the therapist/s agree/s to this care on condition that the client will allow care and protection to be given. The power relations in this kind of therapeutic encounter are, by definition, uneven and potentially subject to abuse by the therapist. TA gives us a clear way of managing this potential through the use of skilful and supervised contracting. Steiner (1971) offers a coherent and now well-established model: 'therapeutic contracts should be regarded with as much respect as are legal contracts in courts of law, and the legal aspects of contracts are fully applicable to therapeutic contracts' (1971: 106). He goes on to state that, to be valid, a legal contract must contain and satisfy four basic requirements: mutual consent, consideration, competency and lawful object. This process binds both the client and the therapist and not, as with some other therapies, simply the client. It follows from this that for all these requirements to be met a valid contract must take place, in ego state terms, Adult–Adult. If this does not happen then contractual and ethical psychotherapy cannot proceed.

Frame of reference
A frame of reference is defined as 'the structure of associated responses which integrates the various ego states in response to specific stimuli' (Schiff et al., 1975: 49). It provides the individual with 'an overall perceptual, conceptual, affective, and action set which is used to define the self, other people, and the world both structurally and dynamically' (1975: 50). In my experience an individual will only conform to the shared 'action sets' of other people and the world, and their shared definitions of reality, to the extent that he perceives he can maintain his own integrity and survival. Since 'over-adaptation' is another key concept of cathexis work (see below) this is an important observation from practice. Also, from an operational point of view, it is only useful to adopt this concept in relation to specific issues and instances, for instance, we might discuss a person's frame of reference about children, about violence or about families, e.g. as in 'Let's see if we can make a shared understanding of the difference between your family's attitude to violence and mine'.

Symbiosis
Schiff et al. (1975) define symbiosis as occurring 'when two or more individuals behave as though between them they form a whole person. This relationship is characterized structurally by neither individual cathecting a full complement of ego states' (1975: 5). Figure 5.1 shows how a parent discounts its own Child ego state and models the discount. The child then mirrors the discount, attempts to take care of the parent's discounted feelings and, in doing so, leaves its own core infant needs unmet, a dynamic which could continue into the next generation.

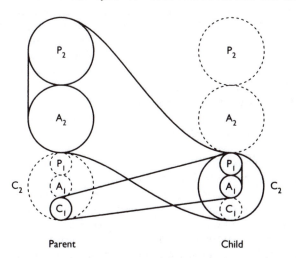

Parent   Child

Figure 5.1 *First and second order structural symbiosis*

In seriously disturbed clients there is often an attempt by a pathologically Excluding Child to recreate an unresolved and unhealthy dependency in a therapeutic relationship. Schiff et al. (1975) suggest that 'the therapist must decide whether the contract goal would be most effectively reached by: (1) accepting the symbiosis and working with it, (2) confronting it, (3) or interrupting it by shifting the problem back to the patient' (1975: 10). In practice, all three options are important and should be available interchangeably as therapy develops. In brief therapy it is useful to be able to recognise invitations into symbiosis because the third option of interruption should be the only one available. The following is a simple invitation sequence:

Client: I think I need a positive stroke.
Therapist: Yes, I think you are very brave for asking.

The therapist is here responding to a question that has not been asked and is therefore accepting an invitation into symbiosis. Transactions are Child–Parent and Parent–Child.

Alternatively:

Client: I think I need a positive stroke.
Therapist: Do you?
Client: Yes, will you do that for me?
Therapist: Yes, I think you are very brave for asking.

The therapist is here declining the invitation into symbiosis and in turn inviting Adult–Adult transacting: the initial Child–Parent transaction is crossed Adult–Adult.

As a working model symbiosis is a very different way of thinking about transference and countertransference phenomena and as such is primarily about long-term therapeutic relationships. A therapist working in the context of a brief therapy contract may usefully develop skills in this area which will allow the safe containment of therapy to facilitate contracts about specific issues. This demands an awareness on the therapist's part of their own unconscious invitations into symbiotic forms of relating. Personal therapy and supervision is thus crucial and integral to the therapist.

Discounting and passive behaviours
I discuss these two concepts together because, as the external behavioural manifestations of internal discounts, passive behaviours are demonstrably integral to discounting theory. Discounting is the means by which an individual maintains a frame of reference. There is a failure to perceive an aspect of reality that does not conform with a particular frame of reference. A conscious mind refuses to admit any failure to perceive and puts in its place a series of rationalisations.

Such false connections then govern the constitution of reality. For instance, if my frame of reference about families is such that 'We are always there for each other and never say no. We never discuss family outside the family and anyone who does deserves to be rejected' then I cannot admit the possibility that there are helpful resources outside the family or that it might be possible to create personal boundaries around privacy within my family.

Discounting (of information) is an internal process and not externally observable. Passive behaviours are the outward behavioural manifestations of discounting and are described as follows (Schiff et al., 1975):

- *Doing nothing* – a non-response to stimuli, problems or options, the ignoring of the existence of a problem.
- *Over-adaptation* – non-identification with one's own goals. Over-adapted people seem obliging, so they get lots of reinforcement from others. This is the most difficult passive behaviour to identify, but is also the most amenable to treatment. This is because people who over-adapt are attuned to accepting objective information from others so that they can reinforce their over-adapting. Care is needed, therefore, in the information that is communicated, for instance, the permission 'You can think' inviting the cathecting of an Adult ego state (rather than a compliant Adapted Child).
- *Agitation* – repetitive, non-goal directed activity, e.g. tapping, obsessing, pacing, etc. are often ways of charging up energy in readiness for impending incapacitation or violence.
- *Incapacitation or violence* – the discharge, one way or another, of energy built up through passivity.

These behaviours represent a process through which an individual will move. Early intervention in the process prevents escalation to violence, and reversion back to the over-adapting stage can be achieved as a method of maintaining safety. In my experience clients are often receptive to new information and skills after an escalation through this process and then de-escalation back down to over-adaptation. For example, during a group therapy session a resident began to agitate by tapping his foot vigorously during someone else's work. The therapist asked the working client to wait and turned to the foot tapper saying 'I find that your foot tapping is distracting attention from the work in hand. Will you stop, please?' At this, the person tapping began to agitate even more and to look sullen and withdrawn. By now the whole group was focused on the foot tapper. The response generally in the group was anger and irritation at the group's attention being hijacked in this way. The therapist then switched ego states from Adult to a clearly defined and authoritative Parent and said 'It may be that you don't understand what is happening now, but if you will allow the group to continue without further interruption we will come back to you and make time to figure out what it is that you need, so calm down' (a complimentary, Parent–Child transaction to a regressive, Excluding Child). There was an uncomfortable moment when no-one was sure if the foot tapper would continue to escalate; he then shifted his sitting position and stopped agitating. Later on in the group he was receptive to an interpretation of the situation which helped him to understand that he could gain some needed attention by asking directly and positively to work in the group rather than by acting out for negative attention.

Power, philosophy and ethics

When I began work 11 years ago in a therapeutic community based on TA philosophy and practice, I was unaware that the Cathexis school of TA had a controversial history (see above). Since then, it has sometimes felt that we have been dogged by the ghosts of past events that have no direct connection with us: as if we (Cathexis and Connect) are the subject of contaminated thinking, emotion and behaviour.

From my reading of the history and my present participation in a therapeutic environment, the basic ethical dispute appears to be about the use, misuse and abuse of power. It is indisputable that people with serious psychopathology are particularly vulnerable in any therapeutic encounter. Schiff et al. (1975) recognised the exchange of power in the therapeutic relationship and, indeed, commented on this in the discussion of their treatment philosophy:

> our policy is to accept the patients' investment of power (transference) to the extent that we believe it is possible to utilize that power for their welfare. Generally our philosophy that the patients know what they need is considered relevant. If the power is useful in developing capacity for relating and trusting and accepting nurturing, that can certainly be considered desirable . . . Ultimately, of course, the power is restored to the patients (1975: 102).

Power and power relationships are not phenomena the responsible therapist can or should avoid or ignore – this, in itself, would be a discount. For this reason the professional and ethical conduct of the therapeutic process, especially in a setting such as ours, must at all times be subject to close supervision, in our case:

Internally   – from members of the TC
             – through supervision
Externally   – through supervision
             – through professional associations e.g. the Institute of Transactional Analysis

   – through independent monitoring i.e. Social Services
Department and Inspectorate Division

Jacobs (1998) has offered some useful reflections on the role of
'bystanding' in situations where people will tend to do nothing even
when they know that abuse is taking place. Any therapeutic community must be awake to these possibilities and hold as a central value the
confrontation of this type of passivity. The questions raised by Jacobs
and others are, for me, essentially about ethics and anyone seriously
interested in Cathexis theory and practice as an addition to their therapeutic tool kit would be well-advised to take account of the ongoing
discussion about their ethical basis. In my own view, no theory can be
intrinsically unethical; how it is utilised as methodology can be.

Connect has come a long way from the early Cathexis 'school' of
TA, its early communities and regressive techniques. We have learned
much from the successes as well as the failures of that early work, not
least the requirement for us to be unimpeachable in our management,
supervision and monitoring of good, ethical practice.

Connect Therapeutic Community – the context for brief therapy

The residential setting is designed specifically for use with long-term
clients and the growth of healing relationships. Along with relationship development comes the re-ordering of disturbed patterns of
attachment which are very often core problems for the mentally ill.
However, within the overall therapy contract with the community, residents can make a brief therapy contract to tackle specific issues with
a particular therapist. The kinds of issues here would be, for example,
a behavioural problem that might be sabotaging her/his chances of
making satisfying, secure relationships. Residents often arrive with an
active, negative stroke economy. This can be behaviourally modified,
for instance, in brief therapy to work with a specific (say) provocative
behaviour such as unconscious threatening and a contract to meet
the need temporarily for negative strokes in a way that is in awareness
and not destructive of needed relationships.

We create a structured and rule-bound (as in bounded) environment into which both residents and staff contract. It is therefore
essential that residents are initially willing to cathect enough coherent
Adult energy to make a realistic contract. The community as a whole
contracts into maintaining the structure of rules and practices by confronting any rule breaking as a discount, thus creating a reactive (not
passive) environment. Our experience has been that most 'acting out'
or 'attention seeking' arises from a need for recognition and the discounting of this need. Where residents can achieve needed recognition

from low-level acting out (i.e. rule breaking) they will tend not to escalate into high-level (dangerous) acting-out in the drive for necessary recognition. For instance, the daily domestic life of the community is organised and run by the residents' peer group. They allocate jobs for themselves in a structured and predictable way and make commitments about what they will do during a particular day. If a job, say, shopping or vacuuming is not done or not done properly this will be noticed and confronted as a discount. It makes sense also to see the discount as a form of unconscious communication, or request, to have something noticed or recognised by the community. It is crucial that all the residents contract in to an agreement to interpret rule breaking or 'forgetting' as discounting. Also it is axiomatic that anyone contracting into this protective framework will be competent to do simple daily tasks in an agreed way. Residents are usually very quick to understand that low level confrontations about day to day living and expectations, although uncomfortable and irritating, offer a high degree of protection from their propensity to discount at life-threatening levels.

A central feature of passivity theory is the behavioural description of a hierarchy of 'acting out' with over-adaptation at its core (see above). Although over-adaptation is in itself a pathology, it is also a psychological stance that by definition lends itself to the 'learning' of new information. We would tend to encourage over-adaptation in awareness as a means of maintaining safety and in the knowledge that we are talking about social adaptation and not profound psychological adaptation. In this case, the 'pathology' can be a useful, learned skill.

The maintenance of a safe, reactive environment is always seen as our first and most important task, and takes precedence over any other concerns in the day-to-day life of the community. After this comes the development of therapeutic alliances and the drive for therapeutic change. The early Cathexis reparenting model arose from intensive work using a family environment as the healing context. A significant development both for Cathexis theory and its practice is the development of Connect into a more clearly defined community model as the context for growth and change. We have, nevertheless, retained our emphasis on long-term relationship contracts (parent or guardian) as the basis for 'holding' residents (metaphorically and literally) through the difficulties and turbulence of impasse work. This presents us with problems on several fronts. Although our experiences support the view that cure of serious pathology is most often achieved when residents make secure attachments to senior staff members (Whiteley, 1994), most potential residents are not able to make such an attachment in the early stages of therapy. In fact some are so unsettled by the realisation of this prospect that they leave before any meaning-ful work can be done. Our way of managing this problem is to make short-term (brief therapy) contracts as a pre-condition of any further long-term relationship work. Thus, any new entrant to the community may make a contract for, say, two months with the goal, for instance, of improving habits of self-care and developing clearer, Adult think-ing. Residents are often institutionalised from long stays in hospital so these are very desirable goals in themselves.

This early contract is defined as brief therapy in itself and may or may not lead to a longer term contract. It has three clear benefits:

- *Theoretical* – that something short of 'full' 'cure' is worthwhile, i.e. social control and symptomatic relief (Berne, 1975a, 1975b).
- *Practical–Personal* – that a resident leaving after a short-term con-tract will do so with a sense of achievement, even although they may still have serious problems living outside an institutional envi-ronment.
- *Practical–Community* – that the community as a whole is not left with a sense of failure when people choose not to carry on into long-term work.

The importance of this was recognised after experiences in which both residents and staff developed strong, emotional bonds with new resi-dents, which could then become painfully anti-therapeutic when experienced as 'trapping' rather than healing. The potential for entrap-ment lay in an unspoken and unquestioned belief that new residents should stay on and become fully 'well' or 'cured'.

A further problem created by our emphasis on long-term relation-ship work was the resistance in the business environment of funders. In effect, as a therapeutic community, Connect would be asking for open-ended financial commitments from statutory services, in an eco-nomic environment that was/is increasingly nervous about long-term financial commitment of any description. Our move to initial brief therapy contracts had the effect of making contracts easier to negoti-ate and less intimidating to purchasers. Experience has proved that when new residents are clearly benefiting from brief therapy, 'roll-over' extensions of funding have been made available. TA principles of OKness in these discussions are invaluable. It has become axiomatic that we see ourselves as working in partnership with medical and social service professionals: the potential for destructive games in this area is clear – new residents are often adept at versions of 'Let's You and Him Fight'.

Below is an example of a 'guest' contract; a guest is defined as anyone engaged in brief therapy and not (yet) a full member of the community. Clauses one to six are the same for every contract and is/are essentially about how people can live together in comfort. In practice everyone makes this contract with everyone else. Clause seven is specific to the individual and three examples are given of this clause. We develop these contracts at an early stage in detail and in writing because most residents have difficulties with thinking and memory, and find security and a sense of belonging with this concrete form.

All of the statements in the 'guest' contract are examples of strategies to allow potential long-term residents the opportunity of experiencing communal life without making a full commitment. They may, in some cases, take several months to arrive at a point where such a contract is possible and meaningful. The community culture is such that it is open and willing to tolerate quite high levels of uncertainty with regard to guests, and its values around hospitality are strongly held. It is also true, however, that staff need to keep a clear awareness of the limits to this tolerance and of the possibility that therapeutic boundaries are being transgressed more often than is healthy for the community as a whole. One advantage of using community consensus as a measure of a new residents' progress in this way is that power does not rest with any single individual but democratically with the community as a whole (see Rapoport, 1960) – whilst we never vote I think our continual search for consensus is democratic in spirit.

Firstly, there are two other categories of our therapeutic work, which can be described as brief therapy, and are also contingent on the existence of a 'holding', reactive environment. Whilst, essentially, they provide specialist therapy and supervision for fellow therapists, they are wholly dependent on the willingness of long-term residents to extend their support and hard-won personal resources.

Brief therapy is available for psychotherapists in training who desire a first-hand experience of Cathexis methods. It is not uncommon for students in the process of training and development to discover a depth of difficulty in their own psychological and emotional development for which they are unprepared. Where conventional supervision and personal therapy are not working, a short spell as a guest of the Community can be of considerable use both in terms of personal problem-solving, and in the development, through experience, of more effective personal resources in working through their problems and those of their clients. The processes of group dynamics and of transference and countertransference are intensified and magnified in a small community, and provide a valuable opportunity to experience and understand the depth of script and game analysis and their potency in practice.

Secondly, therapists in private practice often encounter more serious pathology in their clients than was originally diagnosed. For instance, splitting and dissociation can occur in clients who had originally

CONNECT THERAPEUTIC COMMUNITY
CONTRACT
For One Month from _____ (Date) to _____ (Date)
To be reviewed on _____ (Date)
_____(Name)

1. I will accept and keep the rules.
2. I will behave considerately towards members and other guests.
3. I will confront and accept confrontation from a caring position on issues that concern safety and comfort, I will also accept confrontation that relates to my contract and will respond appropriately.
4. I will keep confidentiality. I will not talk about the problems or personal history of any members or guests with anyone who is outside the boundary of the Therapeutic Community.
5. I will participate in the life and work of the Community.
6. I will do the therapeutic work and make the behavioural changes necessary to fulfil my therapy contract.
7. (a)   I will continue to work on developing my capacity to speak in groups. I will ask for support when I need to do this.

    (b)   I will do check-ins twice a day and will take responsibility for this. I will use these to develop my capacity to articulate my feelings.

    (c)   I will use my individual therapy sessions to begin to verbalise my past experiences which I have difficulties in talking about.

OR

7. (a)   I will use this four week residential period to learn about what I might achieve for myself through therapy.

    (b)   I will seek staff advice about and maintain healthy eating habits in my stay at the community.

    (c)   I will follow the physical exercise regime devised by my key worker.

OR

7. I need support and a safe space to close down my escape hatch options because I want to learn to live with people in a healthy way.

    I often get into a place where, if I think I have nothing to lose, or I have gone too far, I can decide that nothing and nobody matters and I can do anything regardless of the harm I might do. Therefore:

    (a)   I will make a congruent decision to close down my option of threat and violence, whether or not I believe I have gone too far.

    (b)   I will not go crazy.

    (c)   I make my non-contract[1] as follows:-

    If a member of staff says, in any form, that I am breaking my contract, I will state my non-contract simply and clearly.

    'My contract is to ask people if they are willing to hold on for ten minutes while I go out of the situation to calm down and then come back to re-engage in an appropriate manner. May I do this?'

seemed able to undergo a conventional therapy. Exclusion (or spontaneous regression) can also happen in private practice where resources are too limited to manage these phenomena safely. In some cases, the Community may take on a supportive role for both therapist and client on a time-limited basis or a specific piece of work may be contracted. For instance, an excluding Child ego state might be encountered in a therapy process for which both therapist and client are unprepared and ill-equipped. This kind of experience is an everyday occurrence in a therapeutic community, and this fact alone can be enough to provide the safety and confidence to allow therapeutic progress, where premature termination and abandonment might otherwise be the only other option.

Conclusion

It is clear that the Cathexis approach to therapy is essentially about the forming and maintenance of long-term relationships: secure attachments, long-term commitments and learning to hold and make sense of ourselves in relation to others. Nevertheless, in my experience, long-term relationship therapy and brief therapy are complementary and interdependent in our way of working. A practical understanding of how to operate as a therapist using Cathexis methods is, I believe, useful, indeed essential, to a practitioner making brief therapy contracts. The discipline needed from a psychotherapist in regard to maintaining limits and boundaries, is aided by the TA emphasis on contracting, and further supported by a working knowledge of Cathexis concepts. In particular an understanding of symbiosis and techniques for working with unconscious invitations into symbiosis are invaluable for maintaining Adult–Adult relationships. This, in turn, is a pre-condition for the safe maintenance of contractual boundaries in brief therapy.

Notes

1 When contracts are broken it is often in a highly charged and emotive situation, and residents occasionally can end up outside of the safe environment of the community as a consequence. It then becomes difficult to negotiate a way back when the situation is calmer from outside of the physical boundaries of the community. To manage this type of event we have developed a process whereby guests and members of the community can negotiate a personalised 'non-contract' to stay within the environs of the community while they work out a way to remake a therapy contract and reconstruct therapeutic boundaries (Kouwenhoven, 1984).

References

Berne, E. (1975a) *Transactional Analysis in Psychotherapy*. London: Souvenir Press. (Original work published 1961.)

Berne, E. (1975b) *What Do You Say After You Say Hello?* Harmondsworth: Penguin. (Original work published 1972.)

Childs-Gowell, E. (1979) *Reparenting Schizophrenics: The Cathexis Experience*. North Quincy, MA: The Christopher Publishing House.

Jacobs, A. (1994) 'Theory as ideology: Reparenting and thought reform', *Transactional Analysis Journal*, 24(1): 39–55.

Jacobs, A. (1998) *Influence, power and authority*. Keynote speech, ITA Conference, Guildford, Surrey, April.

Kouwenhoven. M. (1984) 'Problem-solving sanctions', in E. Stern (ed.), *TA: The State of the Art*. Dordrecht: Foris Publications. pp. 143–64.

Rapoport, R.N. (1960) *Community as Doctor*. London: Tavistock.

Rawson, D., Buddendiek, H. and Haigh, R. (1994) 'Trident Housing Association Therapeutic (THAT) Community. Community study: Basic principles and values', *Therapeutic Communities*, 15(3): 193–207.

Robinson, J. (1998) 'Reparenting in a therapeutic community', *Transactional Analysis Journal*, 28(1): 88–94.

Robinson, J. (1999) 'Groups in residential settings', in K. Tudor, *Group Counselling*. London: Sage. pp. 145–66.

Schiff, A.W. and Schiff, J.L. (1971) 'Passivity', *Transactional Analysis Journal*, 1(1): 71–8.

Schiff, J.L. (1969) 'Reparenting schizophrenics', *Transactional Analysis Bulletin*, 8(31), 47–63.

Schiff, J.L. with Day, B. (1970) *All My Children*. New York: Evans & Co.

Schiff, J.L., Schiff, A.W., Mellor, K., Schiff, E., Schiff, S., Richman, D., Fishman, J., Wolz, L., Fishman, C. and Momb, D. (1975) *Cathexis Reader: Transactional Analysis Treatment of Psychosis*. New York: Harper & Row.

Steiner, C. (1971) *Games Alcoholics Play*. New York: Grove Press.

Whiteley, S. (1994) '18th S.H. Foulkes annual lecture', *Group Analysis*, 27: 359–87.

Chapter 6

Integrating Views of TA Brief Therapy

Keith Tudor and Mark Widdowson

Transactional analysis can be a multi-faceted system of psychotherapy. Berne's emphasis on the interactional aspect of communication is reflected in the name *transactional* analysis. He saw it as an extension to the in-depth emphasis of psychoanalysis with its singular focus on intrapsychic dynamics. Transactional analysis as a theory of psychotherapy, however, integrates intrapsychic dynamics with interpersonal behaviours in an innovative reactive manner within a humanistic/existential framework of values. (Clarkson, 1992: 1)

Clarkson goes on to suggest that, by virtue of representing the psychoanalytic, behavioural and humanistic traditions, TA is *in itself* integrative. TA's three 'schools' – the Classical, the Redecision and the Cathexis Schools – are still influential and, indeed, it is part of the certifying examination requirements that candidates must demonstrate a knowledge of all three traditions within TA. Furthermore, the Redecision School itself represents an integrative approach to TA, incorporating as it does gestalt and cognitive-behavioural therapies.

Following on from the previous chapters which examine the influences of all three 'schools' of TA and their respective contributions to the theory and practice of brief therapy, this chapter explores the *zeitgeist* of integration – the adding together or combining of parts of different theories – which currently preoccupies much of the therapeutic world and which is equally present within TA. Beginning with a case study of TA therapy with a young man, 'Martin', conducted by one of the authors (MW) over sixteen sessions, this chapter reflects on the integrative – or *integrating* – nature of TA with reference to the case study. It concludes with discussions concerning constructivism as an integrating philosophy for TA therapeutic practice and the importance of personal integration for the TA practitioner.

Case study – Martin

The context
This particular therapeutic contract is set in the context of a youth work organisation which runs a drop-in centre. The therapist (MW) is

contracted and paid by the organisation to be present at drop-in sessions as a point of first contact and to provide therapy with clients who then request it. The client group are all between 16 and 25, are mostly unemployed or in low paid work, and are mostly men with the few women mostly single parents. All the men have been violent or destructive and the majority have used alcohol and/or drugs. In working with this client group and with this particular client, the therapist draws on his previous experience as a mental health worker and a social rehabilitation approach to working with psychiatric patients in the community. Prior to training as a counsellor and a psychotherapist, MW qualified as a shiatsu practitioner and brings to his therapeutic work an awareness of bodywork. With this particular client the therapy contract was limited to a maximum of 20 sessions due to limitations of funding.

Presenting issues

Martin was referred through an organisation that were funding his therapy. Prior to our first meeting I had seen him in the building, being calmed down by a youth worker. He was pacing and shouting about an argument he had just had and seemed extremely agitated. Martin was (is) in his early twenties, unemployed, single, socially isolated and had only a rudimentary education. His initial presentation for his first appointment was placating and apologetic: 'I'm sorry to take up your time' was his opening gambit. He continued by describing his situation as he saw it, together with comments the youth worker had made. There was little emotional content to his descriptions of his situation. Any emotion was either noticeably flattened or inappropriate. The emotion he did show freely was anger. He described how he was having regular violent outbursts, which would manifest in picking arguments, punching walls, trashing rooms, punching through windows or in otherwise extreme physical agitation. On several occasions he had mutilated himself, cutting his arms, chest and thighs with a razor blade. He also bit his fingernails badly, often until they bled. Many of his fingers looked sore and infected. He was extremely keen to establish that I had taken him seriously and that he was serious about wanting to change as 'I don't like getting mad. It's not good. Please help me.' He reported feeling 'really down and depressed' most of the time. Further questioning revealed loss of appetite, apathy and insomnia, exacerbated by his occasional use of amphetamines. All his relationships were markedly strained, with the exception of one friend: 'We disagree, but we never argue.' He had recently begun having panic attacks in supermarkets and had not been to any for a month: 'I've been buying bits from the corner shop, but it's so expensive and I'm out of loads of stuff.' He also disclosed feeling very uncomfortable about his sexuality.

He had recently come out as gay and wanted to 'feel OK about it. I mean, it's not something I can change, is it?' As Martin was unemployed, he was financially in a bad way. He wanted a job desperately but felt lacking in confidence to go through with the application procedure. His poor performance at school and lack of qualifications contributed to his lack of self-esteem. 'I'm just thick' he said on more than one occasion. His description of his childhood was very bleak: 'We were always fed but we never got no attention, except when we'd done wrong. Even then they [his parents] didn't seem to be bothered. And I never got praised for anything, not once.' Both parents were alcoholics and a grandparent he was close with was manic-depressive and had committed suicide several years before. Martin was still extremely upset about this and said 'I want to be over it now.'

Diagnosis and initial contract
Martin was extremely bound up in passivity, and his overadaptation was clear from his placating stance and was reflected in heavy use of a 'Please' driver. This contrasted with his flattened affect and 'Be Strong' driver. These two drivers would alternate in rapid succession, indicating a bipolar structure. His manic-depressive grandparent indicated that such bipolar structure would at least be part of his Parent ego state. His anger racket was clearly a passive behaviour and his inappropriate emotions and lack of emotional vocabulary indicated the need to learn emotional literacy. His feeling down, apathetic, poor appetite and insomnia ('I'm lucky if I get two hours sleep a night') indicated mood disorder. I checked out my diagnosis in supervision, two days after our initial meeting, and confirmed the following multi-axial diagnosis using *DSM-IV* criteria (American Psychiatric Association, 1994):

Axis I – 301.13 Cyclothymic disorder
– 300.29 Specific phobia – situational type
Axis II – No diagnosis
Axis III – Asthma
Axis IV – Inadequate social support, educational problems, unemployment, poverty, family problems
Axis V – Global Assessment of Functioning score: 54 (on initial contact)

His asthma, high level of agitation, physical acting-out and noticeable muscular tension indicated high need for what I refer to as 'somatic decontamination'.

First session
Our first session was spent mostly compiling information and establishing a working alliance. Due to the time-limited nature of our work,

the early establishment of trust and a good alliance in our therapeutic relationship was essential. I used gentle confrontations to check defended areas of script (which were supported by his use of redefining and discounting), and to check his level of Adult functioning in preparation for decontamination and contracting. At the end of our session I taught him a deep breathing exercise and instructed him in two relaxation techniques. I advised him to practice these at least once daily until our next appointment.

Second session
He arrived early for his session and sat in the coffee bar at the Centre reading for a while. He appeared cheerful and took great delight in telling me that he had done his relaxation exercises. The way he responded confirmed my belief in his susceptibility to overadaptation. This had clearly been functional as he reported feeling 'less worked up – it's helped me to chill out a bit when I'm getting mad'. We undertook a racket analysis and talked about escape hatches which he decided to close – for six weeks. We returned to his breathing exercises several times during the session, after or during which I gave him mints to create a kinaesthetic anchor and a tool for getting grounded. I gave him the rest of the packet of mints when he left and advised him to have one when doing his breathing exercises. I explained how he could use mints then to calm himself down by accessing this associated relaxation response.

ANALYSIS   I had decided to use his overadaptation positively as I remembered from my training that one way to facilitate movement out of agitation was through stroking into overadaptation and then stroking autonomous displays. Positive overadaptation would allow sufficient protection by appeasing Parent ego states as he tried out new behaviours and his Adult became increasingly decontaminated. Furthermore, any stroking would be a new experience for Martin, and checks could be made on his stroke filters during sessions which could be immediately addressed. The relaxation and association encouraged grounding and somatic decontamination thus beginning the process of destabilising his racket system. At this stage, we were building our therapeutic alliance and I was collecting information and beginning interventions to decontaminate and invite movement out of racket. At this stage I was using the discount matrix (Mellor and Sigmund, 1975; Schiff et al., 1975) to determine *how* I was decontaminating, in this case inviting the client to move the T_3 to the T_4 diagonal: essentially, from recognising the significance of his problems to the significance of options (see Table 1.1, p. 37).

Third session
We began the session by reviewing his contract and creating behavioural markers. Throughout, I used the discount matrix and we generated behavioural contracts and goals for the next month. We explored his 'Please' system and his way of squashing his own feelings with specific decontamination of script beliefs about self and passive behaviours. I introduced the idea of injunctions and used the 'drowning man' diagram (Lee, 1988) to illustrate his active injunctions. At the end of the session I took an index card and reworded his injunctions into positive statements of rights: 'I have the right to exist, to be me, to be important, to feel and think, etc.' I advised him to use this 'Bill of rights' as an affirmation several times a day (Widdowson, 2000).

ANALYSIS   This session marks increasing decontamination, moving from T_4 to T_5 on the discount matrix, i.e. from the significance of options to Martin's ability to solve his problems and, on occasions, through to T_6 and out of discounting altogether – and, indeed, to *accounting* for himself and his life. The (Type I) impasse, in response to the 'Please' driver was 'Don't Exist' vs. 'I have the right to exist'. The use of affirmations will initiate the creation of an internal Nurturing Parent ego state (from Integrated Adult) and prepare the client for deconfusion, addressing developmental needs and then towards redecision.

Fourth session
The session began with Martin talking about his rackety fantasies. I proceeded with reality-testing decontamination work, aimed at destabilising the middle column on the racket system (Erskine and Zalcman, 1979) i.e. observable behaviours – for example, Martin's agitation; reported internal experiences, e.g. getting angry; and fantasies, e.g. being rejected. This work led to situational planning and behavioural contracting which, in turn, further destabilises the racket system. The work proceeded with further grounding exercises and somatic decontamination. In addition to his use of mints and breathing exercises we used stretching exercises to identify and release areas of bodily tension, notably shoulders, jaw and tightness in his chest. Following this Martin made a series of behavioural contracts involving agreeing to take warm baths, using body lotion and eating nourishing food to install self-soothing and nurturing behaviours, and to reinforce movement out of script with self-stroking. Near the end of the session, Martin revealed he had been sexually abused as a small child by a relative. Due to the fact that we had only 15 minutes of the session left, he told me only brief details and factual content. I avoided eliciting further material due to issues of protection.

ANALYSIS   I was continuing decontamination work with Martin and was moving onto the somatic level which often, as in this case, spontaneously leads, via establishing an internal Nurturing Parent, into deconfusion work (see Figure 6.1).

Fifth session
After a very brief 'check in' Martin began to talk about his sexual abuse. His confusion was evident and he clearly related this to aspects of his script: 'When Mum found out, she went mad and we weren't allowed to see him anymore. I thought it was 'cos I'd been bad or

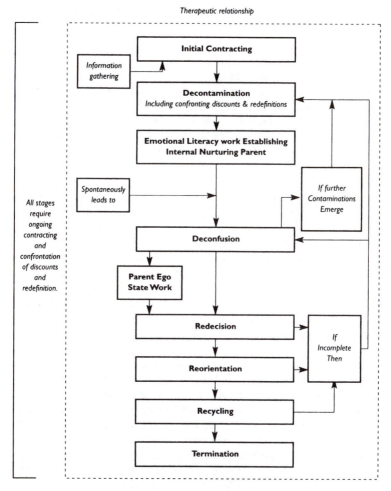

Figure 6.1 *Treatment planning sequence flowchart*

something. My little sister were right upset and she blamed me. You see, even when it were 'appening it didn't feel right. Ever since then I've always felt *I* was bad'. He spoke at length and his feelings were appropriate, congruent and clearly articulated. Following this deconfusion work an area of contamination emerged: he believed the abuse was the cause of his sexuality. I provided him with information about sexual abuse and explained that it was common for survivors of abuse to experience this sort of redefining – both internally (e.g. feeling 'bad') and externally i.e. self-blame and victimhood, reinforced by an often misinformed and discounting societal Parent. The session finished with some two-chair work and 'spot reparenting' (Osnes, 1974) by which we each nurtured 'little Martin' and gave him appropriate parenting including information. I advised Martin to write a letter from him as a grown up to him as a child.

ANALYSIS   In terms of treatment planning we were rapidly cycling through decontamination and deconfusion. Through two-chair work Martin was continuing to develop an internal Nurturing Parent and beginning emotional literacy work. Letter writing is a specialised form of self-reparenting, deconfusion work and facilitates emotional literacy (Parkes, 1990; Retief and Conroy, 1997).

Sixth session
Martin arrived looking very different. He had had a haircut and was wearing new clothes. His posture was more relaxed and his movements freer. He produced a list he had made as he had noticed a number of situations where he was getting into his racket and he had generated nurturing options for himself rather than agitation or violence. We discussed assertiveness briefly and went into early scene work during which Martin explored his 'angry and violent' scripting. We ended the session with more nurturing contracts, and I continued to set further written assignments in line with procedure for working with survivors of abuse.

ANALYSIS   It appeared that Martin had made a redecision of the Type I impasse (see third session, p. 118 above), living out his right to exist, this having been made, as many if not most redecisions do, outside the 'therapeutic hour' (see Woollams and Brown, 1978 on change factors in redecision). He was achieving a level of social control and symptomatic relief (Berne, 1975). He was clearly increasing his level of emotional literacy and his list showed a movement out of overadaptation and into the creation of autonomous options. Clearly the decontamination is helping his cognitive abilities.

Seventh session

During this session Martin wanted to focus on his panic attacks. After I had gathered some information about these and following relaxation exercises I suggested a sessional contract of doing some 'retail therapy' (i.e. shopping) to which he agreed. We spent the next 30 minutes going round the supermarket opposite the Centre. Outside the supermarket we had the following exchange:

> *Therapist (T):* How are you feeling?
> *Client (C):* Tense, a bit scared.
> *T:* You're OK. You're safe. Have you decided what you need to buy?
> *C:* Yeah, but there's too much to carry.
> *T:* OK, so you're going to have to prioritise, decide what's most important.
> *[Client goes through a list.]*
> *T:* Ready?
> *C:* Yeah.
> *T:* Breathe. Let's go for it.

Martin was fine for a while and then began to look distressed after a few minutes. I noticed this and noted his passivity in not telling me. I decided to intervene:

> *T:* What's the matter?
> *C:* That man thinks I've pinched something.
> *T:* What's the reality?
> *C:* He's looking at me; he thinks I'm a thief. He's looking at me funny.
> *T:* So he's looking at you in a way that you don't like. What's the reality?
> *C:* I don't know.
> *T:* Have you stolen anything?
> *C:* No.
> *T:* So whether he looks at you or not, you haven't stolen anything. That's the reality.
> *C:* Yeah.
> *T:* Breathe, relax.
> *C:* [Inhales deeply and slowly exhales, visibly relaxing] I feel better now. Let's go on.

Martin got panicky once more after he knocked something off a shelf. He became very harsh on himself 'What a stupid bastard I am.' I confronted this harsh attack on himself and the grandiosity of viewing a simple mistake as catastrophic. I gave him a mint and he calmed down. I gave him some information: 'It's OK if you knock something over. You can just pick it up. It was an accident. It's not a big deal.' At this point another customer knocked over a tower of cornflake packets and the three of us laughed. Martin helped the other shopper saying 'I've just done exactly the same thing.' I watched them laugh and comment on how easy it is to knock things over, and 'it's a daft place to put them really . . . .' Martin looked totally relaxed and beamed at me. When we finished we went back to the Centre and had a cup of tea. He remained relaxed and pleased with himself.

ANALYSIS This session clearly marked another level of decontamination and challenging script-bound beliefs and fantasies on the racket system. I took the unorthodox step of moving out of the therapy room and taking the client straight into the stressful situation in order to speed up the process of resolution of the anxiety, and to assist the client to take therapy insights out into his life in a more concrete way. I have used a similar approach with a variety of clients now and it has proved to be highly effective. It should be noted that this method is not the same as behavioural implosion therapy and must be understood in the context of its location within the matrix of the therapeutic relationship which offers sufficient protection and permission as well as potency.

Eighth session
Martin turned up for his session with three bags of shopping and the statement: 'See, I feel fine.' Apparently he had occasionally felt anxious in the supermarket but had managed to soothe himself. He said that he felt he had completed half of what he intended to gain from therapy. He had had no outbursts of anger for two weeks and had managed to interrupt his (now) infrequent periods of agitation. His appetite had improved a little and his sleeping pattern had returned to normal, indicating symptomatic relief of depression. He spoke about some bad news he had received prior to leaving the house to come to his session. He expressed authentic sadness and shed a few tears, but after a minute or two noticeably shut down his feelings and got into his 'Be Strong' driver. I honoured his defence as I believed that he would have experienced a confrontation of this at this stage as an assault on his frame of reference. Rather than confront the 'Be Strong' driver I stroked the authentic expression, thus providing a reparative experience whereby feelings were accepted rather than punished. Later, I felt very much as though he were trying to look after me. I reflected this back to him and he talked about 'unspoken vibes' in the family and how he had always had to guess how people were feeling and to lock away his own feelings. We moved rapidly through decontamination into deconfusion. At the end of the session, I mentioned his escape hatch closure. He closed them for another six weeks. I gave him three affirmation cards as he left which said: 'All your feelings are OK with me', 'You can feel all your feelings' and 'You can think and feel at the same time'.

Ninth session
Martin arrived in a very cheerful and relaxed mood. He said he felt he had achieved 70 per cent of what he had intended to get from therapy. We talked about his sexuality and he spoke with updated, relevant Adult information of many new decisions he had made around this. We then went on to make behavioural contracts connected with making new friends, exploring various options and how he would know he had a friend, and how he would know he was being a friend. This led on to a discussion around self-esteem and various positive visualisation exercises and self-stroking. The rest of the session was spent discussing career options and devising a strategy for getting a job. I gave him a final set of instructions for continuing the letter writing at home.

ANALYSIS   Martin was redeciding his 'Don't be important', 'Don't feel', 'Don't be close' and 'Don't think' injunctions in this sessions. The relevant Adult information he gave himself, particularly around gay issues, prevented reinforcement of any of his script messages, especially 'Don't be close' and 'Don't belong' and allowed him movement into a script-free aspect of his personality, assisting redecision. This kind of rapid redecision is common amongst gay people who go through the process of coming out and obtain accurate information combined with acceptance from one or two significant people (Widdowson, 1999). I saw the letter writing as continuing the process of 'conscious empowerment therapy' (Retief and Conroy, 1997).

Tenth session
The first thing Martin did on arriving was to show me his fingers. He had not bitten his nails for about three weeks and was really pleased that they were starting to look nice and that the infection had cleared up and so his hands were no longer sore. He wanted to spend the session exploring coming out to various people including his family. We discussed a number of scenarios, and made contracts concerning how to deal with negative reactions. In the session he decided he would rather tell his parents by letter and asked if I would help him write this. I did help with encouraging him to express his feelings into words, together with some spelling and structure (Martin had had little schooling). When he finished letter writing he asked if I had a prospectus for the local adult education centre. I found one and he quickly looked through it and then asked to use the telephone. He made an appointment to enrol for classes in English, maths and computing. When he came back into the room he was visibly pleased with himself and said, 'There, I've done it now, no more needing other people to

read things for me or help me work out my money, and it will help me get a job'. We celebrated by buying a piece of cake from the Centre coffee bar.

Eleventh session
Martin had enrolled on the courses and was due to start in a few weeks time. He was excited at the prospect of making new friends and learning new skills. He stroked himself (as I did) as he recounted a situation where he had behaved assertively when a family member was seeking to manipulate him into doing chores for them. I helped him analyse the games involved in his main relationships and we spent the remainder of the session discussing the drama triangle and his usual patterns of Rescuer→Victim→Persecutor→Victim switches and explored options for behaving differently.

ANALYSIS   There were now clear indicators of redecision of 'Don't be you' and 'Don't succeed' injunctions. Martin had maintained significant Integrated Adult cathexis over a period of time, and was now thinking clearly and solving problems. Due to holidays I did not see him for three weeks, and a couple of days before our next session after the break he telephoned to cancel, as a family member had been taken ill. I was worried that at this point he may return to script-bound patterns. In the event he had spent the time making further moves towards autonomy, and had maintained high levels of Adult functioning which now appeared to be a lasting change. His earlier redecisions also appeared to have held firm.

Twelfth session
When he arrived Martin presented as grounded and spoke animatedly about new friends he had made at college, together with a potential romantic interest. He also told me about how he had produced a curriculum vitae in computer class and had sent this out to prospective employers. We continued with game analysis and exploring options for dealing with awkward and demanding family members. He reported feeling much better and requested reducing our remaining sessions to fortnightly intervals. We agreed to meet for a further four sessions. He then went on to say, 'I've been thinking a lot over the break and I've decided to look after and care for myself and not harm myself in any way. I'm not going to do anything to hurt anyone else either, and I'm certainly not going to go crackers or anything. It's my life, and I'm going to have it – for me, not anyone else.' With this, he had closed his escape hatches. I checked this with various questions and believed his closure to be a congruent redecision.

ANALYSIS With escape hatches closed, redecision of his injunctions and a stable and developing Integrated Adult ego state, Martin was moving into a stage of reorientation in therapy. My role at this point was clearly a supportive and affirming one, together with providing monitoring and feedback.

The final sessions

These sessions were primarily concerned with generating goals (Stewart, 1996), contracting, updating, exploring and revisiting earlier goals and issues. As we approached the last two sessions Martin brought up the subject of loss and talked through previous losses. He cried a lot during these sessions, mourning his childhood losses and the lack of attention he got from his parents. We created grief rituals involving candles and visualisation (Childs-Gowell, 1992) and contracted to bring goodbye letters for each other to the last session which we spent reading and discussing these letters. His closing comment was, 'I feel so sad and so happy at the same time. I feel so relieved. I'm feeling so good about myself these days and nothing is going to change that. It's so hard to believe I'm the same person who walked in here a few months ago in a real mess.'

ANALYSIS The ending resulted in the usual recycling of issues, particularly to do with loss. This period of evaluation and mourning is essential to provide internal structure which supports and maintains autonomy, and provides opportunity for any transferential clearing that is necessary. For clients terminating at the stage of transference cure this ending is crucial in determining the degree of stability the client's therapist introject has in maintaining script-free behaviour and to propel the client either into (self) script cure or further therapeutic work over time. In terms of the Global Assessment of Functioning (*DSM IV* [APA, 1994]), I assessed Martin as at 75 (compared with 54 on initial contact).

Postscript

I saw Martin three months later as he called into the Centre to see me and say 'Hello'. He told me that he had started a part-time job six weeks previously and had continued at college, shifting the times of his classes to fit in with work. He had developed a wide network of friends and was enjoying a rich and varied social life. He had also started a relationship which seemed to be going well. All his achievements during therapy had held and been integrated as well as his level of functioning and he spoke clearly, confidently and with feeling, and looked better than ever.

Integration, integrating and TA

Insofar as integration means to render entire or complete or to make whole of parts or elements, it appears obvious to state that integration must be the very purpose of therapy or healing: the making whole of distorted, denied, disowned or dissociated parts of the total personality. It follows, therefore, that an integrative approach to therapy is one which brings a whole-istic (holistic) approach to the human being, drawing on different and even differing theories about human nature, the development of the person and the development and maintenance (or otherwise) of psychological health, ill-health and illness or disturbance, the nature of therapy and of therapeutic change or 'cure', etc. It equally follows that *integrating* therapy (which 'integrating' may be read both as a verb and as an adjective) is both an activity and descriptive of a process engaged in by both client and therapist, both of whom (of course) bring the whole-of-themselves-in-context wholly and holistically to this therapeutic relationship and encounter.

However, none of the sentences in the above paragraph *necessarily* 'follows' one from another or may be taken for granted and herein lies the ambiguity of integration for, unlike the terms TA, psychodynamic person-centred, etc., neither 'integration' or 'integrating' specifies an identifiable therapeutic theory or body of knowledge or even the principle by which the practitioner is integrating, for instance, in terms of therapeutic conditions (Rogers, 1990), 'phenomenological considerations' (Thorne, 1967), the therapeutic relationship (Gelso and Carter, 1985), etc. Although there are a number of strands in the literature on therapy integration (all of which are reflected within TA), given that TA already has, principally and traditionally, three component parts or 'schools' within it (see Introduction), any integrative enterprise in TA has to focus firstly on integrating – or *intra*grating (Tudor, 1996) – these internal parts.

The development of different models of integration within TA

Over the past 20 years, a number of models – or, more accurately, metamodels – have been developed by TA theorists and practitioners which are either implicitly or explicitly integrative. These are briefly summarised and assessed in terms of their relevance to brief therapy with specific reference to the above case study.

Groder's (1977) octahedron, comprising six points of view about people – feeling (affective/emotional), doing (behavioural), thinking (cognitive), body (physiological), social system (social/political) and suprapersonal (spiritual) – may be taken as a way of describing and locating different aspects of TA (see Tudor, 1996). It is useful as a holistic organising framework for TA brief therapy in offering a comprehensive 'ecological check' for the integration of all ego states (see Chapter 7) and all aspects of an Integrated Adult. In the above case study the work clearly integrates Groder's six points of view. Erskine's (1975) ABC of effective psychotherapy – the affective, behavioural and cognitive – are present, together with the therapist's emphasis on the physiological, given his own background knowledge and interest and the client's presenting issues. The social point of view is represented not only by the social and political aspects of the client's homosexuality, his acceptance of his sexuality, and his coming out process, but also his return to education. The spiritual dimension is touched upon in the grief rituals.

Kahler's process model, which he has developed over a number of years (Kahler with Capers, 1974; Kahler, 1978, 1979a, 1979b), is integrative in that it draws on and develops a number of TA concepts across all three schools and in that it focuses on another organising principle: that of *process*. Based as it is on the detection of split second driver behaviours (Be Perfect, Be Strong, Try Hard, Please You and Hurry Up), it is not only amenable to use in brief therapy but, arguably, crucial to all TA brief therapy and especially one-session interventions (see Chapter 7). Stewart (1996) provides a useful guide to using the process model which includes a summary of detailed behavioural clues to driver behaviour which in itself is an expression of counterscript and is a 'gateway into script'. He also summarises Kahler's (1979a and b) five channels of communication (interruptive, directive, requestive, nurturative, emotive) which are proactive ways of maintaining contact and the process of communication with clients. Used in conjunction with Ware's (1983) theory of personality adaptations, the process model is not only a sophisticated diagnostic tool, in the form of an assessment matrix (see Stewart, 1996: 150), but also provides a model for moment-to-moment contact within any therapy session. The same emphasis on integration and on process therapy is reflected in approaches to contracting (Lee, 1997) and to groups (Stewart and Lee, 1999). The case study represents many examples of the process model in action: from the initial diagnosis (in the first session), through moment-to-moment analysis of driver behaviour (throughout). In the early sessions the therapist used many channel two (directive) interventions (Kahler, 1979b) to the behavioural 'contact door' (Ware, 1983), e.g. drawing up a racket system with Martin. As the work progressed the therapist used more nurturative and emotive interventions (channels four and five), tracking Martin's increasing emotional literacy.

Drawing on Siegler and Osmond's (1976) work, *Models of Madness, Models of Medicine*, Wilson and Kalina's (1978) splinter chart (named

after Berne's 'splinter in the toe' metaphor) compares different schools
of TA in terms of what the 'splinter' is, how it and the client's symp-
toms/problems are described, what the focus is for removing the
splinter, what tools are used and what the result is. This is useful in
easily identifying the different emphases of the different 'schools' or
approaches within TA. Using it to reflect on how the therapist
described and understood Martin's symptoms we can identify the following (see Table 6.1).

Table 6.1 *Understanding Martin's symptoms and analysis across TA 'schools'*

Symptoms and analysis	TA 'School' and treatment model
Contaminations and Child ego-state confusion	Bernean (medical)
Games analysis, drama triangle	Social Transaction (decisional)
Script types (in this case loveless and mindless), stroke economy and changing stroking patterns, bodywork, homework	Radical Psychiatry (social)
Passivity, discounting, passive behaviours, frame of reference, spot reparenting	Cathexis (family interaction)
Injunctions	Redecision (decisional model)

Table 6.1 shows at a glance the comparative emphasis (within TA) of
this particular therapeutic work, from which we may reflect that it
was influenced by and drew on the radical psychiatry and Cathexis
traditions more than the others. In general, it is a useful model by
which the TA practitioner may reflect on their practice and discover
the influences and relative bias of their work. (Sills and Salter's [1991]
comparative script system is another and an impressive overview of
how theories from the three 'schools' of TA overlap and are paral-
leled. As such it is an extremely useful tool for detailed focus and
therapeutic work on 'specific aspects of the self reinforcing system by
which an individual maintains his or her own script' [1991: 11] and is
applied to systemic integrative short-term psychotherapy [Sills et al.,
1988]).

Steenberger's (1992) metastudy of outcomes of brief counselling
and psychotherapy identifies three phases of treatment: engagement,
discrepancy and consolidation. Drawing on cyclical models of
change (such as Prochaska and DiClemente, 1992), Hewitt (1995)
adapts Steenberger's model and adds a fourth phase to produce a
particularly applicable integrative model for brief therapy (see
Figure 6.2).

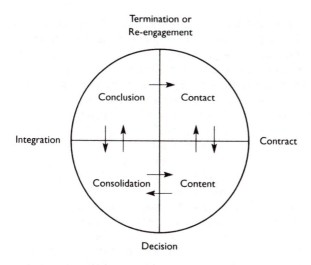

Figure 6.2 *Cycles of psychotherapy (Hewitt, 1995)*

Hewitt develops this by summarising activities of each phase, together with completion markers and the results of premature moves to the next phase and premature treatment termination. Again, with reference to the case study above, Table 6.2 illustrates this model.

Table 6.2 Phases of treatment – cycles of psychotherapy (based on Hewitt, 1995)

Phase	Activity	Completion marked by
Contact	Building empathy, trust and safety (see first two sessions)	Contract made 'To express my anger appropriately' (second session)
Content	Impasse clarification 'Don't exist' vs. 'I have a right to exist' (third session) Other impasses identified later, for instance, about sexuality 'Don't be you (i.e. gay)' vs. 'I am'	Decision or redecision Between fifth and sixth sessions (see pp. 119–20 above) Further redecision (ninth session)
Consolidation	Practice of new behaviour, feeling, thinking, e.g. nurturing behaviours (fourth session)	Integration of change Martin making a list of situations in which he had nurtured himself rather than getting aggressive (sixth session)
Conclusion	Summarising, verbalising, appreciations, goodbyes (last sessions, see p. 125 above)	Mutually agreed termination (sixteenth session)

Finally, drawing on Burrell and Morgan's (1979) paradigm analysis as a metatheoretical, integrative framework, Tudor (1996) locates TA theory within four (psycho)sociological paradigms – the functionalist, the interpretive, the radical humanist and the radical structuralist – and argues that TA's treatment planning sequence may be viewed and experienced as a movement between paradigms. The strength of this analysis is that it identifies the assumptions underlying theory in a sociopsychological perspective which brings together the analysis of the nature of social science and of the nature of society. With reference to the case study we can analyse the following movement (see also treatment planning sequence, Figure 6.1 above) as 'paradigm shifts'. Martin moves from being a passive 'patient' with an internalised external frame of reference defined by others (functionalist paradigm); through greater awareness and meaning making (e.g. the therapeutic work generating insight and options) (interpretive paradigm); on to greater movement, physically and literally, through redecision work and a process of relearning (radical humanist paradigm); finally, through to the restructuring of self (through further redecision) and reorientation (radical structuralist paradigm).

Like any model, these metamodels focus on different elements of theory and, in this case, integration. Groder's (1977) octahedron offers a framework which accounts for *dimensions of human experience*; Kahler's work focuses on *therapeutic process*; Wilson and Kalina's (1978) chart makes explicit the *theoretical assumptions* underlying 'schools' within TA, whilst Tudor (1996) offers a paradigm analysis (from outside TA) of underlying theoretical assumptions and a suggested *movement between paradigms*; finally Hewitt's (1995) model provides a *cyclical approach to TA treatment planning*. In our view, these models are useful in locating different and differing elements of TA theory and practice accurately and quickly – qualities which are of particular use in the context of time-limited therapy.

Integration: A constructivist contribution

Reflecting on the logic of integration in the context of training, Clarkson (1995) suggests that 'a systemic integrative approach to psychotherapy integration does not necessarily seek to provide one true model of integration' (1995: 280). Respecting the vitality of individual difference of both trainees and clients, she argues that training needs to be *integrating* rather than integrative. In many respects this reflects a postmodernist approach to theory, a 'narrative turn' represented in TA by an increasing interest in constructivist approaches (see Schmid, 1991; Allen and Allen, 1995, 1997; Summers and Tudor, 2000) (see also Chapters 3 and 4). Taking the key principles of co-creative, constructionist TA, we reflect on the case study once again:

1. The principle of 'we'-ness

> The therapeutic relationship (or relating) is a more potent phenomenon than the potency (or impotency) of the therapist or client alone. It provides a supportive theoretical framework which emphasises the 'we'-ness . . . of the therapeutic relationship as the medium for human development and change. As such it also emphasises the cultural context of both individual and field. (Summers and Tudor, 2000)

There are a number of points in the case study when the therapist says 'we . . . ' (see p.120 above) or in one instance 'Let's go for it' (see p. 121 above). Whilst this could be analysed as a response to a symbiotic invitation or even such an invitation itself, the *context* of such analysis (by means of the social and phenomenological diagnoses of ego states, especially) demonstrates that this 'we'-ness represents Adult–Adult relating and is very different from the 'we-ness' of transferential Parent–Child, Child–Parent, Parent–Parent or Child–Child relating. In this specific case, the fact that the therapist was and is openly gay also reflects a shared cultural context and field.

2. The principle of shared responsibility

This principle emphasises interdependence, co-operation and mutuality within the therapeutic relationship and is reflected in the co-creation and co-maintenance of potency, permission, protection, support and challenge by both therapist and client, especially in the designing and negotiation of 'interventions' such as going together to the supermarket (see pp. 121–2 above).

3. The principle of present-centred development

Co-creative TA emphasises present-centred human development rather than past-centred child development which, amongst other advantages, 'reduces the possibility of inappropriate infantalising of adult clients (and trainees) which can develop when "growth" is defined within a Parent–Child frame of reference' (Summers and Tudor, 2000). This principle is reflected in this particular case study in the emphasis on the here-and-now development of the client's behavioural options, especially those which focused on his self-support and self-nurturing. The therapeutic focus on supporting the present- rather than past-centred developmental direction of the client is particularly relevant in time-limited therapy.

The following poem, although written in modernist times, reflects with great prescience a postmodernist, constructivist view of change and possibilities.

Everything changes. You can make
A fresh start with your last breath.

But what has happened has happened. And the water
You once poured into the wine cannot be
Drained off again.

What has happened has happened. The water
You once poured into the wine can be
Drained off again, but
Everything changes. You can make
A fresh start with your last breath.

(Bertolt Brecht)

Integration: A personal construction

Finally, in concluding this chapter, we reflect on the meaning of integration and integrating for the transactional analyst. Given the historical and theoretical origins and development of TA (see Chapter 1), and given that many approaches to mental health and psychotherapy emphasise the integration of the personality, it is perhaps not surprising that as therapists we are concerned with integration both theoretically and personally.

Our concern about personal – and professional – integration on the part of the practitioner reflects the fact that a significant number of qualified TA psychotherapists, i.e. clinical transactional analysts (CTAs), registered with the United Kingdom Council for Psychotherapy (UKCP) through the Institute of Transactional Analysis (ITA) refer to themselves as 'integrative psychotherapists' (UKCP, 1999). Of the 129 TA psychotherapists on this register, a significant 24 (19 per cent) describe themselves additionally as 'Integrative Psychotherapists' (a rise of 2 per cent since 1996). Such professional identification, especially by those who do so immediately following qualification, suggests that TA is regarded by its proponents as *in itself* integrative. Professional identity, defined in this case by theoretical orientation, is, of course, a complex matter, influenced by such variables as personal and professional history, training and supervision and the politics of personal and professional organisation, development and change. Such self-redefining may be the consequence of previous professional history or subsequent (re)training and dis- and re-identification. This is no less true of ourselves as KT, a qualified CTA and a Provisional Teaching and Supervising Transactional Analyst identifies much more with the person-centred approach (PCA) whilst MW, a qualified counsellor who, for much of his training identified as person-centred, is now currently in clinical TA training.

In an article discussing the theoretical relationship between TA and the PCA Tudor (1999) concludes that debates about theoretical orientation and professional identity may be placed in a three-dimensional conceptual matrix comprising three continua:

1   Theoretical compatibility, i.e. the degree to which different psychotherapeutic theories are compatible or incompatible
2   Theoretical integration, i.e. the degree to which the integration (intragration or integrating) of such theories is coherent (or not), according to some metatheoretical framework
3   Personal relationship to theoretical orientation, i.e. the degree to which the practitioner identifies themselves personally with their chosen theoretical orientation (or not)

Thus, in our view, in order for a TA practitioner to define themselves as integrative (within TA) they need to address:

1   The degree to which elements of TA theory are compatible or incompatible with each other – there are, for instance, different and differing models of ego states and differing approaches to the notion of and use of transference – and how they relate to such differences both in theory and in practice.
2   The degree to which they have their own model or metatheory of integration (see above pp. 126–30).
3   The degree to which they identify as a transactional analyst and/or integrative and what this means in terms of self-definition, self-identity and personal and professional identity and involvement with, closeness to or distance from particular professional associations, bodies and communities.

References

Allen, J.R. and Allen, B.A. (1995) 'Narrative theory, redecision therapy, and postmodernism', *Transactional Analysis Journal*, 25(4): 327–34.

Allen, J.R. and Allen, B.A. (1997) 'A new type of transactional analysis and one version of script work with a constructivist sensibility', *Transactional Analysis Journal*, 27(2): 89–98.

American Psychiatric Association (1994) *Diagnostic and Statistical Manual of Mental Disorders* (4th edn). Washington, DC: APA.

Berne, E. (1975) *Transactional Analysis in Psychotherapy*. London: Souvenir Press (Original work published in 1961.)

Burrell, G. and Morgan, G. (1979) *Sociological Paradigms and Organisational Analysis*. London: Heinemann.

Childs-Gowell, E. (1992) *Good Grief Rituals: Tools for Healing*. Barrytown, NY: Station Hill Press.

Clarkson, P. (1992) *Transactional Analysis Psychotherapy: An Integrated Approach*. London: Routledge.

Clarkson, P. (1995) *The Therapeutic Relationship*. London: Whurr.

Erskine, R. (1975) 'The ABCs of effective psychotherapy', *Transactional Analysis Journal*, 5: 163–5.

Erskine, R.G. and Zalcman, M.J. (1979) 'The racket system. *Transactional Analysis Journal*, 9(1): 51–9.

Gelso, C.J. and Carter, J.A. (1985) 'The relationship in counseling and psychotherapy: Components, consequences and theoretical antecedents', *The Counseling Psychologist*, 13(2): 155–243.

Groder, M. (1977) 'Asklepieion: An integration of psychotherapies', in G. Barnes (ed.), *TA after Eric Berne*. New York: Harper & Row. pp. 134–7.

Hewitt, G. (1995) 'Cycles of psychotherapy', *Transactional Analysis Journal*, 25: 200–7.

Kahler, T. (1978) *Transactional Analysis Revisited*. Little Rock, AR: Human Development Publications.

Kahler, T. (1979a) *Managing with the Process Communication Model*. Little Rock, AR: Human Development Publications.

Kahler, T. (1979b) *Process Therapy in Brief*. Little Rock, AR: Human Development Publications.

Kahler, T. and Capers, H. (1974) 'The miniscript', *Transactional Analysis Journal*, 4(1): 26–42.

Lee, A. (1988) *Scriptbound*. Workshop presentation, Nottingham.

Lee, A. (1997) Process contracts, in C. Gitle (ed.) *Contracts in Counselling*. London: Sage. pp. 94–112.

Mellor, K. and Sigmund, E. (1975) 'Discounting', *Transactional Analysis Journal*, 5(3): 295–302.

Osnes (1974) 'Spot reparenting', *Transactional Analysis Journal*, 4(3): 40–6.

Parkes, P. (1990) *Rescuing the Inner Child*. London: Souvenir Press.

Prochaska, J.O. and DiClemente, C.C. (1992) *The Transtheoretical Approach: Crossing the Traditional Boundaries of Therapy*. Homewood, IL: Dow Jones-Irwin.

Retief, Y. and Conroy, B. (1997) 'Conscious empowerment therapy: A model for counseling adult survivors of childhood abuse', *Transactional Analysis Journal*, 27(1): 42–8.

Rogers, C.R. (1990) 'The necessary and sufficient conditions of therapeutic personality change', in H. Kirschenbaum and V.L. Henderson (eds), *The Carl Rogers Reader*. London: Constable. (Original work published 1957.) pp. 219–35.

Schiff, J.L. Schiff, A.W., Mellor, K., Schiff, E., Schiff, S., Richman, D., Fishman, J., Wolz, L., Fishman, C. and Momb, D. (1975) *Cathexis Reader: Transactional Analysis Treatment of Psychosis*. New York: Harper & Row.

Schmid, B. (1991) 'Intuition of the possible and the transactional creation of realities', *Transactional Analysis Journal*, 21(3): 144–54.

Siegler, M. and Osmond, H. (1976) *Models of Madness, Models of Medicine*. New York: Macmillan.

Sills, C., Clarkson, P. and Evans, R. (1988) 'Systemic integrative therapy with a young bereaved girl', *Transactional Analysis Journal*, 18(2): 102–9.

Sills, C. and Salter, D. (1991) 'The comparative script system', *ITA News*, 31: 11–15.

Steenberger, B.N. (1992) 'Toward science-practice integration in brief counseling and therapy', *The Counseling Psychologist*, 20: 403–50.

Stewart, I. (1996) *Developing Transactional Analysis Counselling*. London: Sage.

Stewart, I. and Lee, A. (1999) 'Contrasting styles in TA group work', in K. Leach (ed.), *Conference Papers of the Annual Conference of the Institute of Transactional Analysis*. Edinburgh: ITA.

Summers, G. and Tudor, K. (2000) 'Cocreative transactional analysis', *Transactional Analysis Journal*, 30(1): 23–40.

Thorne, F.C. (1967) *Integrative Psychology*. Brandon, VT: Clinical Publishing Co.

Tudor, K. (1996) 'Transactional analysis *intra*gration: A metatheoretical analysis for practice', *Transactional Analysis Journal*, 26: 329–40.

Tudor, K. (1999) 'TA and the PCA – OK? Transactional analysis and the person-centred approach', in K. Leach (ed.), *Conference Papers of the Annual Conference of the Institute of Transactional Analysis*. Edinburgh: ITA.

United Kingdom Council for Psychotherapy (1999) *National Register of Psychotherapists 1999–2000*. London: Routledge.

Ware, P. (1983) 'Personality adaptations: Doors to therapy', *Transactional Analysis Journal*, 13: 11–19.

Widdowson, M. (1999) 'Gay OK: Gay affirmative transactional analysis', in K. Leach (ed.), *Conference Papers of the Annual Conference of the Institute of Transactional Analysis*. Edinburgh: ITA.

Widdowson, M. (2000) 'Affirmations, injunctions, permission and redecision', *TAUK*, 58: 7–8.

Wilson, J. and Kalina, I. (1978) 'The splinter chart', *Transactional Analysis Journal*, 8(3): 200–5.

Woollams, S. and Brown, M. (1978) *Transactional Analysis*. Dexter, MI: Huron Valley Institute Press.

Part II

Applications

Chapter 7

The One-session Cure: On Becoming a Non-smoker

Adrienne Lee

This chapter is about how to cure our clients quickly.

> That's the way to practice psychotherapy. Like you find a splinter and you pull it out . . . and there's only one paper to write which is called 'How To Cure Patients'. That's the only paper that's really worth writing if you're really going to do your job. (Berne, 1970)

The request to take the pair of tweezers and pull out the splinter is Eric Berne's provocative and important demand for the psychotherapist to focus on cure rather than progress, and it becomes the inspirational and philosophical basis for transactional analysis as a successful psychotherapy. The philosophical assumptions of TA also clearly emphasise the 'I'm OK, You're OK' relationship between therapist and client. They accept the client's capacity to think, choose his or her own destiny, and take an equal responsibility in the facilitation of change or cure. The major presupposition of TA is that people can indeed change and that cure is achievable in the completing of contracts that are linked to diagnosis and effective treatment planning. When behavioural contracts are linked to diagnosis they are evaluated and formed to ensure healthy, script-free outcomes that do not endanger the client from the external or intrapsychic repercussions of the cure. When the treatment direction is focused clearly on the relevant diagnosis and the contract, then cure can be economically and directly achieved.

This is the transcript and analysis of a one-session cure using transactional analysis as the core modality for treatment. It also includes techniques from other modalities such as gestalt therapy and Neuro Linguistic Programming (NLP). The client, 'Frank', is 26 years old and has had previous experience of TA therapy, although not with me, and so is familiar with some of the techniques and interventions that are used. I do not think this is particularly significant in terms of judging the effectiveness of this session because the processes are simple and clear and could be experienced easily by a client new to therapy. What is more significant to emphasise is the client's motivation and orientation to change

The session was for one hour. It was videoed, tape-recorded and transcribed, and there was a clear contract that the session would be used for this chapter and for training purposes. The client has seen the transcript and commented on the process of this session (see below, pp. 193-4), comments which have been added independently of my own writing and analysis. I have chosen to present this contribution on cure by relating the transactions on the transcript of the session to TA theory and my thinking at the time. The aim is to demystify the process of TA psychotherapy, a motive close to the heart of Eric Berne; and to provide guidelines to the psychotherapist for facilitating the one-session cure.

There are problems in short-term therapy when behavioural changes are made dramatically without awareness of the more harmful and dangerous parts of the script that may later emerge. In facilitating and promoting brief psychotherapy I think we are well advised to be alert to this, whilst the process of long-term psychotherapy can deal with these issues as they emerge and are ready to be analysed and resolved. As well as addressing the content of the presenting issues the time-limited therapist needs to model a healing process that can be experienced fully in the present and be incorporated intrapsychically to extend *beyond* the therapy session. It is important to understand that the process of therapy does not proceed in a straight line; if anything the process is cyclical, and needs to be so, even in the limited time available in one session (see Figure 7.1). The reader will note that in this session the client, Frank, and I keep returning to the issue and behaviour that needs to be changed and seek to find out where it is rooted in the life script, in the past, and gradually bring this to awareness where it can be understood, felt and processed. Each time one issue or significant factor is brought to the surface and dealt with, another, developmentally often an earlier one, emerges. It is as though the therapeutic process releases the hidden, embedded issues and, as one is cleared, it frees the system to allow another to be released. I strongly believe that the ethical and effective therapist must stay with this 'sluicing' until the intrapsychic waters, so to speak, run clear. This healing processing is described by many therapists who are also familiar with grounding and meditation techniques and over the years I have often heard Elizabeth and Ken Mellor speak of this process. In TA terms, it is as though many different ego states 'hold' the behaviour, feelings and thoughts related to different experiences, and that making significant behavioural changes like giving up smoking will impact on different parts of the psyche. I think of Parent and Child ego states as parts of the psyche that are fixated until they are brought into the here-and-now where they can be

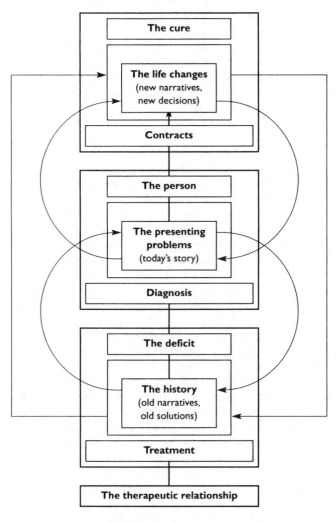

Figure 7.1 *The treatment process*

processed or released, and that the energy required to maintain the fixated ego states can then be released to enable change and healthy living. The old narrative or script story is reconstructed and a new experience and new narrative takes its place.

Becoming 'script-free' and autonomously choosing new behaviours requires an honouring of the positive intentions that the old behaviour served and an honouring of the different ego states as though they are separate people in a community and have an investment in how the whole person lives his life. Even in one session, as is demonstrated here, it is possible to do significant therapy with several different ego states. I think that cure can be achieved when there is an ecological awareness of the needs of the different ego states integrated into the contracting and treatment. I demonstrate this process in this session and this enables both me and the client to be assured that the implications of the life changes have been thoroughly accounted for so that cure is achieved and stable under stress.

The treatment process

In transactional analysis treatment, there is a clear and on-going link between the diagnosis, the contracting and the treatment (see Figure 7.1). The diagnosis is what we see revealed in the person of the client in the present as they tell their story. It contains the adaptations and decisions made in the past that the client is remaking and repeating in the present each time he encounters discomfort or the presenting problem. To understand diagnosis we need to explore its roots in the past where the earlier decisions were conceived (originally as solutions to present problems or impasses) and became part of the life script.

It is in response to the client's history that we devise our treatment planning. We explore the deficits and honour the positive intentions in the old feelings, thinking, behaviours and determine ways to free and release these embedded issues in the present, in ways that are healthy and responsive to the client's current need, development and evolution. The contracting process ensures that any future development, even for the next moment (Lee, 1997), is chosen in the present. By focusing on what the client wants to become in the future, the new meaning that he wants his life to have, as well as the new experiences and behaviours he wants to actualise, he is already in the process of changing his past and the present. Each new contract for change will result in new decisions, new behaviour, new narrative and new meaning which, in their time, will also become redundant and part of history (his story).

So the cycle will begin again. In treatment this whole process is contained within the therapeutic relationship where the links between past, present and future; diagnosis, contracting and treatment; the history, the presenting problem and the life changes: all can be formed and performed and creatively reformed. What is really important for the therapist and client to affirm is that all this can be processed in one session – and is reprocessed and reformed session by session, moment by moment, as new experiences or problems emerge. This cyclical process of cure within a limited time frame modifies the potential grandiosity of the one-session cure.

Transcript and analysis of the session[1]

The first transactions that take place before the start of the session are not recorded here but include warm greetings, to show the client that he is welcome, and invitations to be comfortable. These **initially give the client unconditional permissions 'To Be'.**

1 *A* Welcome!
So what have you come here to do?

The initial contract question invites the client to **take responsibility for the work on an equal basis. A question like this creates an orientation to change.**

2 *F* I've come to stop smoking. [*smiles*]

The contract is clearly defined in terms of a behavioural outcome and seems decisive, but is accompanied with a smile that possibly signals a script message or discount (Mellor and Sigmund, 1975a) of the desire to change. I am wondering already what scripting is fulfilled by smoking. **Note discounts as clues to the hidden intrapsychic process and invitations to support the script.**

---

1 The transcript is organised transaction by transaction, numbered for ease of reference. *A* is me Adrienne, the therapist; *F* is 'Frank', the client. The second column contains my reflective comments (normal type) as well as clinical notes and points (bold type) particularly for the clinician and trainee interested in this way of working. Theoretical concepts are referenced the first time they appear.

3 *A* I notice that when you say that, you smile.

I choose to confront the smile straight away with the aim of stimulating the client to redistribute cathexis and cathect an uncontaminated portion of the Adult ego state (Berne, 1966). **Confront the discounts if the client seems not to be aware of the inconsistency and is able to shift ego state.**

4 *F* Yes. It's exciting!

Frank responds using feelings first in response to my behavioural transaction. I hypothesise a histrionic personality adaptation and therefore assume he will be most responsive to therapy in the sequence of feeling, thinking and then behaviour (Ware, 1983). I also notice some 'Please you' driver behaviour (Kahler, 1974) that supports the histrionic diagnosis as well as some grandiosity of feeling, particularly euphoria, which may be his racket feeling (Berne, 1966; English, 1971). **Useful to begin diagnosis based on open doors and driver behaviour because the evidence is immediately available. Initial diagnosis will need to be confirmed.**

5 *A* What would be exciting for you in giving up smoking?

I choose to combine feeling with the behavioural outcome question in order to go to the client's 'open door' (Ware, 1983). I am also seeking to find out if the client has emotional investment in making the change. **Note and identify the positive gains in the change. Intensify the impasse so that the client is consciously aware of it.**

6 *F* Having money to spend on shoes and things that I wouldn't spend it on! And for health reasons.

Yes, there is emotional energy in the secondary gain of extra money. This is a Child ego state response and there are still euphoric feelings being expressed. Frank's Adult ego state or probably Adapted Child seems to tag on the health benefit as an after-thought. This will need to be explored.

7 *A* When you got really excited about buying shoes I noticed that your eyes lit up.

Specifying (Berne, 1966) the physical response reflects the information I have gained from observation and encourages Frank to keep 'grounded' (Mellor, 1996). **Form an alliance with the Child by stroking the anticipated pleasure in the new behaviour.**

8 *F* [*laughs*].

The laughter seems to confirm the 'feeling first' sequence (Ware, 1983) and the Child ego state pleasure at having been seen and stroked.

9 *A* And then your voice dropped a bit when you talked about the health reasons. So what is it about the shoes? Why do you want to spend money on them?

The comment on the dropped voice is a confrontation of the possible Adapted Child response that could sabotage the contract, but mostly continues the process of 'grounding'. **Useful to focus on the here-and-now physical responses to the transactions to maintain 'grounding'. This encourages release of the energy tied up in maintaining the problem.**

10 *F* I like it. Because shopping is my favourite hobby.

11 *A* How much extra money would you have if you become a non smoker?

Important to ensure that the significance of the gains from therapeutic change are fully specified.

12 *F* About £70 quid a month.

13 *A* What would it mean for you having that extra money to spend?

I am eliciting information to determine the significance of the gain.

14 *F*   I'm sure I'd find something to do with it! [*smiles*]

At present the transactions are playful and using social diagnosis (Berne, 1961) I note the mischievous Child ego state invitations and his redefinition (Mellor and Sigmund, 1975b) but choose not to confront it at this stage.

15 *A*   [*Smiles and then pause*] What about your health then?

The previous alliance with the Child can now free the Adult to respond and although this is a straight question to elicit more information it also serves as a confrontation of the discount noted earlier. **Ensure that other important gains are accounted especially those relating to healthy living and safety.**

16 *F*   I think it's important. It is important for my career. I get an awful lot of sore throats, colds and sore throats and things. I'm sick of it. I'm fed up with having coughs and sore throats all the time. I'm sure it's down to smoking because I've done everything else. I can't stop.

His response shows that he may be discounting the life threat by focusing on less significant symptoms. It sounds like Adult but Child ego state is more likely. Note the Child language. There is evidence here of his awareness of his Child helplessness and need of Adult resources. It will be important to hear his Child and move on as quickly as possible to Frank's empowerment in his Adult. **Form an alliance with the Child before moving to the resources that are in the Adult.**

17 *A*   How long have you been smoking?

The request for information is also intended to assist Adult cathexis.

18 *F*   10 years.

19 *A*   Do you remember when you started?

I choose to focus now on the original scene that gave rise to smoking as its elements will need to be incorporated in the redecision work that will come later (Goulding and Goulding, 1979). The elements of the early scene will be significant when new behaviours will be found to meet the same need.

20 *F* Yes.

21 *A* Do you remember what that occasion was?

The early scene that gives rise to the problem needs to be identified.

22 *F* I was out with some friends.

It is likely that being with friends will be the strongest stroke resource for the smoking today. It may therefore be the area for potential sabotage.

23 *A* What happened?

Elaboration of the scene makes it real and present. Bringing the past into the present makes it available for change. I could have changed the tense of the verb here and encouraged the account to be told in the present tense for more immediacy.

24 *F* We'd had a lot to drink and we got these really long menthol cigarettes [*voice gets animated*] and we were all passing these around and we thought 'this is great!' We looked good. I felt really happy. It was a good night. And that was it. A few nights later my friend offered me a cigarette and that was it!

The scene is described with excitement and animation and smoking, the problem behaviour, is seen as a peer group permissions 'To Belong' and 'Be Important' as well as 'To Enjoy' (Goulding and Goulding, 1976). I am now wondering if the smoking originated in the antiscript (Berne, 1972) or if there are also script messages to encourage smoking. There is a certain Child glee present here that alerts me to pursue script analysis (Berne, 1961).

25 *A* So what could you have done differently at that time?

This is an important question that can introduce options (Karpman, 1971) and invite the resources of the here-and-now Adult to be used to change the past. **Invite the client to consider their options and a new response to the past decision.**

26 *F* I could have said 'No'.

The option is accounted for. Frank's Adult is available now for the process of change.

27 *A* If you could replay that scene of 10 years ago, knowing what you do now and how much money it has probably cost you, if you want to, and you could just replay that scene now, can you see how it could be different?

Invite client to replay the early scene with the new option or behaviour to see how it could be different. This also provides an orientation to change and most of the therapy is already done when this can be experienced as a viable option because it also verifies that the client could act differently and choose a new destiny. I am inviting the significance of options on the discount matrix (Mellor and Sigmund, 1975a).

28 *F* Oh yes.

29 *A* If you could travel in time and look at those 10 years, what differences would it have made to your life if you did not smoke?

I could have asked the client here to elaborate the differences but the tone of his answer seemed to be positive enough and I chose to **emphasise the significance of the new options.**

30 *F* I think healthwise I'd be much fitter than I am, and I think that financially I'd be in a much more comfortable position than I am, I guess that's it.

The significance of the non-smoking behaviour is accounted in Adult. The type I impasse (Goulding and Goulding, 1979) between 'I want to have more money and be healthier' and 'Pleasing peers' seems to be clarified. **See if a type I impasse at the counterinjunction level has been identified.**

31 *A* This is an odd question really, but who do you think you would have pleased by smoking?

This question is intended to check out if 'Pleasing' the peer group is more deeply imbedded in the script itself. Is mother or father pleased by this behaviour?

32 *F* Probably most of my family. All my family smoked.

'Please' driver is confirmed. Script reinforcement by the whole family of origin is confirmed.

33 *A* So what was it like being a little boy growing up in a family where everyone smoked?

I decide to focus on the earlier scenes of childhood that precede the teenage smoking. **This is a key question to ask to form alliance with the Child through gentle inquiry (Erskine and Trautmann, 1996). Identify the early life decision by getting client to associate into the experience rather than intellectualise it.**

34 *F* I didn't like it. I didn't like the smell of it. I thought the smell of it was disgusting. I remember when I was about 8 my mother left a cigarette burning in the ashtray, and I had a quick drag and she caught me and she told me off and asked me to smoke the rest of the cigarette and I went green and threw up.

I note the emphasis again on feelings to access the memory, confirming my earlier diagnosis. The child-like language indicates the shift from Adult to Child ego state. **Note the use of language to give evidence of ego state shifts.**

35 *A* What do you think about that now?

Invitation back into Adult (probably too fast). I missed the opportunity to **clarify the early life decision** and could have asked 'What did you decide then?' or 'What was your secret response then?'

36 *F* I think it was a bit of a shock treatment, but it didn't work! It worked at the time, but not afterwards.

37 *A* So the message in your family is . . . it sounds as though there were two messages: that it was OK to smoke, because everybody did; and not OK to smoke. Did anyone else not smoke?

Crystallisation (Berne, 1966) from my Adult to Frank's Adult inviting him to be aware of the paradoxical script messages. **Invite client to generate Adult options for resolving the** impasse. The last question seeks to find a parent figure in childhood who is available to support the non-smoking behaviour.

38 *F* My maternal grandmother.

If possible identify an early introject in Parent who will support change.

39 *A* Did she have any thoughts about it?

40 *F* When I did start at about 16 there was some disapproval at first and then she just started to laugh.

There is no ally there. The laughter reinforces the negative behaviour in the script.

41 *A* So what did you decide at that time?

Identify early life decisions.

42 *F* That it was OK to smoke.

Decision confirmed. Client needs to hear it clearly from all ego states.

43 *A* So in some way you pleased your family.

The interpretation (Berne, 1966) facilitates deconfusion of the Child.

44 *F* Yes.

45 *A* And now you want to give up smoking? What do you think about that?

The type I impasse is fully clarified and resolution confirmed.

46 *F* As I told you, I don't really care what they think anymore.

Is this a Rebellious Child response or does it come from Adult?

47 *A* Is that true?

Important question to check Adult reality if there is any possibility of an adaptation to the therapist, especially given the context of this session.

48 *F* Yeah. Pretty much. I think it's really sad that it has come to that, but I've had an awful lot of experience of that in my family.

The acceptance of the reality is thoughtful and congruent, though I have some alert to his use of words like 'pretty much' that suggest some discounting.

49 *A* So if all your family right now were sitting over there, smoking, and saying to you 'Frank, it's OK to smoke in our family, we don't mind if you carry on smoking', what would you say to them?

It is probably not potent enough to enable the client to make an Adult decision about new behaviour if the script could be reinforced through internal dialogue with Parent introjects, so I encourage Frank to externalise the intrapsychic conflict and put his family on empty cushions. By speaking for them, I am provoking Frank to get in touch with his feelings and take the power away from the parents in the script. **Two-chair work will dramatise the impasse and facilitate redecision work.**

50 *F* I don't have to.

Frank's voice is soft, probably still in Child. It will be a true redecision when he changes 'I don't have to' to 'I will not'.

51 *A* Do they hear you?

My question is really a permission to be important and to be heard. **Give permissions to support the empowerment of the Child.**

52 *F* No, they don't seem to be listening. [*laughs*] No.

Note the gallows laughter (Berne, 1972) on 'not being important enough to be heard'. We are beginning to identify a type II impasse.

53 *A* So what needs to happen for them to hear you?

There are permissions to 'Be Important' and 'Be Heard' implied in this question. Invitation to his own Adult to resource his Child.

54 *F* I don't need you to hear me, I'm doing what I want.

Frank's voice is quiet and subdued and so the assertion lacks potency. The script apparatus is still in place.

55 *A* They don't seem very convinced by that.

Of course he doesn't need to convince them but this confrontation is intentionally provocative to encourage more energy in the dialogue and hence more potency in the redecision for autonomy. **Invite potency in response to old introjects.**

56 *F* [*laughs*]. You're right! I'm just remembering what my Mum said the other day when I told her I was coming here she said 'Oh good. Let me know if it works!' And I thought, 'Cheeky cow – of course it will work!'. [*voice stronger*]

Frank uses the confrontation to access the present continued script reinforcement from his mother. His grown-up present self has more potency than the Child and he is able to tap into his OK Free Child alongside his Adult to overcome the script message from his mother. He is also identifying a 'Don't Succeed' injunction (Goulding and Goulding, 1976).

57 *A* So what you are aware of now is a double message.

Crystallisation of the impasse.

58 *F* Yes. Yes. I guess if I was at home it would be OK for me to smoke but I don't want to do it anymore. I'm giving it up whatever.

The redecision is clarified and now there is real energy in his voice. **Clarify the impasse and note changes in energy to encourage resolution.**

59 *A* How about you say it again and hear your own voice as you say it. Hear yourself.

It is apparent that his family will refuse to hear him but this is an invitation for Frank to hear his own voice and use self-reparenting (James, 1974) to overcome the 'Don't Be Important' and 'Don't Succeed' injunctions.

60 *F* 'It's OK for you to smoke but I don't want to do it any more. It's not what I want to do.'

His voice is strong and this sounds like an assertive redecision but I have an alert to the message 'It is OK for you to smoke' even though he separates himself from them. There may be a potential sabotage here that will undermine the cure if not addressed.

61 *A* Tell them why it is important to you.

Ensure there are no discounts in the redecision.

62 *F* Because my health is important. Smoking is damaging to my health. I don't want to do that. I want to look after myself.

Frank's voice is stronger now and he is clearly emphasising the benefits to his health in terms of positive statements and what he does want, not what he doesn't or what he is not going to do. **The redecision is restated but is not activated until it is behaviourally affirmed.**

63 *A* Is that true?

Final test of the redecision and confirmation of Adult ego state.

64 *F* Yes. Yes.

The response is clear. It seems that he has decided that he does not want to smoke. Now we need to focus on how he will achieve this.

65 *A* So what needs to happen for you to give up smoking?

We are now ready to **form the behavioural contracts for the new behaviour.**

66 *F* I don't know. I've been here before.

The confusion here and the powerlessness are indicators that the decision to 'Be Important' and 'Please myself' instead of others may be masking a more catastrophic injunction like 'Don't Exist'. We cannot yet assume that the redecision has been achieved. **Are the 'escape hatches' closed? (Holloway, 1973) Check!**

67 *A* Is it safe for you?

This is an important question that acts as a 'bull's eye transaction' (Karpman, 1971) and goes to several different ego states at once to check on the possible 'Don't Exist' injunction and the open escape hatch.

68 *F* Yeah. It's important to keep myself safe.

Is this Adult ego state or an adaptation?

69 *A* What do you mean?

My question seeks clarification and offers opportunity for Frank to articulate his closure of the escape hatches.

70 *F* I need to keep myself safe. I've made a commitment to keep myself safe and I will keep myself safe and this is the only way that I don't.

He affirms his closure of the 'no suicide or harm to myself' escape hatch and his decision to keep himself safe and yet is still aware that smoking raises questions about his safety.

71 *A* I believe you. Will you say more about that?

I choose to support his closure of the escape hatches including his reservation and also invite elaboration to ensure that there is no discounting or sabotage.

72 *F* I've made a commitment to keep myself safe and people around me safe. I may have been careless but not deliberately harmful. I need to be responsible for my actions and for people around me and this is the only thing left that is panicking me.

The escape hatch closure decision is still in place, I think, and the emphasis on responsibility is clearly autonomous. The use of the 'Be Strong' driver in not owning that he is responsible for his own feelings of panic is, however, another alert for a discount that I need to address.

73	A	So if you've made a commitment not to damage yourself or others – giving up smoking or becoming a non-smoker is going to keep you safe and other people safe. Is that true?	The use of specification (Berne, 1966) to declare and reflect on the information we have gained is to fix the significant information in both our minds.
74	F	Yes.	
75	A	So how come you've not done it before?	This is a check on his passivity (Schiff and Schiff, 1971) which may have maintained the script.
76	F	I think for a long time I didn't want to. I didn't particularly want to, and then I believed that I couldn't. I'd want to, and then I'd not do it, I'd not do it. And I feel great having a cigarette, I still do. It's just that I don't want to do it anymore. I've decided, this is it. I'm not doing it anymore. I've decided, this is it. So what's changed for me is I had the feeling I *ought* to stop and now I *want* to. I've decided I want to.	This is a clear and insightful self disclosure that shows that Frank is accessing his Adult as well as his Child. There is no adaptation. He is clear about what is adaptation ('ought') and what is autonomous ('want'). The type I impasse has now been resolved. **It is now necessary to move from 'wanting' to 'doing'.**
77	A	You want to?	This is a confrontation. The use of the words 'want to' instead of 'I will' demonstrate that Frank is not yet fully off the discount matrix.

78 *F*   Yes.

79 *A*   So what will it be like not smoking?

The change to the future tense assumes that the cure has already taken place. By moving the focus to 'doing' the new behaviour I can **check for any possible discounts from a different perspective.**

80 *F*   I think it will be difficult, particularly around my friends because a lot of them smoke but they'll be supportive. I'm really scared about getting miserable that's another reason I didn't stop by myself. I get irritable and snappy with people and I don't want to do that. I get in a foul mood.

Frank identifies the practical difficulties that ensue from ceasing smoking and it is important here to note the return to the peer group pressure 'To Belong' via smoking that was present when he started smoking as a teenager. He also indicates a lack of control over his feelings. Both of these issues will need to be dealt with before the therapy is complete. *The client always tells us what needs to be done. Take one issue at a time.*

81 *A*   So it sounds as though you have been very thoughtful about some of the side effects.

I stress thinking here. It is an important permission for someone with a histrionic adaptation to be able to think and feel at the same time. The success of the therapy will require both.

82 *F*   Yes.

83 *A*   And you've had some difficulty in the past?

I am checking on possible sabotage in the past.

84 *F*   Yes, I have, and I want to give up now.

85 *A*   It certainly sounds as though you do want to give up.

I am supporting his Child decision here.

86 *F* Yes.

87 *A* So what alternatives to smoking are there that would provide for you what smoking has done for you?

This is a technique from NLP called 'the six stage reframe' (Bandler and Grindler, 1979) where the positive intention of the smoking behaviour is recognised and creative alternatives to provide the positive intention without the original behaviour are sought. It can be equated in TA with seeking viable options on the discount matrix and with finding a new source of strokes to prevent sabotage. **Identify alternatives to the old behaviour that will satisfy the positive intention of the old behaviour and provide strokes.**

88 *F* I've thought about it for the immediate, but I'm not sure about the long-term stuff. I've bought loads of chewing gum. It's in my pocket. I've thought about eating fruit and stuff and nourishing myself instead of poisoning myself. My partner's said he's got a nice incentive for me as well – he's said I'll have a very lickable tongue. So when I get a craving for a cigarette I'll get my tongue licked instead! [*laughs*] Which is much better than a cigarette!!

Frank names some short-term alternatives but they are unlikely to be effective on their own as they are very behaviour oriented and for Frank this is his 'trap door' so it unlikely to be stable under stress. The phrase 'nourishing myself instead of poisoning myself' is his own crystallisation of his new decision and will be important for him to use again in his redecision work. He has identified food and erotic stimulation as an alternative source of strokes.

89	*A*	That sounds like an incentive to you!	Acknowledgement of his Free Child incentives.
90	*F*	Yes it does! My partner is a non-smoker. I'll get more kisses!	**The enjoyment and pleasure in the gains for all ego states need to be celebrated.**
91	*A*	So your partner's a non-smoker. I bet that will make a real difference.	The **support in the social network** is important for holding the cure, so it needs to be emphasised.
92	*F*	Yeah.	
93	*A*	So tell me something, Frank, what do you think has been served by your smoking?	Awareness of the positive advantages in the smoking behaviour now need to be clarified and substituted.
94	*F*	I've used it to structure a bit of time. I've spent a lot of time in the last few weeks noticing when I have cigarettes and it tends to be before and after things, like I think I've got these pots to wash so I think: 'I'll just have this cigarette first, I'll just have this fag and then I'll wash up' and then afterwards I'll have a cigarette to relax. I can sit down and give myself 10 minutes for myself.	The significance of time structure as a hunger is confirmed and this will demand new resources to substitute for the cigarettes. He also uses smoking as a 'bribe' or 'prize' for his Child to do unpleasant tasks and a substitute for the 'goodies' will need to be found.

95 *A* So it sounds to me then as though smoking gives you a very important time structure, an important space that you've taken before doing something or taking a pause afterwards, is that right?

Crystallisation – the summary provides us both with focus and direction.

96 *F* Yes.

97 *A* So I'm really glad to hear about some of the other things that you can do instead, but what might provide some of that same rest space and stimulus space that the smoking provided?

I am still seeking creative alternatives to the smoking behaviour to meet the same positive intention.

98 *F* I can still take that time for myself. I can afford five or ten minutes out just to sit and relax and breathe deeper. If the weather's nice I can go out for a look in the garden and enjoy the flowers.

New options are affirmed and recounted with animation and feeling. He has sufficient personal resources to get the nourishment he wants. Are these 'goodies' going to be enough?

99 *A* And will you do that?

Frank now sees that he can act differently and is accounting in all areas and modes on the discount matrix. The final area is action. **Form contracts for viable new behaviours.**

100 *F* Oh yes. I think I'll water the plants or something.

101 *A* So will you just go through one of those scenes when you see the washing up in the sink and you think of a new option and say 'Oh I can do that'? Go through that process.

The tense of the verb is now significantly the present tense. This becomes a fantasy 'dress rehearsal' for the new behaviour. **Imagine the new behaviour in the present.**

102 *F* There's a pile of pots waiting for me in the sink for when I get in!

The new behaviour can be used as soon as he gets home! The fantasy can become real!

103 *A* So go through it. What might you have done when you lit a cigarette and what you will do instead?

The animation above is only a slight redefinition but it hooks my Parent and I seek to hold him on track. I may invite adaptation, so I include questions to cathect an Adult–Adult relationship again.

104 *F* I'll go and sit in the armchair with a book and a cup of tea, read, draw, listen to a bit of music.

105 *A* And then what will you do?

The 'future pacing' (NLP) is an important part of problem solution.

106 *F* Get on with whatever.

107 *A* Get on and do the pots?

108 *F* Yeah.

109 *A* So you've done the pots, then what do you do?

I am encouraging him to **elaborate the scene with the new behaviours clearly defined.**

110 *F* I phone a friend. I make a cup of tea. Put my feet up for 10 minutes with a cup of tea.

111 *A* What interests me is, before when you've had a cup of tea, did you normally have a cigarette too?

I check to see if the smoking behaviour is anchored to drinking a cup of tea and I look for ways of resolving this. We are now at the 'relearning' stage of treatment (Woollams and Brown, 1978).

112 *F* Yeah.

113 *A* So will you take us through that. Your body remembers certain signals, certain anchors and certain messages like sitting down with a cup of tea. What hand do you hold the cup in?

Focus on specific physical responses that may be anchors for old behaviour.

114 *F* This one [*the right hand*].

115 *A* What did you hold the cigarette in?

116 *F* This one, the left hand.

The left hand will still 'want' to hold the cigarette!

117 *A* So what do you think you could do differently?

118 *F* I could hold my cup in the left hand. I usually do if I've got a cup of tea and I've not got a cigarette.

Alternative behaviour found.

119 *A* So just imagine yourself doing that, is there anything else that you might need? How is that experience for you?

He needs to **access the new behaviours physiologically.** This is difficult as behaviour is his 'trap door' (Ware, 1983).

120 *F* Feels a bit weird.

121 *A* A bit weird?

122 *F* Yeah.

123 *A* So it feels weird to put your cup in the other hand.

124 *F* I keep wanting to do something with my hand.

What will he do to replace the cigarette in his hand?

125 *A* It sounds to me as though that could be important for you to actually know that there are alternatives. Is that right?

The potential sabotage in the changing of deeply rooted behaviours is apparent unless the discomfort is recognised and new options offered.

126 *F* Yes.

127 *A* So what alternatives can you come up with?

128 *F* I've just remembered that a couple of years ago a friend bought me some worry beads back from holiday so I'll have to fiddle with those instead!

129 *A* Fiddle with beads!

130 *F*   Yes.

131 *A*   Where will you keep
        them?

132 *F*   In my trouser   The creativity of this suggestion is
        pocket – in the same   worth noting, but so is the potential
        pocket where I keep   sabotage in the tense of the verb. This
        my cigarettes.   discount could be an invitation into a
                               game of 'Kick Me' (Berne, 1964).

133 *A*   The pocket where   The sabotage and discount are con-
        you *used* to keep   fronted.
        your cigarettes.

134 *F*   Yes [*smiles*].   Did he get the 'kick' anyway?

135 *A*   So as we start to   **Check that the new behaviours will be**
        look at some of the   **maintained under stress.**
        behavioural options
        that you have, what
        do you think about
        them? Are they
        viable for you?

136 *F*   Yes. I can see myself It looks at this point as though the
        doing all those   work is finished and he is off the dis-
        things.   count matrix but there are concerns
                               raised earlier that will need to be sorted
                               (see transactions 72 and 80).

137 *A*   What else do you   This is another 'bull's eye transaction'
        need?   that goes to all ego states and
                               provides a good reality check on com-
                               pletion and will open any unresolved
                               issues.

138 *F*   I'm still anxious   Anxiety surfaces about his ability to
        about things like   maintain the redecision in environments
        being in a club and   where the smoking is strongly anchored
        having had a bit to   and supported by his peers. Strategies
        drink and it will be and reassurance are needed to protect
        smoky. I think I'll   the new decision.
        be all right because

I think the smell of
it will put me off.

139 *A* Will you want to go
into those clubs if
the smell puts you
off?

140 *F* I want to see my
friends.

Will becoming a non-smoker withdraw
the permission 'To Belong' that is
achieved through smoking? A new
problem is identified that will need to
be checked through the discount
matrix again.

141 *A* That might be
crucial.

The significance of his friends needs
affirming.

142 *F* Yeah, yeah I
think so. I'm
thinking about
being with friends
now and having a
drink and wanting
a fag and messing
things up.

Frank identifies the potential sabotage
strongly here. If this had been
bypassed it is possible that the redecision work would have collapsed under
this stress.

143 *A* So what could you
do instead?

Adult invitation.

144 *F* I want to spend as
much time with
non-smokers as
possible.

He reframes 'belonging' by applying it
to a different set of friends i.e. non-
smokers.

145 *A* Some of your friends
are non-smokers?

146 *F* Yes, some, about
half and half really.

This is a potential resource. **Identify
resources.**

147 *A* Do they go to these
clubs?

148 *F* Some of them do yes. I've got about two or three different groups of friends.

149 *A* So one option is to spend time with your friends who don't smoke. There may be friends in these clubs that you do like to visit that you do want to see, so what are you going to do then? I can see that this is something that causes you some anxiety.

Clarification of options and viability of options are checked.

150 *F* Yes, I shall remind myself of my reasons for choosing to not smoke and they'll be respectful, they are respectful people. They'll not offer me cigarettes.

The information about friends has been updated from those of his past. However the responsibility is given to them. What if they are not respectful and do offer him cigarettes.

151 *A* So if you ask them not to, and you tell them what you are doing they'll respect you.

Emphasis here is on his ability to ask them not to offer him cigarettes.

152 F Oh yes. Quite a few of them have said so already.

I think he is off the discount matrix now.

153 *A* OK. So what I invite you to do now . . . it sounds as though you've got some good behavioural

Another crystallisation before consolidating the script change. It invites Adult as well as beginning a process that is a part of the six stage reframe called the 'ecological check'. Here the strategies, it sounds as though you are very aware of what the script messages are about smoking, it sounds as though you've made a clear decision about wanting to be healthy and not harm yourself and not harm other people and you've been very congruent about what you've said, so what I invite you to do is to do an internal check. Take a few moments just to be inside yourself and say 'Is there any part of me that might object to the non-smoking behaviours? To becoming a non-smoker?' Pay attention to any parts of you that respond.

client is invited to **pay attention to any unconscious objections to the new behaviours** that will usually be signalled through some physiological response. In TA terms this is an opportunity for any discounted ego states to respond now rather than sabotage the new behaviours outside the therapy room. **It is possible that an earlier impasse may be revealed before the script change can take place.**

154 *F* [*Points to his diaphragm*] Just there. Something there does not feel happy, feels scared. Just there.

This seems like a Somatic Child response and may well reveal a type III impasse that is very early developmentally and is expressed at the visceral level (Mellor, 1980).

155 *A* So there is a part of you that feels scared at the thought of not being a smoker?

Specification that reflects back the information gained and also helps to **form an alliance with the young Child ego state by means of an empathic intervention.** My voice tone has lowered, and my pace is slower.

156 *F* Yes.

157 *A* Would you like to get in touch with that part of you?

A contract is invited for a new therapeutic process.

158 *F* Yes.

159 *A* What has that part got to say?

I invite him to dialogue with this scared Child.

160 *F* It's being really critical.

Frank is ready for a new internal dialogue.

161 *A* What does it say?

162 *F* 'Oh, for Christ's sake, you're not really going to be serious about that!'

This sounds like P_1 or the 'Pig Parent' (Steiner, 1974) and the scared feelings in C_1 are apparently being covered with anger.

163 *A* You are not really going to be serious about what?

Seeking clarification while reflecting and matching the language in order to build rapport.

164 *F* 'You can smoke, you know it won't hurt! You know it's a lot of fuss about nothing!'

The language sounds vicious and is probably what Berne (1972) calls the 'Little Fascist' or what I call the 'saboteur'.

165 *A* What do you say back to it?

Facilitate the intrapsychic dialogue.

166 *F* It will. It is harmful. And it *is* hurting.

Frank is potent and clear in his own confrontation of this internal discount. There is no longer any contamination of his Adult and the impasse can be felt strongly. The dialogue is being articulated in the language of a type II impasse but I retain the possibility that it defends a developmentally earlier impasse because the initial experience was visceral rather than at a feeling or thinking level.

167 *A* And what does that part of you reply?

Both sides of the dialogue needs to be activated to clarify the impasse.

168 *F* It's being a bit quiet. It looks like 'Rumplestiltzkin'! And he's stamping his foot! [*laughs*]

It is as though this Child ego state knows we are on to him and is resisting. Frank is able to separate his Adult here and now self from this Child ego state and be amused by the impact he is having on this 'relationship' with a part of himself.

169 *A* So will you take that part of you on to your hand?

Externalising the internal dialogue makes the whole process clearer and gives permission for this ego state to exist and be included in the therapy. **Curing the 'Don't Be Important' injunction requires the new permission to be given to all parts of the psyche.**

170 *F* Mmmnnn. [*Mimes taking something from his diaphragm onto his right hand and looks at his hand.*]

Frank accounts the invitation to accept the 'reality' of this part of his psyche. This is also a way of redistributing cathexis or energy in the ego states.

171 *A* Is he there?

If the therapist accepts the reality of the psychodrama then the client will not be shamed by accepting it too.

172 *F* Yes.

173 *A* So we take it outside of you – is it true that it is outside of you?

I need to be sure that I am not co-authoring a fantasy: it needs to be the client's process made symbolically tangible, not mine.

174 *F* Yes.

175 *A* So what does that part of you say?

It is likely that the quality of the internal dialogue will change when it is externalised. The potency of any sabotages or messages is radically decreased and the potency is shifted to the Adult ego state of the client.

176 *F* I can hardly hear it.

The potency of this critical voice is already diminished by 'exposing it to the daylight' of here-and-now reality.

177 *A* You can hardly hear it.

178 *F* It an only whisper now. It looks silly, it looks really silly!

Frank is genuinely surprised and delighted by how easily he has dealt with the 'saboteur'.

179 *A* Is there anything you want that part of you to know?

This is an invitation for him to parent this part of himself, though my question is open so that Frank can choose where to go with it. **Create opportunities for self-reparenting.**

180 *F* You can scream and shout all you like but I'm not going to take any notice of you! I know better than you do.

Again a declaration of his potency. I am aware that he is giving parenting to a two-year-old child who is now being oppositional and I am alert to what other parenting may be needed to release the fixation of this ego state.

181 *A* And what does that part say back?

Keep the dialogue between different ego states going to ensure that all transactions are completed. If there is an incomplete transaction it leaves a space for old script decisions to complete the gestalt.

182 *F* Nothing. He's folded his arms. He's looking in a bit of a huff!

For reasons stated above it is important, I think, to maintain the dialogue.

183	*A*	What does that part of you need?	**We recognise that this part is a Child ego state with needs and we now have the opportunity to do some self-reparenting** of the two-year-old who is learning how to individuate. This is also the time developmentally when the child sees himself as an important individual in a world of others who are also important, so this part of the work is crucial to deal with the healing of the childhood deficit (Weiss and Weiss, 1984; Clarkson, 1992).
184	*F*	He wants looking after. He wants to be a bit naughty as well! [*laughs*] He likes to make a bit of mischief, I think!	An alliance has been formed with the 'saboteur' and his experience is now being accounted in an age appropriate way. Frank is making a new relationship with this part of himself.
185	*A*	What do you think about that?	I am inviting Frank to keep thinking and stay in Adult as well as maintaining the dialogue.
186	*F*	Well he can make mischief anyway without a cigarette.	This seems like a potential invitation for even more dangerous sabotage if the cigarettes are withdrawn so I am alert and I must **be careful now not to collude with a new decision that could be dangerous.**
187	*A*	True?	I deem it best to engage his Adult to assess this decision. My question is a confrontation.
188	*F*	There are lots of ways. It's true isn't it?	I am now being asked directly to collude and affirm that this decision is OK . This is an awkward moment!
189	*A*	In safe ways, that's right.	I deem it appropriate to **put in a Parent intervention that emphasises the need to be safe and responsible.**

190 *F* He can be naughty in 'Safeways' ! [*we both laugh*] He can put something in someone's trolley or ring someone's doorbell and run away!

The joke is seductive and the creative use of the pun is witty and funny. I join in the laughter deciding that it is important to enjoy and play with the Child not just confront it, but I have an alert (even though I have evidence here that this child is just a bit mischievous rather than dangerous) and will return to the safety issue soon. **Beware of colluding with potential sabotage.**

191 *A* So, it's very young this part, then, I guess?

It is important to enable the client to understand the developmental age of his ego states in order to provide appropriate care to heal the deficit. This is essential in the self-reparenting process.

192 *F* Yes, yes.

193 *A* So what does that part say now?

194 *F* Let's have fun!

195 *A* Is it OK to have fun without smoking?

This is an important check to see if the 'Don't Be Important' or 'Don't Grow Up' script messages are archaic, Little Professor ways of giving Frank permission 'To Enjoy'.

196 *F* Yeah.

197 *A* Is that true?

There is something not quite congruent here and it is possible that we may be opening up another impasse.

198 *F* It seems a compromise, but . . .

Frank's hesitant response supports this lack of congruence.

199 *A* That's not quite right. That's tricky. Not quite sound. It is an important part

I voice my concern and decide to encourage the dialogue with this Child ego state to ensure that there is permission to 'Enjoy' incorporated of you. So what does he want?

alongside the new permissions to 'Be Important', 'Be Responsible' and 'Be Grown Up'. **Check that all the needs of the Child ego states are being expressed**.

200 *F* He wants to know that I won't let him down, that I'll let him have fun.

I was correct. Frank has now clarified the impasse and formed an alliance with his Child ego state. I see this as an important deconfusion process.

201 *A* So he needs to know that you won't let him down and you can have fun.

My reflective repetition is intended to encourage the alliance with this ego state and I show that I have heard him. **Deconfusion of the Child (Berne, 1961).**

202 *F* Yes.

We are in rapport.

203 *A* What does 'not letting him down' mean?

It is now important to clarify the meaning of these requests so that the intrapsychic contracting can take place. This is part of the self reparenting process.

204 *F* Not keeping my promise.

The response is expressed in child-like language and is still not clear.

205 *A* What promise is that?

The question is a genuine request for information but is expressed in the tone of inquiry rather than 'interrogation' (Berne, 1966).

206 *F* That I will look after him. I will have fun in ways that are safe without hurting other people.

Now it is clear that safety has been incorporated in the new decision, my alert now subsides. Frank's Child ego state is contracting now for the new parenting that he needs from Frank's Adult.

207 *A* How will you do that? Will you look after him?

I invite behavioural markers for the care **as part of the contracting process (Stewart, 1997).**

208 *F* I'll look after myself and I'll look after him, he is part of me.

I don't get very clear behavioural markers but the contract sounds like a profound validation of the core self and I am loathe to interrupt this with what might seem like unnecessary 'Be Perfect' categorisation. The 'promise' is being made now and witnessing it is very moving.

209 *A* Yes. What I invite you to do is to really tell him that. OK? Tell him that he is an important part of you.

I am seeking to **confirm how significant and important this process is**, and how important both Frank the responsible grown-up and Frank the open Child are.

210 *F* OK [*pause, Frank looks at his hand*] He's sat down now and he's quite happy about that. He's a bit surprised about it.

I note that Frank chooses to talk to his Child internally: he takes his time focusing on his Child in his hand and shows with a nod and smile of deep satisfaction that the communication has taken place and been heard.

211 *A* He seems surprised?

212 *F* At first, Yeah. He's pleased though.

213 *A* What does he need now?

I check to ensure that this piece is complete.

214 *F* He needs to be important and have some comfort.

The client knows the permissions he needs.

215 *A* And some comfort. It sounds really important, Frank . . .

We are still reinforcing the new permissions and decisions 'To Be Important' and now the permission to 'Be Close' has been added.

216 *F* Yes.

It is interesting here to see how quickly Frank comes in to get the affirmation for 'Being Important'. This is significant evidence for the integration of this new permission.

217 *A* ... to have that part of you acknowledged and comforted and taken good care of.

218 *F* That's right, that's right.

219 *A* And is he willing now to let you stop smoking?

The 'saboteur' has become an ally intrapsychically.

220 *F* Yes.

221 *A* Is that true?

It seems laborious to keep checking this but I think this question is always crucial in ensuring that Adult ego state has been cathected.

222 *F* Yes.

223 *A* It sounds very clear. So what do you need to do with him now?

We still have an ego state sitting on Frank's hand! We obviously can't just drop him or pretend that he isn't there or the work will be destroyed by a negative parallel process. **If a part of the self has been actualised concretely it needs to be reincorporated intrapsychically.**

224 *A* Put him back.

Frank is invited to choose how to take care of him . . .

225 *F* Will you go ahead and do that? [*Frank puts him symbolically in his diaphragm*]

. . . however he still needs the permission from me to go ahead and do it. I think this is a perfectly normal and healthy response because it acknowledges that we have shared a special creative experience and **the closure needs to be agreed and harmonious** (and hence the 'we's in the commentary on 223 above).

226 *A* How do you feel now?

This question invites a closure of the moving experience we have just shared and allows it to be 'grounded' in the present. **Ensure that client is grounded.**

227 *F* My breathing feels easier. I don't feel scared.

The somatic and feeling responses are important diagnostic clues for the integration of this work and the reparative parenting that has been received.

228 *A* Think about that for a moment. That scare. You have given a real affirmation a real acknowledgement to a very important part of you that it might have been easier to discount. So what are you learning? What sense are you making of all this?

I also invite Frank to include thinking in his process. This is necessary for the healing of his histrionic adaptation and to move the work into the cognitive 'meta-position' or Integrated Adult (Erskine, 1988). Making the learning overt is a way of consolidating the therapy and ensures that the new gestalt of this experience includes an integration of the corrective experience. **How we make meaning out of our experience is where the cure will be recognised and integrated.**

229 *F* That it is very important for me to have a bit of mischief and a bit of fun and that I can have all those things in ways that look after me and are good for me.

Evidence of this piece being satisfactorily completed.

230 *A* That is true. [*pause*]

I confirm and stroke the new decision.

231 *F* Yes. [*pause*] That is true. [*pause*]

We are both reflective and experience satisfaction and closure. There is a pause here.

232 *A* So let's go and do another check intrapsychically. We are aware that we have many ego

Accepting that we have dealt with this part does not rule out the possibility that there are other parts that still need attention. I'm still aware that there is a piece unfinished regarding control of states, many parts, and what we are looking at now, Frank, is for congruence.

his escalated feelings so the ecological check is still necessary. I regret not contracting from Adult here, my control over this process could be experienced as Parental and I may get an overadaptation to 'Please' me.

233 *F* OK.

234 *A* In terms of a new decision you want to make in your life. We are checking it out in script, we have checked it with your health, we are checking it out with the whole of you intrapsychically. So as you now take to yourself the decision that you have made to give up smoking, you can see for yourself new behaviours in the future and ways in which you'll take care of yourself. Is there any part of you . . . ?

I am crystallising the work we have done so far and the process we are now engaged in. The fact that Frank interrupts me here is important feedback for me as it shows that I have been Parental and he is not being compliant in his Adapted Child! **If the client confronts the therapist be alert to the counter-transference** (Clarkson, 1992).

235 *F* [*laughs*]

I hear this as a confrontation of my process rather than a possible sabotage.

236 *A* What were you thinking about?

I don't know yet where he is coming from and need the information.

237 *F* I'm craving an apple or something! [*laughs*]

The Free Child response doesn't feel rebellious but it does disarm me.

238 *A* Craving an apple!

I am disarmed!

239 *F* Yes.

| 240 *A* Is it OK for you to crave apples?! | I feel that my own Parent has been possibly over concerned with the safety issues. I am experiencing my own discomfort now and am not sure whether this is because I have been appropriately confronted or because another issue of safety has arisen that may need to be dealt with. **Pay attention to the countertransference and keep it in consciousness if useful or clear it if not.** |

| 241 *F* Oh yeah, it's good! | I experience this as a 'bull's eye' transaction coming from lots of different ego states in Frank. |

| 242 *A* Let's do another check though, even so, I might be labouring this, but I just want to really be sure. | I am still disarmed and decide to be open about my concerns about safety. In a way I am saying, 'This safety check is for me Frank not just for you', and this seems acceptable to him. I have made my countertransference open. It is important for me to know that I have ensured the safety of my clients by using processes that invite them to take due care of themselves. My investment, however, needs to be open now. |

| 243 *F* OK. | Frank accepts this. |

| 244 *A* So as you go inside now and take that decision to become a non-smoker and to stop smoking . . . notice I keep reframing it as 'To become a non-smoker'. Is that OK with you? | I continue with the ecological check for integration of all ego states. My checking out the changed use of language with him restores our Adult–Adult relationship. I am also considering that it is **important to frame the new behaviour in terms of something he becomes rather than something he stops doing.** |

245 *F* Yeah.

246 *A* See if there is any other part of you that objects or experiences discomfort.

247 *F* There's a small part of me that's a bit scared about snapping at people and getting irritable.

This discomfort has been anticipated. Frank has used cigarettes to suppress and control his feelings and their escalation (see transaction 80), so what will he use instead?

248 *A* What does that part need?

Again the focus is not on the feelings that need to be controlled but the Child ego state that may need some more reparenting.

249 *F* He needs to know that I'm safe being a bit tearful. I can feel irritable and not shout and be horrible to people. I can feel it and not be unpleasant.

He is asking if it is OK for him to feel what he is feeling and still be safe, and to know that he is in charge of himself and can regulate his responses if necessary. Voicing this concern comes from Child not Adult. His Adult already knows the answer!

250 *A* It sounds as though this is a part of you that you 'feel' with, that has feelings?

A somatic Child (C_1) is now apparent.

251 *F* Yes.

252 *A* You said tearful, that you were feeling a bit tearful. Is that right?

Although Frank had talked about his irritation I am thinking that this is possibly his racket feeling and that the repressed sadness underneath may need to be acknowledged and expressed. **Check for repressed feelings.**

253 *F* Yeah.

254 *A* That doesn't sound like irritation to me. Does it to you?

255 *F* No.

256 *A* What does it sound like to you?

It is important to let him access this sadness himself rather than have me name it.

257 *F* Sadness.

Frank is emotionally literate and can track well with his feelings. Some **clients may need more time to access and understand the feeling sensations before naming them.** If this were the case I would **invite the client to intensify what they are feeling.**

258 *A* So there may be a part of you that is sad and another part of you that is angry and this gets soothed with a cigarette. Is that possible?

I can offer this interpretation because I already have an alliance with Frank's Adult. I am offering a way of understanding the function of the cigarettes and inviting his Adult into the dialogue with me.

259 *F* Yes, I wonder what else is being put away.

Frank expands the possibility that other feelings may also be repressed.

260 *A* So will you check too with that part of you if there are any other emotions that get bypassed or missed when you smoked? That get stopped.

It is important to **track closely with suggestions from the client to expand the interpretation. The client always knows!**

261 *F* I suppose happiness. I can't go around feeling really happy with a fag in my hand!

We discover that underneath the scare is his anger, underneath his anger is his sadness, and underneath his sadness is his happiness that is very different from any possible racket euphoria that may have been present earlier (e.g. transactions 4 and 90). **Note that feelings may be layered.**

262 *A* Is that true?

263 *F* Yes, I think so. I was thinking about the sadness in me and my anger and I was thinking about times when I've felt really angry and when I've felt really sad – I've gone straight for a cigarette! Hmm.

The interpretation in transaction 258 is confirmed.

264 *A* So what does that part of you need, to make up for having the cigarette taken away?

We are now looking for new strategies to replace the function of the cigarettes. I think it is at this point that we have identified the positive intention behind the smoking behaviour.

265 *F* To say 'It's OK.' I can still hold on to those feelings if I need to. Apart from if I'm in a situation where it's not OK or not really safe for me to burst into tears or scream and shout then I can take that away until I've got a space to bring it out.

His new Integrated Adult can be the regulator of his feelings. He is combining thinking with his feeling and is demonstrably in charge but he is describing escalated feelings like screaming and shouting. He seeks safe regulation of his **feelings that will be stable under stress.** I think it appropriate to explore this further.

266 *A* It sounds to me as though this is really important.

267 *F* Hmmmm.

268 *A* It sounds to me as though the cigarettes have been useful to dampen down your emotions into some sort of acceptable strength that you might otherwise have gone bursting into tears or been too loud or extravagant with your enjoying or fun, or irritation.

A crystallisation of the earlier interpretations. I am thinking my way through the discount matrix. The significance of the problem is accounted. **If a new problem or aspect of a problem emerges, check it through the discount matrix.**

269 *F* I'm aware that I've lit up when I've felt irritation on more than one occasion in the past week!

Frank relates this to recent experience to test the validity of the interpretation.

270 *A* So your emotions could go like this [*indicates rising level with hand*] but with cigarettes they come down [*indicates downward more level movement*]. Is that right?

Further crystallisation. I am introducing a **behavioural metaphor** as I think this may be a useful resource later that he could use to communicate between his new Nurturing Parent and his Somatic Child.

271 *F* Yes.

272 *A* So now we have a part of you that is worried that if you give up the cigarettes you won't be able to cope with your emotions. So how can you deal with that? What resources do you have?

Invitation into Adult thinking about the viable options for the solution of the problem. Asking two very different questions at once is not very useful and could invite 'Try Hard'.

273 *F* I know myself that it is not true.

He demonstrates that he does not have apparent Child contamination of his Adult ego state, but it is still possible that there is a Parent contamination. Nor does he have a 'Try Hard' driver!

274 *A* It could be true!

The point of this confrontation is to bring into awareness the reality of the need to regulate his emotions and incorporate thinking with them.

275 *F* I think I could deal with them.

276 *A* The cigarette could be used by a Parent ego state, as some form of moderator that says 'Turn it down!' to keep you safe. I'm suggesting it, but it may not be true and I want to check it out with you. Do you think there is something like that going on?

I am making an interpretation to check out if smoking is used in anyway by his Parent ego state to keep him safe. I make a clear invitation for his Adult to participate with me in this hypothesis.

277 *F* Yes.

278 *A* So there is something that is served by you smoking that helps to control or keep your feelings to some acceptable limit. What are you going to put in the place of cigarettes to do that?

New strategies.

279 *F* I don't know.	I think this is a real lack of information and a resource that people with a histrionic adaptation generally lack. **There may be an opportunity to heal a Parent deficit** here.
280 *A* If you are ever with somebody who is too much, too loud what do you want to do?	I am exploring his own viable options to solve the problem.
281 *F* Say 'Shut up!'.	This seems to indicate a lack of moderation. His Parent ego state seems to have limited resource as a moderator of his Child feelings or disturbing behaviour. 'Shut up!' could even reinforce a 'Don't Exist' injunction.
282 *A* Say 'Shut up!'. Do you do that?	
283 *F* I tend not to.	I notice that he has not fully accepted this anyway.
284 *A* So you are not likely to do that for yourself?	
285 *F* No.	
286 *A* If it was a television what would you do?	
287 *F* I'd just turn it off?	This, again, is an 'all or nothing at all' option that can also indicate a 'Don't Exist' injunction if applied to himself. I think it appropriate to do some decontamination work at this point. It is also possible that an earlier schizoid adaptation is being presented.

288   *A*   You'd turn it off?

289   *F*   Yes.

290   *A*   But suppose it was   I bring the analogy with the television
          a programme you   back to his own feelings. I speak up for
          still wanted to see? his Child feelings and **confront the**
          Because if I were   **internal Parent on his behalf.** This illus-
          you, if I were your   tration is intended for both his Child
          anger or if I were   and Parent to hear and is intentionally
          your excitement, I   provocative. It confronts the 'Don't
          wouldn't want you to Exist' injunction.
          switch me off!

291   *F*   No.

292   *A*   And if I'd been using   I continue the analogy and the provo-
          cigarettes to keep in   cation to enable the **decontamination**
          moderation, then   **process.**
          I'm going to want to
          keep smoking rather
          than be switched off!

293   *F*   There is something   Frank has experienced the decontami-
          really good about it   nation though he still refers to himself
          so I'd just want to   as 'it' so, even if this is a slip of the
          turn it down a bit.   tongue, I think the permission 'To Be' is
                                 not yet fully integrated.

294   *A*   You'd want to turn   Again there is a **behavioural marker**
          it down? So how   **required to make the intention realis-**
          would you do that?   **able.**

295   *F*   Yeah. Just so that it   The gesture has been taken in from the
          was comfortable.   television analogy and I am remember-
          Like that [*makes a*   ing that he made a gesture earlier that
          turning knob down   also anchored his soothing things
          gesture].   down.

296   *A*   As you think about   This is another ecology check to ensure
          yourself at the   that he is integrating the new permis-
          moment in   sion that 'It is OK to feel and to think
          situations where you   at the same time'.
          might get really

angry, really happy, really excited, you feel the full flow of that feeling, what do you feel as you turn it down a little?

297 *F* I feel detached from it.

Frank's response shows that he is still in the 'all or nothing at all' position. If he can not feel with full intensity he may dissociate. I am again alert to the possible 'Don't Exist' injunction here.

298 *A* Will that work? It may not be a good idea to detach from your feelings. I don't think that's OK. It's OK to acknowledge the fact that your feelings are very important to you. You don't need to do anything to detach you from your feelings. Your feelings are important, and who you are and what you feel is important.

I decide quickly to **do some spot reparenting** (Osnes, 1974) at this point and say very strongly that both he and his feelings are important and give him the unconditional strokes that I think people with a histrionic adaptation or disorder crave. I am concerned to make it really clear that soothing his feelings does not mean that he is not OK.

299 *F* Hmmm.

I'm not sure that he has accepted this yet.

300 *A* So how can you feel what you are feeling and for that to be OK, without a cigarette and for that to be controlled enough for you to feel OK without a cigarette?

I am aware that time is short and we have an important piece still to do . If toning down his feelings is equated with being 'switched off' then there is a major redecision piece still to do. I gauge that Frank has enough Adult available to pursue this now.

301 *F* I need a rational part of me around to say 'Shhhh!' [*makes a soothing down gesture with his hand*]

He is fully aware and has found his own physical and auditory anchor and moderating mechanism. I also note that he has integrated my gesture (from transaction 270). He is actualising a new internal Parent in place of the archaic one and reveals that he is no longer in the contamination.

302 *A* Notice what you just did. This seemed to be the gesture that you just used, just now [*demonstrates soothing down gesture*]. What does that gesture say to you? I invite you to do it again. [*Frank repeats the soothing down gesture*]. And when you do that and say 'Shhhh', what does that part say?

I am drawing attention to what he did spontaneously; my aim is to enable him to become fully conscious of the gestures so that they are fully in focus and intensified.

303 *F* I know you're there!

I think this is an interesting response because it reveals the parenting and Child deficit that has now been repaired. If his Parent is present to soothe him then he knows that he exists and has permission to feel and be alive and be important. If there is no Parent limiting him he has no permission to exist and if his feelings get too loud and he has to be 'switched off' he also gets no permission to exist. He says the words 'I know you're there' gently and lovingly.

304 *A* 'I know you're there'. What are you aware of when you say that? As you say it you smile. [*pause*]

I repeat his words to confirm and heighten the significance of them. I seek to **intensify his experience** now and also draw attention to his smile which seems to be one of pleasure.

| 305 | F | Good, gentle. [*pause*] | He is experiencing that he can have feelings that are gentle and still exist and be important. I think we are resolving the type III impasse here. |

306 A It seems as though this is a very important part of you that is full of feeling and doesn't want to be switched off.

I am articulating his decision to exist via an interpretation. He has gone very quiet and looks open and happy. **I say the words for him because he may be experiencing a very early Child ego state that is pre-verbal** at this point.

307 F Yeah. [*nods*]

308 A You sounded very loving to that part.

I am acknowledging his love for his own Child ego state.

309 F [*Laughs happily*]

He is quite reluctant or unable to speak at this point, probably because he is **experiencing a new permission to exist and be safe and happy. The type III impasse is resolved.**

310 A It sounds like something you might say to a little child who is perhaps a bit boisterous. You don't want to send him away but be there and enjoy him.

This part of his work is very slow and gentle and my own crystallisation is made in a quiet soothing voice that also offers some spot reparenting.

311 F I enjoy having him, I want to enjoy him there without getting a headache!

He is moving to **a new Parent ego state who clearly gives permissions to his intrapsychic Child.** Enjoyment is now linked to the permission 'To Exist'.

312 A You don't need cigarettes to do it!

313 *F* No.

314 *A* What do you need instead?

315 *F* I could just say to myself "You are OK. I enjoy having you".

Confirms the permission to exist again and also combines it with enjoyment again.

316 *A* What are you aware of when you are saying that to yourself? You are smiling.

317 *F* It's like giving myself a hug!

The new permission has been received!

318 *A* It is, isn't it? It is really loving.

319 *F* Hmmmm.

320 *A* It sounds really loving to hear you say that to yourself. [*Frank looks happy and content*] Lovely.

The dialogue has mostly been internal and visceral and is a resolution of the type III impasse. The work is very tender and moving and I'm thinking that all the earlier work has been leading up to this.

321 *A* So if you were now thinking about what might happen if you were irritable what do you imagine you could do about that?

I am aware of a need to bring this piece to an end and **focus back on the 'here-and-now' problem and its solutions.** I am seeking to transact now Adult to Adult and have changed the tone of my voice.

322 *F* The first thing is for me to listen carefully to what I'm saying to people I care about.

Frank has cathected Adult and is also relating his new permission to listening to others. He has just had the experience of listening to himself quietly and understanding the significance of that.

323 *A* Good for you! **I stroke him for this healthy new decision.**

324 *F* To listen to everybody, really, to listen carefully to what I'm saying and to engage my brain before my mouth takes over so as not to say anything horrible.

He realises that listening applies to hearing himself as well as others.

325 *A* Sometimes your mouth will just take over!

I want to be sure that he does have realistic expectations of himself and know that he doesn't have to be Perfect in order to be OK.

326 *F* Oh yeah!

327 *A* Sometimes it might, because you are going to be spontaneous and it is OK to think and feel at the same time.

I take another opportunity to give this key permission again.

328 *F* Yes.

329 *A* And sometimes you will feel tense perhaps and then when you might have taken that cigarette to dampen your feeling what will you do instead?

We are rehearsing again his new scenario. This is **the relearning phase of the treatment.** Because we only have this one session the relearning has to be done imaginatively.

330 *F* I'll not go to my critical side but I'll ask for a hug. And if I say something a bit sharp to someone then I can apologise.

He has **integrated his new behaviours,** and given himself permission to make mistakes knowing that he can stay in contact with people and repair mistakes in contact.

331 *A* That's true. So there   I am confronting his earlier grandiosity
          is no need to   about the strength and effect of his
          frighten yourself   feelings
          with losing control.

332 *F* Oh no.

333 *A* You know you are
          not going to do
          anything horrible.

334 *F* I don't do horrible! I   We are now being playful, but the con-
          don't do that! I don't   frontation has been heard.
          think I'm horrible,
          maybe a bit
          unpleasant at times!
          A little bit bristly,
          but not really
          horrible [*laughs*].

335 *A* So will you check   **Final closure** on this piece.
          again with the part
          of you that maybe
          had some of that
          responsibility for
          soothing down your
          feelings. Can you
          tell that part of you
          that you are not
          going to smoke
          anymore but what
          you will do instead
          is say 'Hush. You
          are OK. I enjoy
          having you and you
          don't do horrible'.
          What does that part
          of you say back?

336 *F* It just smiles.

337 *A* Is that OK?

338 *F* Yes.

339 *A* And does that
part of you
accept you not
smoking?

340 *F* Yes.

341 *A* Sounds good!

342 *F* I feel human. I feel
very relaxed.

343 *A* Good. OK. So let's
check again. Are
you in for this?

Final check.

344 *F* Yes.

345 *A* So go internally
again with your
decision not to
smoke any more. Just
go in and check that
that is acceptable
with the new options.

Because each time we have done this
there has been an internal objection to
the new behaviour we have had to **keep
returning to the internal check until we
get the 'all clear'! This is a really safe
way of ensuring that the work has been
done at all levels.**

346 *F* No objections. Just
get on with your
life!

'Get on with your life!' is a creative and
effective summary of all the work he
has done in this session

347 *A* Say that again.

This decision is worth anchoring or
heightening.

348 *F* 'Just get on with
your life!'

349 *A* 'Just get on with
your life'.

I repeat it so that he hears the same message in another voice as well as his own.

350 *F* Yes.

351 *A* And will you?

**Saying it is one thing – it has also to be
acted on to finally get off the discount
matrix.**

352 *F* Oh yes. I don't
need my 'ciggies'
for that. I'll just
go on and do my
thing!

353 *A* Is there anything   **It is important for the client to experi-**
else that you want?   **ence satisfaction.**

354 *F* No. I'm happy.
Thank you.

355 *A* So have you still got   I am aware that **there may be a final**
a cigarette pack   **symbolic act for ending** smoking that
with you?   we can do together.

356 *F* Yes I've got some in   He has already prepared to do this so it
a packet and a   is important to have acknowledged this
lighter and I deliber-   in the session and use it to maximum
ately held on to them   therapeutic effect!
so I could throw
them in the bin.

357 *A* So do you want to
do that?

358 *F* Yeah. Where's the
bin?

359 *A* There's a big one on
the way out that you
can put them in as
you leave – is that
OK?

360 *F* Yes.

361 *A* And what will that   The meaning that he gives to this
mean when you put   action may be significant and worth
them in the bin?   accounting for.

362 *F* That's it. I'm done. I   Making new meaning reconstructs our
don't need it   life; the therapist can invite this (Allen
anymore.   and Allen, 1987).

363 *A* And what have you
          got instead?

364 *F* I've got me, I've   He says this with vitality and pleasure.
          got my feelings,
          and I've got my
          health.

365 *A* You've got you.   I repeat his own words exactly as they
          You've got your   are healthy and life affirming and come
          feelings and your   from an Integrated Adult . . .
          health.

366 *F* and I've got more   . . . and a happy Child.
          money in my
          pocket. Which I'll
          spend!

367 *A* Finished.   **The work is done.**

368 *F* Yeah.

369 *A* Good for you!   **Celebration.**

370 *F* Brilliant!

371 *A* That's it then.

372 *F* Done?   **Closure**

373 *A* Done.

374 *F* Fab!

          As Frank leaves the   **Cure!**
          building he throws
          the cigarette packet
          and the lighter in
          the wheelie bin with
          the rubbish and
          says, 'I don't need
          those anymore!'

Postscript

As I re-read this transcript and analysis I am aware of many alternative interventions that I could have made. The therapist has to be satisfied with doing it 'well enough'. I now open the letter from Frank and conclude with some of his comments.

Frank's written responses to the session confirm much of my thinking and analysis. He says he became aware for the first time of 'double messages' in his family of origin about smoking and says at transaction 59, 'I started to feel a bit angry in a healthy way. Some energy was beginning to shift and I started to feel 'bigger', as if I'd drawn myself up to stand up to a bully'. Experiencing his own potency in standing up to Parent introjects will be important in choosing to come out of script. The transactional analyst looks for these energy or ego state shifts as evidence of intrapsychic restructuring.

He reports that 'the words about nourishing myself instead of poisoning myself have stayed with me. I have kept reminding myself, affirming to myself that I am choosing to nourish and nurture rather than poison myself'. In the session I regretted not coming back to these important words and was pleased to learn that Frank had integrated them anyway. I am reassured that the therapist doesn't have to take care of everything and the client can share responsibility for claiming and keeping what will be significant even if the therapist misses it.

He notes that he 'started to feel scared around transaction 248 . . . and liked how you really validated this scare and acknowledged my anger'. He also confirms his realisation that the smoking served his script decision not to feel anger or sadness. I think it is obviously important for the therapist to validate and affirm the feelings and thinking the client has disavowed. The therapist will, I think, always pick up enough of the transference to be a major resource in spot reparenting and is certainly a model for new permissions that can be introjected and later integrated. Commenting on transactions following 301 Frank says, 'I'd found a way to nurture, you then started to model nurturing. I felt very warm and connected with you here. I felt like a tentative baby and parent when the child takes its first steps'. I think that when this is experienced in the therapeutic relationship the client is simultaneously taking this in and being the nurturing Parent to his own new Child ego state. This opportunity to recycle the past and restructure ego states with new resources is one of the efficient techniques TA has developed. It facilitates brief and effective psychotherapy because when integrated, the client can perpetuate the new experience without the presence of the therapist. 'On reflection', writes Frank, 'the whole thing seems to have been self parenting'.

Following the session Frank reports, 'I felt fine, and surprisingly, didn't crave. About three days later I was a little grumpy but it was OK and manageable. I went out with friends and felt fine. The occasions which were very difficult were about a week later when I was in a club and rather tiddly and someone offered me a cigarette which I took without thinking. When I realised, I thought, 'Oh well'. It tasted vile! Yuk! and I put it out! This has happened a few times since and I've thought 'What on earth did I see in it?' I really wasn't aware of how I was poisoning myself. In conclusion, he writes, 'On the whole I feel very satisfied with myself. My health has improved and I've been spending money on surrounding myself with beautiful things! I'm enjoying the good life'.

The one-session cure? If Frank can sustain his new self reparenting and the new decisions he has made without the reinforcement from a therapist, there is no reason why this session shouldn't be enough. Frank's own redecision in the session echoes Berne's challenge to us all: 'Just get on with your life!'. I've done my job Eric!

References

Allen, J. and Allen, B. (1987). 'To find/make meaning: Notes on the last permission', *Transactional Analysis Journal*, 17(3): 72–81.

Bandler, R. and Grindler, J. (1979) *Frogs into Princes*. Moab, UT: Real People Press.

Berne, E. (1961) *Transactional Analysis in Psychotherapy*. New York: Grove Press.

Berne, E. (1964) *Games People Play*. New York: Grove Press.

Berne, E. (1966) *Principles of Group Treatment*. New York: Oxford University Press.

Berne, E. (1970) *Keynote Address* at Golden Gate Group Psychotherapy Society Conference, San Francisco, California, June.

Berne, E. (1972) *What Do You Say After You Say Hello?* New York: Grove Press.

Clarkson, P. (1992) *Transactional Analysis Psychotherapy: An Integrated Approach*. London: Tavistock/Routledge.

English, F. (1971) 'The substitution factor: Rackets and real feelings', *Transactional Analysis Journal*, 1(4): 225–30.

Erskine, R. (1988) 'Ego structure, intrapsychic function and defence mechanisms: A commentary on Berne's original theoretical concepts', *Transactional Analysis Journal*, 18(1): 15–19.

Erskine, R. and Trautmann, R. (1996) 'Methods of an integrative psychotherapy', *Transactional Analysis Journal*, 26(4): 316–27.

Goulding, M.M. and Goulding, R.L. (1979) *Changing Lives through Redecision Therapy*. New York: Brunner/Mazel.

Goulding, R.L. and Goulding, M.M. (1976) 'Injunctions, decisions and redecisions', *Transactional Analysis Journal*, 6(1): 41–8.

Holloway, W. (1973) *Shut the Escape Hatch, Monograph IV*, in *The Monograph Series I–X*. Medina, OH: Midwest Institute of Human Understanding. pp. 15–18.

James, M. (1974) 'Self-reparenting: Theory and process', *Transactional Analysis Journal*, 4(3): 32–9.

Kahler, T. with Capers, H. (1974) 'The miniscript', *Transactional Analysis Journal*, 4(1): 26–42.

Karpman, S. (1971) 'Options', *Transactional Analysis Journal*, 1(1): 79–87.

Lee, A. (1997) 'Process contracts', in C. Sills (ed.), *Contracts in Counselling*. London: Sage. pp. 94–112.

Mellor, K. (1980) 'Impasses: A developmental and structural understanding', *Transactional Analysis Journal*, 10(3): 213–220.

Mellor, K. (1996) *Personal balance at home and work*. Melbourne: International Master Practitioners' Council Inc.

Mellor, K. and Sigmund, E. (1975a) 'Discounting', *Transactional Analysis Journal*, 5(3): 295–302.

Mellor, K., and Sigmund, E. (1975b) 'Redefining', *Transactional Analysis Journal*, 5(3): 303–311.

Osnes, R.A. (1974) 'Spot reparenting', *Transactional Analysis Journal*, 4(3): 40–6.

Schiff, A.W. & Schiff, J.L. (1971) 'Passivity', *Transactional Analysis Journal*, 1(1): 71–8.

Steiner, C. (1974) *Scripts People Live: Transactional Analysis of Life Scripts*. New York: Grove Press.

Stewart, I. (1997) 'Outcome-process contracts', in C. Sills (ed.), *Contracts in Counselling*. London: Sage. pp. 79–93.

Ware, P. (1983) 'Personality adaptations (doors to therapy)', *Transactional Analysis Journal*, 13(1): 11–19.

Weiss, L. and Weiss, J.B. (1984) 'The good child syndrome', in E. Stern (ed.), *TA: The State of The Art*, Dordrecht: Foris Publications. pp. 119–26.

Woollams, S. and Brown, M. (1978) *Transactional Analysis*. Dexter, MI: Huron Valley Institute.

Chapter 8

Short-term Therapy for Post-trauma Stress

Steve Dennis

This chapter describes a combination of short-term interventions designed to prevent the development of Post-traumatic Stress Disorder (PTSD). It is intended for use as a crisis intervention model with people who have experienced a recent traumatic incident. The model was originally designed for short-term interventions in workplace counselling, however it can easily be adapted for use in a wide variety of settings.

I developed the model while working as the principal employee counsellor within a large Local Authority. The Employee Counselling Service provided short-term counselling for 24,000 workers in eight departments representing a wide variety of trades and professions. As the service grew in reputation increasing numbers of people were seen who were experiencing the signs and symptoms of Post-trauma Stress (PTS) following single traumatic events. Initially, the service had expected to receive referrals for post-trauma symptoms from employees most at risk such as social workers or firefighters. It soon became clear that other employees such as highway workers, who clear debris following road traffic accidents, could also experience post-trauma reactions. Many of the people who approached the Employee Counselling Service for assistance were desperate for help. For some this was their 'last resort' having been prescribed various drugs and relaxation methods that had failed to fully address the problem.

There is some variance in the definitions of post-trauma phenomena. Parkinson (1993), for example, defines PTS as 'the normal reactions of normal people to events which, for them, are unusual or abnormal' (1993: 24). Parkinson works mostly in the immediate aftermath of incidents and uses the Dyregrov (1989) method of psychological debriefing to which I will return later in the chapter. He differentiates between PTS and PTSD, viewing the latter as a more advanced version of PTS. He states that when the signs and symptoms of PTS persist and intensify for 'more than a month' the person can be identified as having PTSD. The American Psychiatric

Association's (1995) *Diagnostic and Statistical Manual of Mental Disorders* (*DSM-IV*) defines the essential feature of PTSD as:

> the development of characteristic symptoms following exposure to an extreme traumatic stressor involving direct personal experience of an event that involves actual or threatened death or serious injury, or other threat to one's physical integrity; or witnessing an event that involves death, injury, or a threat to the physical integrity of another person; or learning about unexpected or violent death, serious harm, or threat of death or injury experienced by family member or other close associate (Criteria A1). (1995: 424)

Parkinson goes on to say that 'the feelings, emotions and physical reactions described here can also be found in Post-trauma Stress' (1993: 46). I find the differentiation between PTS and PTSD useful because it takes into account the factor of time and acknowledges that only a few people will go on to develop the *disorder,* characterised by 'extreme distress and disruption of normal living' (Parkinson, 1993: 46) whereas many more will experience post-trauma stress at some point in their life as a normal reaction to bereavement or loss.

Scott and Stradling (1992) refer to three variations of PTSD, these being: acute, chronic or PTSD from prolonged stress and make reference to various rating scales that are included as appendices in their book. There also exists the complication of delayed onset of PTSD, one example being the London firefighter who developed PTSD ten years after attending the Moorgate tube disaster. Scott and Stradling point out that 'pre-trauma personality, psychological disorder and post-trauma beliefs will influence the symptoms experienced by the client' (p. 28). This may help to explain why some people pass off an incident as a 'one off atypical event' while others feel extremely and immediately affected. Within a transactional analysis (TA) frame of reference script analysis may have much to offer a study of which people may be predisposed to PTSD, for instance, in relation to the process script types: Until, Never, Always, After, Almost (Type I and II) and Open-ended (see Berne, 1972; Kahler, 1979 and Stewart, 1996b) (Table 8.1).

The approach described in this chapter assumes that any client who has experienced an incident 'outside the range of normal human experience' is at risk of developing PTSD. There does not appear to be any virtue in predicting whether a person is going to develop PTSD, nor is it useful to assume that every person who experiences trauma is going to develop PTSD. At best, we may regard PTSD as a possible outcome and ensure that effective methods for reducing the likelihood of PTSD are available. This is similar in principle to having a vaccination as a precaution against influenza rather than 'hoping' it does not develop – which, in TA terms, is 'magical thinking' coupled with passive behaviour which promotes illness and pathology.

Table 8.1 Characteristics of different process scripts in relation to post-traumatic stress (developed from Stewart, 1996b)

Name	Driver	Greek myth/figure	Pattern	Motto regarding trauma
Until (Before)	Be Perfect	Jason	Stops self from getting something pleasant until something unpleasant has been completed (Golden Fleece)	'I won't let myself think/feel about it until I've finished all my work'
Never	Be Strong	Tantalus	Doesn't get started, doesn't get anywhere	'I can't get it out of my head: I'll never get over it'
Always	Try Hard	Arachne	Stays with situations even when negative (condemned to a life of spinning webs)	'I can't get it out of my head: I just keeping going over it again and again'
After	Please Others	Damocles	Gets something pleasant but then punishes self with something unpleasant (having something [a sword, suspended by a thread] hanging over you)	'Just as I was beginning to get over the bad memory, something the other day reminded me of it'
Almost I	Please Others + Try Hard	Sisyphus	Gets started but doesn't quite finish (condemned to roll a stone up a hill)	'If only I could crack this and stop thinking about it I'll be all right'
Almost II	Please You + Be Perfect	Hercules	Finishes and goes on without pausing to another task (Twelve Labours)	'I can't think about it. I'm too busy'
Open-ended	Please You + Be Perfect	Philomen and Baucis	Reaches a certain point in life and then 'hits a blank' (What Next?)	'The trauma's behind me now; it's just that I don't see any purpose in life'

An anthropological view of post-traumatic stress

The therapeutic approaches I first became aware of when working in the Employee Counselling Service were designed for people who were experiencing the long-term effects of trauma such as childhood abuse. I began to question whether there should be variations in approach where the incident was a one-off experience or where the person was a witness or professional helper. As their role in the event was different from that of a casualty, for example, then it was likely that the treatment approach could be different too.

I reminded myself of some of Berne's most challenging maxims, in particular, the metaphor of 'pulling out the splinter', i.e. taking the most direct and succinct route to therapeutic outcomes (Berne, 1971). He also warned the therapist that 'he should not poke into any traumatised areas until he is ready to finish what he begins' (Berne, 1966: 62). One of Berne's most illuminating stories of brief practice is his account of 'Amber McArgo', a woman who travelled a very long distance to see Dr Q and who had to fly back home that night. Dr Q therefore had the 'interesting challenge' of curing her in one session. In describing how the cure took place Berne (1972) emphasises 'the Three P's of script antithesis: potency, permission and protection' (1972: 358). In terms of potency the therapist asks herself 'Am I powerful enough to prevail over the person's script messages?' Permissions need to be worded very carefully as 'the Child behaves like a smart lawyer looking for loopholes in a contract' (1972: 359). As regards protection, an important issue in short-term therapy is the possibility of kickback from harmful script messages (script backlash). Perhaps the most interesting element of the story is the potency of Dr Q as perceived by Amber McArgo who made her pilgrimage based on her belief in the doctor's competence. The factor of *belief* in short-term therapy is also well illustrated in the story of Quesalid. Quesalid (as he came to be known) was an anthropologist studying the Kwakiutl Indian people from the Vancouver region of Canada in the first half of the last century. In observing the work of the tribal shaman he came to the conclusion that their curing rituals were a complete sham and then set out to prove his theory. The best way of exposing this con, he decided, was to undergo the shamanic training and then expose the impostors from within. So, he apprenticed himself to a master shaman, and, at some financial expense, learned many tricks of illusion such as how to get his staff to levitate by impaling it on a tree branch with a rusty nail. He learned to act, to feign a trance or seizure and appear mysterious and gifted. Most important of all he learned how to conceal a feather in his mouth and at the point of healing would bite his tongue and produce a blood smeared feather as a representation of the illness or evil which was affecting his patient. To his astonishment, his patients got well which caused him to grow in confidence to such an extent that he began to believe in his own powers. He lost sight of the original reason he had ventured into shamanism and went on to discredit his rivals, whose tricks were not as convincing as the bloody feather technique, and thereby become a revered master shaman in his own right.

There are several interesting points in this story recounted by the structural anthropologist Levi-Strauss (1968). Most notable is the theme of Quesalid overcoming his own scepticism due to his burgeoning self-confidence and faith in his methods. The sense of theatre, performance, the apprenticeship and the exchange of money (similar to Steiner's [1971] valid consideration) are not far removed from the training of counsellors and psychotherapists today. Whilst genuine empathy for clients is essential, a degree of acting and performance does exist in the therapist role, for example, when the therapist invites a client to place a person in their imagination on a chair (as in two-chair work) and then behaves (responds, participates) as if the ensuing dialogue is 'real'. Perhaps the most surprising aspect of the story is that the cure worked even though Quesalid was sceptical. This is because he went through the motions, did the right thing and, most importantly of all, the client believed in him.

This illustrates an important aspect of ritualised symbolic healing. We do not necessarily have to know why a particular ritual works because the key to its success is participation and the willingness to suspend disbelief (Dennis and Stock-Hesketh, 1998). For example, people may not know the symbolism of 'cutting of the cake' as part of the wedding ritual in Western culture; however if it did not take place guests might feel unease that something had been 'left out', literally and symbolically.

An anthropological examination of the phenomena of post-trauma stress and its treatment requires an observation of our own cultures rather like Berne's concept of 'thinking Martian'. This means observing and making sense of our cultures as if we were an alien making a visit to Earth. We might observe that traumatised people think, feel and behave in ways that echo the extraordinary experiences they have encountered. By virtue of being outside the range of usual if not 'normal' human experience, the carnage or suffering witnessed is outside the range of 'normal' conversation and thus becomes 'unspeakable'. The traumatised person is thus 'at odds' with their immediate social group and often behaves in ways which label them as different or 'unacceptable' – a process which sets up a self-fulfilling defensive and protective 'racket system'. They have in short been through an abnormal transformation experience that alienates them from their social group. Some of the most disturbing examples of the transformative effect of trauma can be seen in ex-military personnel who served in Vietnam. These combat survivors reported feeling disconnected from loved ones and from society in general. As a result they often turned to drugs and alcohol to numb psychic pain and could no longer integrate with the accepted societal norms presented to them on their return. Many turned to a life on the highway, drifting rootless from state to state often winding up with third degree game payoffs such as psychiatric care, prison or suicide. These reactions were compounded by the fact that they returned to the United States from fighting what had, in their absence, become an unpopular war.

Viewing trauma as a transformative experience helps to highlight certain curative factors which may need to feature in the treatment plan. In other words, the way out of the perceived problem may be best approached through careful study of the way into it. The therapist therefore sets about creating a symbolic healing process or 'rite de passage' (Van Gennep, 1960) in order to 'normalise' the experience. While investigating what could be done to best assist people who had experienced recent one-off incidents, I became aware of the claims made by practitioners who used neuro-linguistic programming (NLP) regarding the speed and effectiveness of their techniques. I was instructed in how to conduct a technique for helping people process traumatic episodes called the *Double Dissociation Phobia Cure*. Like Quesalid I was initially sceptical, but decided to try out the method and discovered it to be effective. The clients who experienced this guided visualisation reported an immediate change in the way they perceived the event. While they still remembered the event, the traumatic feelings associated with it seemed to be drained from it. A typical response following the Phobia Cure is 'OK, this happened to me, but it is in the past and I can now get on with my life'. Any assumptions about the necessity for long-term therapy were further challenged as such profound changes usually followed a much longer period of work.

Definitions of post-trauma stress and post-traumatic stress disorder

Parkinson (1993) describes the kind of reactions, which stem from involvement in a traumatic incident as 'normal reactions to abnormal events'. Among these normal reactions, Parkinson stresses the theme of loss:

- *Physical loss* through loss of possessions, changes to our surroundings or our own bodies.

- *Emotional loss* through bereavement, loss of self-esteem, security or purpose.
- *Spiritual loss* through losing faith in a benign presence, or existential dilemmas.
- *Social loss* such as family or friends, work, income or identity.

Psychiatric symptoms can be characterised by three themes: *re-experiencing*, *avoidance* and *arousal*. There are many possible reactions, the most common being denial, a sense of pointlessness, increased anxiety and vulnerability, intrusive images and thoughts. Common feelings are shame, anger, regret, blame, guilt and bitterness, sense of isolation and loneliness, fear of closed or open spaces and fear of the same thing happening again. Traumatised people commonly experience *behavioural changes* such as sleep disturbance and nightmares. Avoidance or isolation is common as the person struggles to eliminate any stimuli that may trigger a re-experiencing of the event. Inability to concentrate or make decisions, impulsive actions, irritability and tendency toward anger and violence are also frequently reported. Many people also report *personality changes* such as intense irritation or anger at seemingly trivial problems, withdrawal or isolation, feelings of pointlessness and a loss of meaning to their lives. They can feel emotionally 'numb' which can lead to relationship problems, as they often find difficulty feeling affection or love. They frequently become withdrawn and isolated and as a result feel depressed. They may have lost trust in others or their own judgement. Some report feeling as if they are going mad. It is important to bear in mind that traumatic incidents can 'stack up' in their unresolved state to become a large 'psychic bank account' of accumulated feelings. Trauma can cause fundamental *changes in values or beliefs* such as loss of faith or deepening of purpose in life. In terms of *physical effects* dependence on substances, such as alcohol or non-prescribed drugs that induce a temporary feeling of OKness and release from distress, is frequently reported. So too are illnesses, both major and minor, listlessness, excitement, hyperactivity and increased or decreased physical or sexual desire. Self-harm and suicide risk should always be assessed as fully as possible as well as any desire the person may have to harm or kill others.

Having introduced the relevant terms (PTS and PTSD) and sketched my anthropological approach, I now turn to a description of the brief therapy model I developed in the Employee Counselling Service in response to working with people who experienced traumatising events. It comprises four sessions preceded by an intake/assessment process and theoretically is based on my background and training in transactional analysis and its understanding of people, health and pathology (diagnosis), therapeutic method (contracting) and therapeutic process (treatment direction). The model also integrates particular techniques from NLP.

Intake/assessment – process and considerations

The first contact may be by telephone or in person where an impression can be gained about the suitability of this method. It is important to ascertain how long ago the incident occurred, the person's involvement in it and whether they have had previous similar experiences. This brief approach to trauma may be used in instances where:

- The person had no personal loss or bereavement
- The person experienced a one-off traumatic event, and
- Where the event happened recently, i.e. less than one month ago.

Trauma reactions to these kinds of events are experienced as unwanted intrusions into the present. It is important to differentiate between those with PTS reactions and those who are grieving normally due to a personal loss and want to 'get rid of' their distress. In the latter scenario, the counsellor or therapist working competently would not normally encourage the client to dissociate from their feelings as they are normal feature of the grieving process. One example of an appropriate referral is a woman who had stopped to help the casualties of a road traffic accident and had become traumatised. Although she did not witness the actual crash, her distress stemmed from becoming actively involved in the aftermath of the accident. She did not know anyone involved in the incident and she was not physically injured herself.

The brief method would *not* be suitable:

- Where there is a natural process of bereavement or personal loss taking place
- Where there are multiple or 'stacked up' traumas
- Where there is a high risk of the client acting out harmful behaviours
- Where the person has developed post-traumatic stress disorder

In these instances, the person would need alternative interventions such as bereavement counselling, post-traumatic stress counselling methods such as those developed by Bourne and Oliver (1999), or the assistance of psychiatric services. In my current post as Welfare Officer in the Fire and Rescue Service, trauma related to operational incidents is more likely to be as a result of a sequence of traumatic events accumulated over a period of time. In some instances a member of the emergency services may experience a trauma in their personal life which can trigger the stack of previous work-related traumas in becoming active. The therapeutic work in these circumstances becomes complex and often long term. The brief methods described here are not suitable for these types of experience.

Assuming that the person's issues are suitable for this short-term model, this can now be outlined to them. The therapist explains that the work is limited to four sessions with the first being a 'get to know you' session, followed a week later by a one-to-one critical debriefing of the incident. The third session comprises the Double Dissociation Phobia Cure, a specific method drawn from Neuro-linguistic Programming (NLP) which aims to assist the person to put the event in the past where it belongs. The fourth session aims to restore the person's self-confidence using the Circle of Excellence, another NLP technique. If this meets with their approval they are invited for an initial session.

In my experience the descriptions of the sessions and their aims resonate positively for people who express a desire to 'feel normal again'. It is important to give information on post-trauma responses. The phrase used by debriefers: 'Your reactions are normal reactions to abnormal events' is particularly helpful. If there is any indication of psychosis or other phenomena which the professional does not feel competent or experienced enough to deal with (such as extreme paranoia) then it is important that the person is referred through their GP for psychiatric assessment.

The same precautions need to be exercised with regard to alerts on self-harm or homicidal intentions. Traditionally TA places particular emphasis on issues of harm, both in assessment and ongoing work, and on the importance of assisting clients to close off those routes or 'escape hatches' to harm. Suicide risk always needs to be borne in mind when assessing clients with post-trauma responses. However, if we regard self-harm as a continuum scale with suicide being at the extreme end, it is possible to imagine the myriad ways a person can act out harmful behaviour, such as having 'accidents', or drinking alcohol to excess. Again, if the therapist is not competent to help the client deal with issues of harm, they would be advised – and, indeed, it is ethical – to refer on.

Within TA it is assumed that such destructive drives exist in all of us to a greater or lesser degree. It is possible that involvement in traumatic incidents may trigger our script potential for harmful behaviours, which may not otherwise have been acted out. A TA practitioner may facilitate the client to close off the escape routes to harmful behaviour for good. In the absence of such a decision, the client may decide to opt for a time-limited contract for keeping themselves safe and sane for the period they are in therapy. This has the effect of calling a person's potential drive toward harmful behaviours into their conscious awareness in which options for alternative behaviour can be chosen. The process of 'closing the escape hatches' (Holloway, 1973) or shutting off the routes to harm may become incorporated into the person's psyche as lasting script change or may at least begin the process of deciding to keep themselves safe. Therapists have different views on the necessity or urgency of such no-harm contracts and will no doubt approach the issue in line with their own professional practice (see Mothersole, 1996, 1997). The clients I have worked with using this method have congruently opted to keep themselves safe. If I encountered a client who was not willing to do this I would address this issue before attempting the short-term trauma method.

Jim referred himself for counselling following his involvement with a road traffic accident. He was driving his car when he came across a multiple car accident which had happened a few moments earlier. Jim stopped to assist the casualties and was handed a small child to look after whose mother was trapped in a vehicle. Even though Jim had no personal connections with anyone involved in the incident, he began to experience post-traumatic reactions. He presented for counselling three weeks after the incident reporting restlessness, intrusive thoughts, sleep disturbance and nightmares. This was causing considerable strain on him and his family and at work his performance was deteriorating. Jim had reached desperation point and he saw counselling as his last hope. Jim fitted the criteria for the method described here as he had experienced a one-off incident that did not involve a personal bereavement.

The first session

In essence this is a familiarisation session. As the work is brief, a deep therapeutic alliance is less likely; however I have found that a good enough alliance can be achieved in a short space of time, together with high levels of trust. One possible reason for this is the desperation felt by the individual seeking help. People experiencing PTS are frequently in crisis, believing that their lives are falling apart and their self-image, relationships or professional ability will never be restored. They are frequently on long-term sick leave from work, exhausted from lack of sleep and very scared. Counselling or psychotherapy is frequently regarded as their last hope of getting well after prescribed drugs or alcohol has had only limited success. The person is frequently so desperate that they will try anything. They want the therapist to work some magic which will 'get rid of their distress'. I use this session to instil hope. Yalom (1995) describes this as a key 'curative factor' in psychotherapy. Without making any unrealistic or false claims about the efficacy of any therapeutic endeavour, it is important to convey optimism to the client. I like to keep this factor in mind whenever I work and I believe that hope is particularly important in short-term work.

> *Jim sought reassurance in his first session. His main fear was that he was 'going mad'. As Jim had no previous history of psychosis and was able to cathect his Adult, I felt confident that he was sane and that his reactions were normal. I used this opportunity to provide Jim with information on his symptoms as being congruent with someone who was experiencing a shock or post-traumatic reaction to an abnormal event. 'Normal reactions to abnormal events' is a reassuring phrase to use and can be repeated as often as necessary. It was important to provide Jim with an opportunity to unburden himself as he was keeping much of his reactions to himself so as not to frighten his family and friends. By the end of the session Jim looked relieved to have been open about his experiences and to have gained some information which helped him to order and make sense of the incident.*

The second session: critical incident debriefing

Critical incident debriefing (CID) is a method of debriefing professional helpers use following the kind of incidents that are defined as being outside the range of normal human experience. Typically these incidents involve death or serious injury to members of the public or to members of the emergency services or helping professions. Here I describe a model of CID based on the Dyregrov (1989) method, commonly used in the emergency services, which I have adapted for use in a one-to-one situation. It bears many similarities with the 'narrative reprocessing' model devised by Bourne and Oliver (1999) and as a method of one-to-one debriefing I find this model is a combination of theirs and the traditional Dyregrov CID method. It comprises five stages:

Introduction
This is where the purpose of the CID is explained. The stages are briefly outlined together with the warning that the person may feel worse during or after the session and that this is normal. The role of the therapist is to ask questions that will enable the person to thoroughly recount the story of the incident. It is important to avoid interpretation or empathic responses, as these may encourage the client into strong affect too prematurely.

Expectations and facts
This is the stage where the client tells the story of what happened. I find Bourne and Oliver's ideas useful here. They stress the need for

the story to stay in chronological sequence and to keep the narrative in the past tense. This helps the client to stay with the facts and suppress feelings for the time being. They also suggest helping the client to establish an 'anchor point', i.e. a point just before the experience began when things were still OK for them. This helps the person retain a link with how they were before the trauma. Thoughts and impressions are important here. Some examples of the type of questions asked here are 'What did you expect to happen', 'What did you think was happening' and 'What did you do next'? This enables the person to achieve a 'cognitive grip' on the experience, that is, to update Adult information and make sense of what happened in the past.

Sensory experiences
In this stage the person is invited to retell the story, this time recounting their sensory experiences. They are encouraged to mention everything they remember seeing, hearing, smelling, tasting or physically feeling. The reason for this is that unwelcome re-experiences of the event or 'flashbacks' are triggered by sensory stimuli, particularly smells. For example, a road traffic accident may elicit sensory memories such as the feel of a cold car door handle, the smell of leaking petrol or the sight of blood. Any future re-experiencing of these stimuli may trigger a traumatic response. Recounting the sensory information assists the person to contain them within the incident and to be prepared for the possibility of out-of-context triggering.

Emotional responses
This stage tends to follow naturally from the sensory stage above. Recounting sensory experiences invariably triggers a re-experiencing of affect. This part of the process looks and sounds somewhat like counselling with the exception that the facilitator resists his or her natural urge to give empathic responses. However, summarising, paraphrasing and focusing are all fine techniques to use here. The range of questioning covers the transition of feelings throughout the incident and after the incident, including those triggered by the reaction of family or friends who were not involved. According to Parkinson (1993), the reactions of others can cause difficulties for the person, one example being the soldier who returned from the Falklands conflict to a hero's welcome and party. For him there was no cause for celebration because when juxtaposed with the reality of battlefield carnage, he felt physically sick. In TA terms this part of the CID encourages deconfusion of the Child ego state.

Normalisation

This part of the CID is about providing Adult information on the range of reactions and feelings which may arise as a result of the incident and the debriefing process. Valuable permissions are given to feel all feelings however unpleasant they may be. Reassurance is given that all feelings are normal and that the person is not mad or stupid for feeling as they do. This is also an opportunity to encourage the person to seek the support of family and friends.

> *Jim was initially hesitant about recounting his story of the incident. He said he had done this several times with his partner and a close friend and had hoped this would 'put the experience behind him'. However, by telling it over again his symptoms just seemed to worsen. I explained that seeking the support of his family and friends is important however I would be inviting him to tell his story in a different way. This time he would be describing his experience in fine detail including everything he saw, heard, felt, smelt or tasted and that he would probably remember elements of the event that he had forgotten. Jim agreed to go ahead. As his story progressed Jim began to re-experience his feelings of helplessness and anger which he had unknowingly suppressed. By the end of the debriefing, Jim felt tired but relieved that he had 'told the unspeakable'.*

The third session: the double-dissociation phobia cure

This technique is a powerful means of *removing the affect* from a remembered past situation. In TA script work, it can be used to help the client neutralise the emotional charge attached to past memories; the *content* of the memory is not changed, but it will no longer have an emotional 'trading stamp' attached to it. In work with simple phobias, this technique can be used on the client's memory of some recent scene in which he or she felt the phobic response. The technique is also useful in cases of PTSD, where the person can remember the traumatic scenes from which the disorder arises.

What follows is an outline of the process as described by Stewart (1996c), a transactional analyst and an NLP master practitioner, who, in turn, draws on an original NLP audiotape presentation (Andreas and Andreas, 1989; NLP Comprehensive, 1991). Here I go through the steps of the technique, in terms of what the client is asked to do. We start from the point where the client has specified a past traumatic scene, and you (as the practitioner) have agreed a contract for the relief of the related phobic response, PTSD or current racket pattern.

First, *talk* the client right through the stages that follow, instructing her/him *not to do it yet.* Then have the client relax with closed eyes and guide her/him through the procedure again, this time with the client actually doing each stage in imagination. Throughout, watch your client's affect. If s/he appears to be getting into the painful feelings associated with the past scene, stop the technique and do whatever the client needs to get grounded before continuing.

1   Imagine you are seated in a cinema. Up in front of you, you can see the cinema screen. For the moment, it's blank.
2   Now, leaving yourself sitting in the cinema seat, float up easily and safely into the projectionist's cabin of the cinema. You are now the projectionist in the cinema. As you look round the projectionist's cabin, notice how you can look down through a clear but very solid plexiglass window, down into the cinema. Down there, you see *that other you* still sitting in her/his seat, looking at the blank screen, waiting for the show to start.
3   You're going to show a black-and-white film of that past painful situation, with yourself appearing in it. The film will start with a still shot, showing a point in time when things were still OK, *just before* the part of that past scene that began to be painful. You turn down the house lights, and turn on the projector, so the first still shot comes up on the screen. Then you start the projector in motion, and the black-and-white film begins. From the projectionist's cabin, you can watch *that other you* as s/he watches the black-and-white film, with yourself appearing in it, unfolding on the screen.
4   Now the film of that past painful scene is coming to its end . . . and the film runs on just a little further, to a point just beyond the end of the painful scene itself, when things were OK again (even if only for a while). Momentarily, the black-and-white film goes into a 'freeze frame'.
   (NB to counsellor: When the client is actually doing the following steps 5–6–7, talk her/him through the steps at a rapid rate, congruent with the quick pace you are asking from the client.)
5   At that instant, very fast, you move safely down out of the projectionist's cabin, back down into the cinema seat, so you merge again with the *other you* who has been watching the film . . . and immediately, still very fast, you . . .
6   . . . jump right into the film that has been in 'freeze frame' up there on the screen, so you now become the *you* who has been taking part in the film itself. Now *inside the film*, you immediately give the scene full colour and sound . . . and, even faster than before, you . . .
7   . . . run the entire film through *backwards*, extremely speeded-up, in full colour and sound, with yourself inside it . . . everything happening backwards at amazing speed . . . until you shoot out of the

scene backwards, and come to rest back at the time just *before* the painful scene started, when things are still OK.

8   Now bring your attention back to this room. Open your eyes, look around you, notice where and when you are. (NB to counsellor: It is most important to include this step.)

9   Now test. Recall that past scene, the one that was painful for you. Do you feel any different about it now?

If the client still has painful affect attaching to the scene, you may repeat the whole sequence up to five times. If you do repeat it, ask the client to run the 'backwards' part of the procedure *faster* each time. (You do not need to speed up any of the other stages.) After each repeat, be sure to have the client 'come back to the room' as in step 8 above.

This double-dissociation phobic cure (DDPC) allows the Child to make new meaning of the scene very rapidly. The process strips the original meaning the Child had placed onto the painful incident. The original meaning is then scrambled by the reversal part of the process and in effect, makes it meaningless. As it is not possible to attach affect onto something that is meaningless, the affect is no longer required and the incident passes into memory with no unpleasant affect.

In TA terms, this cure could invite clients to discount what happened to them. If there are script origins for a person's traumatic reactions then the DDPC is unlikely to be a complete script or transference cure. In these cases the method tends not to work and the client reports a residue of bad feelings connected with the incident. There is a case for assuming that every stress reaction has its origins in life script, and if this is so, then the DDPC is a method for helping the person to achieve 'social control'. This may be useful for those who do not wish to resolve their issues at the script level or who cannot afford the longer-term therapy required. However, the wisdom of this could be questioned. If there was no short-term alternative then many traumatised people could slip through the net and develop more chronic problems at a later date. It is hoped that clients who experience a positive outcome from short-term interventions such as those described here feel more inclined to return and take out a new contract for script-change work at a later date.

Jim smiled when told of the process of the DDPC. He was intrigued by its novel approach and he agreed to take part. During the process of watching the story on the screen from the safety of the cabin in his imagination, Jim's eyelids twitched, his brow furrowed and he anxiously fiddled with his wedding ring. [Any changes in facial expression or other behaviours often indicate points at which the client replays the most traumatic parts of the story.] *Jim raised a thumb to indicate he had reached the end of the 'film'. I quickened my speech, adding a sense of urgency to the instruction to play the film in reverse. It took just a few seconds for Jim to do this and in this time his facial tensions and furrows disappeared. As Jim opened his eyes, I had a good sense that something had changed for him. I asked him the test question 'How do you feel about the incident now?' He said 'Well, it happened . . . I know it happened but I just don't feel it's so important now.'*

The final session: the circle of excellence

In TA terms this structured positive visualisation exercise enables the client to apply their age-appropriate Adult resources, and authentic feelings to a future situation. People who have been traumatised frequently report a loss of faith in their judgment and abilities. They may feel racket feelings, notably anxiety, about future events. In terms of the racket system (Erskine and Zalcman, 1979), such 'catastrophic expectations' form part of their script fantasies. The Circle of Excellence technique appeals to the Child like a piece of magic and at the same time engages Adult resources. Here I briefly outline the process as described by Stewart (1996a) from original NLP sources (NLP Comprehensive, 1991). You can do the exercise effectively by using a purely imagined 'circle' on the floor. Alternatively, you may use a circle drawn on a flipchart pad, or a circle of coloured thread. The steps of the exercise are as follows, in terms of what the client is asked to do (instructions to the counsellor are in parentheses).

1   Stand a few steps away from the circle. Bring to mind the upcoming situation you've been feeling bad about. See it in your mind's eye; hear the sounds, feel the way you're expecting to feel.
2   Now, make that situation into a video, with full visuals, sound and 'feelies' (i.e. kinesthetic sensations). Run the video back a bit, to a point just *before* you expect to start feeling bad. Now run it forward again in slow motion. Identify, as closely as you can, the *cue* that lets you know 'Now is the time for me to start feeling bad'. Is that cue something you see in the imagined scene, or something you hear, or something you feel? (Note: The cue for anxiety in future scenes is often visual – check for this, but do not assume it must be so. When the client has identified the cue as clearly as he can, continue.) Now put that imagined scene on one side for a while.
3   Look around the room for a second or two, and be aware of your surroundings.

4   Now think of a past scene in your life, one in which you *did* have all the positive resources you needed, in which you got a result you really wanted, in which you felt very good indeed. (Wait for the client to get in touch with a good scene. If necessary, have her/him make one up. Then continue.)

5   Now, step into the circle. Let yourself get fully in touch with that good scene you've just been remembering. Be right there in that good scene – see it, hear the sounds, get the feel of it. Now, let all the good feelings and positive resources in this scene flow down through you, so they completely saturate the circle. Give yourself as much time as you need to do this. When these good feelings and resources are completely filling the circle, step back out of the circle, *leaving it saturated with those good feelings and positive resources.*

6   Step a few paces away from the circle. Look at it, and notice how it is still completely saturated with those good feelings and positive resources.

7   (Note: Tell the client you are going to explain this step, and will then ask her/him to do it.) Now, get ready to bring back that other scene, the up-coming scene you've been feeling bad about. I'm going to ask you to begin running it through again like a video. Just at the very moment when you come to that 'cue for feeling bad', then please *step forward, into the circle.* (Ensure the client knows the sequence, then continue.) OK, now before you start, step just to the edge of the circle. Get ready to run the scene, and step into the circle when you're ready. Go!

8   (As the client steps into the circle, watch for changes in physiology. Give the client time in the circle. Then continue.) OK, please step out of the circle again. Now test. Think of that up-coming situation, the one you were feeling bad about. How do you feel about it now?

It was a week since Jim went through the DDPC and so I checked out how he was doing. Jim said that ever since the incident he had felt nervous about talking in meetings at work. His job as a social worker required him to do this frequently. He readily agreed to carry out the circle of excellence. His highest point of anxiety came whenever he was due to speak at these meetings and at this point he imagined the faces of his boss and colleagues all staring at him. For his antidote to this bad feeling, Jim chose a memory of a performance in a school play where he received a standing ovation for his portrayal of a character. When Jim had imbued himself with these good feelings, he said that he felt much calmer about facing his colleagues. As he said this he actually looked and sounded more confident.

Some reflections on the brief method

TA has a great deal to offer our understanding of various post-trauma reactions and possible interventions. Scott and Stradling (1992) refer to the 'high levels of co-morbidity' associated with PTSD such as personality change, anxiety, depression and addiction. A study by Friedman (1990) revealed that 40 to 60 per cent of combat veterans who seek treatment also have a personality disorder. In terms of the script apparatus, any of the above reactions could be predisposed in the script. It seems at least possible therefore that a traumatic experience causes some people to flip into script. Ideas on which people are more or less likely to flip into script would depend largely on the makeup of the script itself. So, it seems that some people are more vulnerable than others to being hooked into an unresolved script issue through being traumatised. As nobody comes through childhood psychologically unscathed, we all have the potential for a post-traumatic reaction. One reason some remain more stable under duress than others may be to do with their ability to self-soothe. This ability is likely to stem from early childhood experiences of good enough parenting and healthy levels of emotional literacy and self-awareness. Another factor may be the individual's ability to dissociate from their experiences.

Delayed onset of PTSD, for example, may be the result of a protective Be Strong driver which enables the person to remain functioning in the belief that such incidents do not have any effect on them; that is until they have an experience that is 'the straw which breaks the camel's back'. This accumulative effect of trauma is a particular feature in emergency workers who often believe that they become 'hardened' to gruesome sights through experience. In reality the reverse is more likely to be true. Remembering Berne's (1975) concept of the 'pile of pennies' to symbolise the psyche, a traumatic experience is like a bent penny in the stack which eventually causes the entire pile to become unstable and topple.

Bergmann (1982) describes the decisions made by American Vietnam veterans following battle trauma. One example is 'I knew the minute I got here I would survive. Yes! *Any* means to get back on that plane and go home'. Bergmann views this kind of decision as 'highly functional' in equipping the soldier to get home alive. Other survival decisions he notes, such as 'I must always be alert' or 'Don't get close' (because if I do they'll get blown away), were necessary for survival in war. On return to civilian life these later life decisions gave rise to many of the typical symptoms of PTSD, such as inability to establish relationships, hyper-vigilance, paranoia and sleep disorders. Decisions I have heard in my own practice include 'The world is a dangerous place' and 'You can't trust anyone'. TA methods of facilitating clients to make redecisions clearly has a role in the rehabilitation of people with PTSD.

Bergmann (1982) suggests that the hurried return of Vietnam survivors to civilian life contributed to their psychological difficulties. Fast jet aircraft travel meant that soldiers could be discharged and back on the streets of America within 36 hours of leaving Vietnam. This did not give sufficient time for them to integrate their experiences and make a clear physical and psychological break between combat and civilian life. Following previous wars, the slow troopship method of travel allowed more time for such integration and transformations to take place. It may be useful to view brief methods for treating post-trauma stress as a form of 'troopship' experience, providing the person with respite from the world outside while the therapeutic space (or *temenos*) provides a time and place to 'say the unspeakable' (Gersie, 1991) rather than remaining in silent turmoil. One of my colleagues recently told me of Native American tribal people who segregated their warriors after combat into a separate tepee where they were free to process their experiences before returning to the larger group. It is a hopeful sign that in recent years post-traumatic reactions are becoming accepted as genuine and significant. I trust that the research and interest in these phenomena will continue so that we may become as wise as the tribal people who went before us.

Note

I would like to thank Ian Stewart for his generosity in permitting me to reproduce here in full his aide-memoir for the Double Dissociation Phobia Cure and the Circle of Excellence; to Valerie Heppel for her account of Native American warriors; to Barbara and John Monk-Steele for their ideas on PTSD and script; and to Keith Tudor for his editorial work and encouragement in developing my ideas about process scripts and PTS.

References

American Psychiatric Association (1995) *Diagnostic and Statistical Manual of Mental Disorders IV.* Washington, DC: APA.

Andreas, C. and Andreas, S. (1989) *Heart of the Mind.* Moab, UT: Real People Press.

Bergmann, L. H. (1982) 'Significant adult decisions of Vietnam veterans', *Transactional Analysis Journal*, 12(2): 115–20.

Berne, E. (1966) *Principles of Group Treatment.* New York: Oxford University Press.

Berne, E. (1971) 'Away from a theory of the impact of interpersonal interaction on non-verbal participation', *Transactional Analysis Journal*, 1(1): 6–13.

Berne, E. (1972) *What Do You Say After You Say Hello?* New York: Grove Press.

Berne, E. (1975) *Transactional Analysis in Psychotherapy.* London: Souvenir Press. (Original work published 1961.)

Bourne, I. and Oliver, B. (1999) 'The telling of terror: Helping trauma survivors construct a therapeutic narrative', *Counselling*, 10(2): 135–8.

Dennis, S. and Stock-Hesketh, J. (1998) A willing suspension of disbelief: The theatre of religion and therapy, *ITA News*, 50: 15–18.

Dyregrov, A. (1989) *Caring for Helpers in Disaster Situations: Psychological Debriefing. Disaster Management 2.*

Erskine, R. and Zalcman, M. (1979) 'The racket system: A model for racket analysis', *Transactional Analysis Journal*, 9(1): 51–9.

Friedman, M.J. (1990) 'Interrelationships between biological mechanisms and pharmacotherapy of post-traumatic stress disorder', in M.E. Wolf and A.D. Mosnaim (eds), *Post-Traumatic Stress Disorder: Phenomonology and Treatment.* Washington, DC: American Psychiatric Press.

Gersie, A., (1991) *Storymaking in Bereavement.* London: Jessica Kingsley.

Holloway (1973) *Shut the Escape Hatch: Monograph IV*, in R.R. Holloway and W.H. Holloway, *The Monograph Series: Numbers I–X.* Medina, OH: Midwest Institute for Human Understanding.

Kahler (1979) *Process Therapy in Brief.* Little Rock, AR: Human Development Publications.

Levi-Strauss, C. (1968) *Structural Anthropology.* London: Allen Lane.

Mothersole, G. (1996) 'Existential realities and no-suicide contracts', *Transactional Analysis Journal*, 26(2): 151–160.

Mothersole, G. (1997) 'Contracts and harmful behaviour', in C. Sills (ed.), *Contracts in Counselling.* London: Sage. pp. 113–24.

NLP Comprehensive (1991) *NLP: The New Technology of Achievement* (Audiotape Presentation). Chicago, IL: Nightingale-Conant.

Parkinson, F. (1993) *Post Trauma Stress.* London: Sheldon Press.

Scott, M. and Stradling, S.G. (1992) *Counselling for Post Traumatic Stress Disorder.* London: Sage.

Steiner, C. (1971) *Games Alcoholics Play.* New York: Grove Press.

Stewart, I. (1996a) *Circle of Excellence.* Workshop presentation, The Berne Institute, Kegworth, Nottinghamshire.

Stewart, I. (1996b) *Developing Transactional Analysis Counselling.* London: Sage.

Stewart, I. (1996c) *Double Dissociation Phobia Cure.* Workshop presentation, The Berne Institute, Kegworth, Nottinghamshire.

Van Gennep, A. (1960) *The Rites of Passage.* London: Routledge & Kegan Paul. (Original work published 1909.)

Yalom, I. D. (1995) *The Theory and Practice of Group Psychotherapy* (4th edn.) New York: Basic Books. (Original work published 1970.)

Appendix

TA Script and Therapy Check Lists

The following list is a condensed version of Berne's script check list which was designed to give a quick way of finding the active elements in a person's script. It includes only those items related to script analysis and is followed by a therapy check list, the questions to which, if answered in the affirmative, confirm whether the client is out of script and, according to Berne, 'completely cured'. (The numbers in the list refer to the numbers in the expanded versions of the lists.)

Condensed script check list (Berne, 1975: 435–7)

1B.1	What kind of lives did your grandparents lead?
1C.1	What is your position in the family?
1E.2	Who was around when you were born?
1F.3	Whom were you named after?
1F.4	Where does your surname (family name) come from?
1F.5	What did they call you as a child?
1F.6	Do you have any nicknames?
2A.4	Were you constipated as a child?
2F.1	What happens to people like you?
3A.1	What did your parents say to you when you were little?
4A.1	What was your favourite fairy tale as a child?
4A.3	What did the reader say about it?
4B.1	How did your parents react when things got tough?
4C.1	What kind of feelings bother you the most?
4F.1	What did your parents talk about at the dinner table?
4F.2	Did your parents have any hang-ups?
5F.2	Tell me any dream you ever had.
5F.3	Have you ever had any delusions?
5G.4	What do you expect to be doing five years from now?
5I.1	What would you put on your sweatshirt so people would know it was you coming?
6A.8	Have you ever attempted suicide?
6B.1	What will you do in your old age?
7B.1	How long are you going to live?
7B.2	How did you pick that age?

7D.1   What will they put on your tombstone?
7D.2   What will you put on your tombstone?
7F.1   Are you a winner or a loser?
8A.1   Do you know how your face looks when you react to things?
8B.3   Does your real self always control your actions?
8C.1   Do you have any sexual hang-ups?
8D.1   Are you conscious of odors?
8E.1   How far ahead do you begin to worry about things?
8E.2   How long do you worry about things after they are over?
8F.1   Do you like to show that you are able to suffer?
8G.1   What do the voices in your head tell you?
9B.2   How did you choose me?
9C.3   What did you learn from your previous therapist?
9C.4   Why did you leave her/him?
9C.9   Can you tell me any dream you ever had?

(Questions the therapist asks her/himself:
10A.1   What is the script signal?
10A.2   Is s/he having hallucinations?
10C.1   What is the most frequent respiratory expression?
10C.6   Where do the OK words come from?
10C.8   What is the metaphor scene?
10C.10 What are the security phrases?
10D.1   What is the gallows transaction?
10E.1   Is s/he consulting her/his grandfather/mother?
10F.1   What is the story of her/his life?)

11A.1   How do you think your treatment will end?
11B.5   What has to happen before you can get well?
11D.1a Would you rather get well or be completely analysed?
     b Would you rather get well or leave the hospital?

A therapy script check list (Berne, 1975: 437–9)

1F.7   Do your friends now call you by the name you like?
2B.1   Are you an OK person?
2C.1   Does the world look different to you now?
2C.2   Are you free of delusions?
2C.3   Have you changed your childhood decision?
3A.1   Have you stopped doing destructive things your parents ordered you to?
3A.4   Can you now do constructive things your parents forbade you to do?
4A.4   Do you have a new hero, or see the old one differently?
4C.1   Have you stopped collecting trading stamps?

4C.3	Do you react differently than your parents did?
4D.1	Are you living right now?
4D.2	Have you given up saying 'if only' or 'at least'?
4E.1	Have you given up playing the games your parents played?
4I.1	Have you taken off your sweatshirt?
5F.1	Has your dream world changed?
6A.6	Have you given up your script: prison, hospital, suicide?
7B.1	Are you going to live longer than you used to think?
7B.5	Have you changed your last words?
7D.1	Have you changed your epitaph?
8A.1	Are you aware of how your facial reactions affect other people?
8B.1	Do you know which ego state is in charge at a given moment?
8B.3	Can your Adult talk straight to your Parent and Child?
8C.1	Can you get turned on sexually without artificial stimulation?
8D.1	Are you aware of how odors affect you?
8E.1	Have you cut down your reach-down and after-burn so they do not overlap?
8F.1	Are you happy rather than just brave?
9B.5a	Have you changed your reason for coming to therapy?
b	Have you stopped doing what used to get you into the hospital?
10A.1	Is your script signal gone?
10A.2	Are you free of hallucinations?
10B.1	Are your physical symptoms gone?
10C.1	Have you given up coughing, sighing and yawning for no apparent reason?
10C.4	Do you use verbs, instead of adjectives and abstract nouns, when talking about people?
10C.8	Do you use a wider variety of metaphors?
10C.9	Are your sentences crisper?
10C.10	Have you stopped hedging when you say something?
10D.1	Have you stopped smiling and laughing when you say something?
11A.1	Do you see your therapist differently?
11B.1	Have you stopped playing games with her/him?
11C.1	Are you able to stop playing games before they begin?
11D.1	Do you think you have gotten cured rather than just made progress?

Reference

Berne, E. (1975) *What Do You Say After You Say Hello?* London: Corgi.

Glossary

This glossary provides the reader with a handy reference for key terms used in the book. It is not intended as a comprehensive or defining account of TA terms – for which readers are referred to Berne (1963, 1966), Stewart and Joines (1987) and Tilney (1998). A further caution, informed particularly by a constructivist perspective, is that definitions not only are disputed but also change over time, evidenced, for example, by Berne's different and developing definitions of *games* and *scripts*.

administrative contract also referred to as the business contract, the contract which deals with the practical arrangements of therapy such as the purpose, fees (if any), time, place, confidentiality and its limits.

Adult ego state 'is characterized by an autonomous set of feelings, attitudes, and behavior patterns which are adapted to the current reality' (Berne, 1975a: 76), and is therefore present-centred; see *Child ego state* and *Parent ego state*.

agitation repetitive, non-goal directed activity (e.g. tapping, obsessing, pacing, etc.), often a way of charging up energy in readiness for impending incapacitation or violence; one of the four passive behaviours originally identified by Schiff et al. (1975); see *doing nothing, over-adaptation* and *incapacitation* and Chapter 5.

antiscript literally, the antithesis or inversion of the script, it has a compulsively defiant and rebellious quality which is equally script-bound, e.g. if the parent says 'Don't drink', the client drinks, if the parent says 'Drink', the client does not drink.

autonomy 'manifested by the release or recovery of three capacities: awareness, spontaneity and intimacy' (Berne, 1968: 158) (following on from the definition of antiscript I have heard it defined as when a person does something, even though their parents would approve!).

blocking transaction literally, a transaction which has the effect of blocking or avoiding the stimulus usually by disagreeing about the definition of the issue at stake, e.g. *A*: 'Do you love me?', *B*: 'Ah, what is love . . . ?'; a type of *redefining transaction*.

bull's eye transaction a direct Adult comment which effectively is aimed at or reaches all three ego states in the other person at the same time, verified by a switch in ego states in the recipient to Adult.

cathect (verb) to invest an intrapsychic structure such as an ego state with psychic energy (see Berne, 1966).

Cathexis the Institute and 'School' of TA, founded by the Schiffs (Schiff et al., 1975) and based on their work with psychotic clients, so called because in treatment clients were encouraged to de*cathect* their 'crazy Parent' ego state.

Child ego state 'a set of feelings, attitudes, and behavior patterns which are relics of the individual's own childhood' (Berne, 1975a: 77). See *Adult ego state* and *Parent ego state*.

confrontation an intervention, one of Berne's (1966) therapeutic operations, designed to disconcert the Parent or Child ego state by highlighting an inconsistency (see Chapter 1).

contact door a 'way in' to working with people in therapy through prioritising behavioural, feeling or thinking contact, and linked to identified personality adaptations (Ware, 1983); see *trap door*.

contamination the intrusion of archaic material (introjected [Parent] or experience [Child]) into the present (Adult), usually characterised and illustrated by certain types of prejudice or delusions; see *decontamination*.

contract 'an explicit bilateral commitment to a well-defined course of action' (Berne, 1966: 362); see also *administrative contract, escape hatch closure, guardian contract, guest contract, hard contract, parent contract, soft contract, stop contract, treatment contract*.

contractual method one of the guiding principles of TA practice, whereby client and therapist define, negotiate and agree the goal/s of therapy.

counterscript a set of decisions made by the child in compliance with the counterinjunctions or *drivers*.

deconfusion the identification and expression of unmet needs and feelings in the *Child ego state*, synonymous with psychoanalytic cure (see Chapter 2).

decontamination interventions and a process designed to clarify archaic ideas (attitudes, behaviours, feelings, etc.) and to strengthen the boundary between Adult and Child or Adult and Parent, it forms an early and crucial stage/phase in TA *treatment planning*.

discounting 'ignoring information relevant to the solution of a problem' (Schiff, cited by Stewart and Joines, 1987: 173), a process which is out of awareness and an internal mechanism of which the external manifestation is observable in *passive behaviours, redefining transactions* and *gallows laughter*, etc.

doing nothing a non-response to stimuli, problems or options, the ignoring of the existence of a problem, one of the four passive behaviours originally identified by Schiff et al. (1975); see *agitation, over-adaptation* and *incapacitation*.

drivers the five commands: Be Strong! Try Hard! Please Me! Hurry Up! and Be Perfect! which either reinforce the early *injunctions* or are a conscious *counterscript* given by the parents in later childhood, which essentially reflect a position of conditional OKness ('I'm only OK if I am strong . . .'), and which represent 'distinctive behavioural sequences' (Stewart and Joines, 1987: 328) played out in time frames of split seconds and a few seconds (see Stewart, 1996) (see Chapter 1).

drowning man a diagram, presented by Lee (1988) showing a figure weighed down by his *injunctions* and held up by balloons which represent his *driver* messages.

ego state 'phenomenologically . . . a coherent system of feelings related to a given subject, and operationally as a set of coherent behavior patterns; or pragmatically, as a system of feelings which motivates a related set of behavior patterns' (Berne, 1975a: 17).

ego-state model a model of the personality representing the Parent (P), Adult (A) and Child (C) *ego states* (Figure G.1), the structural version of which has been developed to represent subdivisions within and the development of the personality (Figures G.2 and G.3) (see Chapter 2).

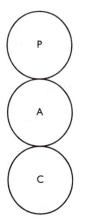

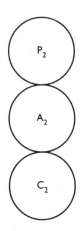

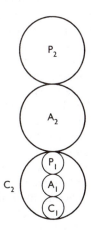

Figure G.1 *Ego-state model*

Figure G.2 *Ego-state model – structural (first order)*

Figure G.3 *Ego-state model – structural (second order)*

escape hatches the three tragic script outcomes: harming or killing self, harming or killing others, and going crazy (mad).

escape-hatch closure the decision made by the client, with the therapist as witness, never, under any circumstances, to harm or kill themselves, harm or kill others, or to go crazy; a decision which is the basis for script change (Holloway, 1973).

excluding ego states a stereotyped, predictable attitude, maintained in the face of threat which has the effect, in ego-state terms, of excluding another or the other two ego states (see Berne, 1975a).

frame of reference a filter on reality, a structure of responses which 'provides the individual with an overall perceptual, conceptual, affective and action set, which is used to define the self, other people and the world' (Schiff et al., 1975: 50).

Free Child a functional metaphor which characterises behaviour from a person's childhood free from Parental rules or limits.

gallows laughter the kind of self-deprecating laughter, indicative of discounting, which invites collusion on the part of the audience and which reflects an incongruence (for instance, between the laughter and the words).

game 'an ongoing series of complementary ulterior transactions progressing to a well-defined, predictable outcome' (Berne, 1968: 44), often (though by no means exclusively) leading to a negative payoff in the form of a familiar 'bad' feeling; see *racket* and *racket feeling*.

grandiosity 'an internal mechanism involving an exaggeration (maximisation or minimisation) of some aspect of the self, others, or the situation' (Schiff et al., 1975: 18).

guardian contract a therapeutic contract defining a long-term relationship akin to that of a guardian, developed and used in the Connect Therapeutic Community (see Chapter 5).

guest contract a therapeutic contract defining a short-term (brief therapy) relationship, analogous to that of a guest, also developed and used in the Connect Therapeutic Community for those residents or regular visitors who are not (yet) full members of the community (see Chapter 5).

'hard' contract a bilateral commitment (see *contract*) which is defined in behavioural and observable terms and which is finishable in an mutually agreed time frame; see *'soft' contract*.

impasse a concept originally developed in gestalt therapy (Perls, 1975) to describe a stuck point when two parts of the personality are pushing against each other or in opposite directions; TA describes three types of impasse, the first (Type I) involving counterinjunctions or *drivers*, Type II involving *injunctions*, and Type III representing early developmental conflict which is pre-linguistic and often experienced somatically and represented symbolically (see Mellor, 1980).

incapacitation often paired with violence as a way of discharging energy built up through *passivity*, one of the four passive behaviours originally identified by Schiff et al. (1975); see *agitation*, *doing nothing* and *over-adaptation*.

injunction a negative message from the parent to the child which forms the basis for the child's negative early decision. Goulding and Goulding (1972) identified twelve such messages: 'Don't Be (Exist)', 'Don't Be You', 'Don't Be a Child', 'Don't Grow Up', 'Don't Make It', 'Don't (Don't Do Anything)', 'Don't Be Important', 'Don't Belong', 'Don't Be Close', 'Don't Be Well (Don't Be Sane)', 'Don't Think' and 'Don't Feel' (see Chapter 4).

Integrated Adult (also Integrating Adult), a term used to describe and emphasise the here-and-now, present-centred, integrating function of the *Adult ego state*.

life script see *script*.

Little Fascist a term originally used by Berne to describe the negative, destructive, authoritarian part of the Child ego state – in terms of second order structural analysis of ego states, the Parent in the Child (P_1) (see Figure G.3); a term now fallen into disrepute; many transactional analysts, for example, Lee (in Chapter 7), prefer the term 'Saboteur'.

Little Professor a term used to describe the creative and intuitive strategies for problem-solving – in ego-state terms, the Adult in the Child (A_1) (again, a second order structural analysis, see Figure G.3).

Martian 'the willingness to intuitively see through the images and beliefs that nurtured us during our personal and social struggle to survive' (Groder, 1976: 365) (see Chapter 1).

metaphor scene the notion that metaphors are indicative of script scenes; Berne (1975b) describes a client who was 'all at sea', 'couldn't fathom anything', 'could hardly keep her head above water', 'had stormy days', etc.

miniscript a process model of script based on *drivers*, developed by Kahler and Capers (1974) (see Chapter 1).

no going crazy contract see *escape hatch closure*.

no homicide contract see *escape hatch closure*.

no suicide contract see *escape hatch closure*.

OKness a concept which describes the positive existential life position 'I'm OK, You're OK' (I+U+), it contrasts with the other three life positions (I+U–, I–U+ and I–U–); later Berne (1975b) extended these two-handed positions to include the three-handed position 'I'm OK, You're OK, They're OK'.

options the idea, developed by Karpman (1971) and based on the functional metaphor of ego states, that people have choices as to how they transact with other.

over-adaptation a non-identification with one's own goals in favour of accepting others', one of the four passive behaviours originally identified by Schiff et al. (1975); see *agitation, doing nothing* and *incapacitation.*

parent contract a therapeutic contract defining a long-term relationship akin to that of a parent (see *parenting*), used in the *Cathexis* school of TA (see Chapter 5).

Parent ego state 'a set of feelings, attitudes, and behavior patterns which resemble those of a parental figure' (Berne, 1975a: 75); see *Adult ego state* and *Child ego state.*

parenting the method or process of fulfilling a *parent contract* whereby a therapist acts as a parent to their client.

passive behaviours the external, 'acting out' (rather than active) behaviours which manifest some level of *discounting*; Schiff et al. (1975) identified four such behaviours: *agitation, doing nothing, incapacitation* (or violence) and *over-adaptation.*

permission a positive transaction which has the effect of countering or even cancelling the *injunctions* which help to maintain the script, this may be offered or given by the parents or, more commonly, by the therapist; and which, together with potency and protection, form the three 'P's of therapy (Crossman, 1966) which the therapist needs in order to give the client new Parental messages (see Chapter 4).

Pig Parent also referred to as the internalised oppressor, a term which, along with others (such as the Ogre and the Witch Parent), describes, in terms of second order structural analysis of ego states (see Figure G.3), the harsh aspect of the Parent in the Child (P_1); a term generally fallen into disrepute, although Steiner (1988) offers a strong defence of its usefulness.

potency refers both generally to the therapeutic authority and effectiveness of the therapist and, specifically, to the notion that, for the client to accept the therapist's *permission/s*, the client's Child needs to perceive the therapist's Parent as more powerful or potent than their own actual parents from whom the original negative messages derive; see *permission, protection* and Chapter 4.

process scripts the generalised broad categories of script patterns (see Chapter 8).

program the script messages to the child from the parents' Adult ego states which focus on 'how to do things'.

protection a quality of the authoritative and effective therapist which the client needs in order to deal with the potential intrapsychic (Parental) backlash from becoming script free; together with *permission* and *potency*, the third 'P' (Crossman, 1966).

protocol the original experiences which pattern a person's life, from which the *script* derived.

racket a set of script behaviours whereby a person experiences a racket feeling, and the process whereby a person sets that up (out of awareness), so called after the notion of the (criminal) 'protection racket' which gives some sense of the positive intention inherent in this concept.

racket feeling 'a familiar emotion, learned and encouraged in childhood experienced in many different stress situations, and maladaptive as an adult means of problem-solving' (Stewart and Joines, 1987: 209).

racket system a model which explains the nature and maintenance of life scripts, developed by Erskine and Zalcman (1979) (see Figure G.4).

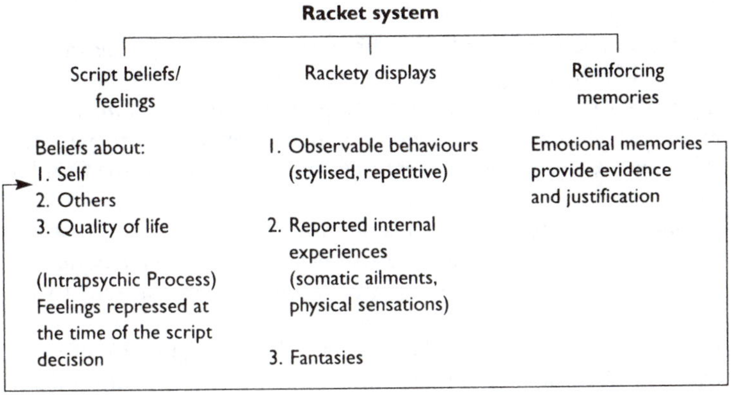

Racket system

Script beliefs/ feelings	Rackety displays	Reinforcing memories
Beliefs about: 1. Self 2. Others 3. Quality of life (Intrapsychic Process) Feelings repressed at the time of the script decision	1. Observable behaviours (stylised, repetitive) 2. Reported internal experiences (somatic ailments, physical sensations) 3. Fantasies	Emotional memories provide evidence and justification

Figure G.4 *The racket system (Erskine and Zalcman, 1979)*

radical psychiatry a tradition within TA, represented particularly by the work of Steiner (Steiner, 1987; Roy and Steiner, 1988), which emphasises the social context of illness and pathology, oppression and alienation and the analysis of power and oppressive and conflictual relationships (sometimes used synonymously with *social psychiatry*).

Rebellious Child a functional metaphor which characterises behaviour from a person's childhood in a rebellious adaptation to Parental rules or limits.

redecision a new decision made in order to move out of script by changing the early (script) decision (see Chapter 4).

redefining transaction a transaction in which the response shifts or changes from the one being addressed by the stimulus e.g. *A*: 'What do you *feel* when I ask if you love me? *B*: 'Well, I *think* . . . '; see also *blocking transaction* and *tangential transaction*.

regression a term originally used by Freud to describe a defence mechanism, a 'diffusion of instinct' through a regressive form of expression; more broadly describing a reversion to an earlier stage of development and, following Berne (1975a), who formulated it as a way of integrating archaic Child material into Adult, used by some transactional analysts as a therapeutic technique.

reparenting 'involves the total decathexis of the originally incorporated Parent ego state, and the replacement of that structure with a new Parent structure' (Schiff et al., 1975: 88).

script 'an ongoing program, developed in early childhood under parental influence, which directs the individual's behavior in the most important aspects of his life' (Berne, 1975b: 418).

script analysis the analysis, usually in therapy, of the *script* (see Appendix).

script apparatus the complete mechanism of the script, defined by Berne (1975b) as consisting of: the *script payoff* (or curse), the *injunction* or stopper, the provocation or come-on, the *antiscript* or spellbreaker, the *counterscript* slogans or prescription, parental behaviour patterns and instructions, and the demon or the Child in the child (C_1).

script matrix a diagram, originally developed by Steiner (1966), which shows the *counterscript* messages (or *drivers*) and *injunctions*, as well as the *program*, originating in the parents and being sent to the child.

script payoff the outcome of the script which, Berne (1975b) observes, are generally four: 'be a loner, be a bum, go crazy, or drop dead' (1975b: 110).

script signal 'a characteristic posture, gesture, tic, or symptom which signifies that [a person] is living "in his script," or has "gone into" his script' (Berne, 1975b: 315).

script types the various classifications of scripts, originally: winning, losing and non-winning (Berne, 1975b), there are also script process types (see Stewart, 1996 and Chapter 8).

self-reparenting the generating of a new Parent ego state to replace the existing one, a technique developed by James (1974).

social psychiatry originally synonymous with transactional analysis – the subtitle of *Transactional Analysis in Psychotherapy* (Berne, 1975a) is 'a systemic individual and social psychiatry' (also and somewhat confusingly used synonymously with *radical psychiatry*).

'soft' contract a phrase increasingly used to describe a more open, less defined and open-ended commitment or agreement which does not fulfil the requirements of a *'hard' contract*.

spot reparenting the technique, developed by Osnes (1974), whereby the client in therapy recalls and relives a specific (negative) experience at which point the therapist intervenes with a new, positive nurturing message.

stop contract a commitment a person makes to stop behaving (or not to behave) in a way which harms or endangers themselves or others; see *escape hatch closure.*

stroke a unit of recognition.

stroke economy the pattern by which people decide how they organise the giving, receiving and processing of strokes; according to Steiner (1971) there are a number of restrictive Parental rules which describe a negative or restrictive stroke economy: 'Don't give strokes when you have them to give', 'Don't ask for strokes when you need them', 'Don't accept strokes if you want them', 'Don't reject strokes when you don't want them', and 'Don't give yourself strokes'.

stroke filter describes the way in which people discount or filter out strokes, usually on the basis of the restrictions of their personal *stroke economy.*

symbiosis whilst healthy symbiosis is a natural and necessary occurrence in a dependent child/nurturing parent relationship, pathological symbiosis describes the situation when 'two become one' in ways which do not enhance autonomy for either; sometimes described in TA as when two people have only three ego states between them, a situation which involves *excluding ego states* (see Schiff et al., 1975).

tangential transaction describes a stimulus-response exchange or sequence in which the people concerned address different issues or different aspects of the same issue which has the effect of missing or 'talking past' each other, e.g. *A*: 'Do you want to make love?' *B*: 'I'm really tired tonight'.

therapeutic contract a bilateral commitment which defines the desired therapeutic outcome (as distinct from the administrative arrangements) of therapy.

therapeutic operations eight interventions/interpositions which originally (Berne, 1966) described the technique of transactional analysis (see Chapters 2 and 9).

time structuring six ways which, according to Berne (1966, 1973), people structure time (withdrawal, rituals, pastimes, activities, *games* and intimacy).

trading stamps based on the concept of trading stamps given by shops and collected by customers (in the era before 'reward points'), the idea that people collect psychological trading stamps (which could be angry, jealous, sad, etc.) and then at some point cash them in by means of a row, divorce, etc.

transaction 'a transactional stimulus plus a transactional response' (Berne, 1966: 370).

trap door in terms of the feeling, doing and thinking sequences developed and described by Ware (1983), the 'door' to avoid in working with people in therapy; see *contact door*.

treatment contract synonymous with *therapeutic contract*.

treatment direction 'the informed choice of interventions to facilitate the client in achieving the agreed contract, in the light of the [therapist's] diagnosis of the client' (Stewart, 1989: 9) (see Chapter 1).

treatment planning the planning of 'treatment' or therapy so that, in Berne's phrase 'at every stage you [the therapist] knows what you are doing and why you are doing it' (quoted by Stewart, 1989: 9).

ulterior transaction a stimulus-response sequence in which there is a social level transaction and, at the same time, a psychological, hidden or ulterior level to this transaction, e.g. 'Would you like to come up and see my etchings?'

References

Berne, E. (1963) *The Structure and Dynamics of Organizations and Groups.* New York: Grove Press.

Berne, E. (1966) *Principles of Group Treatment.* New York: Grove Press.

Berne, E. (1968) *Games People Play.* Harmondsworth: Penguin. (Original work published 1964.)

Berne, E. (1973) *Sex in human loving.* Harmondsworth: Penguin. (Original work published 1970.)

Berne, E. (1975a) *Transactional Analysis in Psychotherapy.* London: Souvenir Press. (Original work published 1961.)

Berne, E. (1975b) *What Do You Say After Hello?* London: Corgi. (Original work published 1972.)

Crossman, P. (1966) 'Permission and protection', *Transactional Analysis Bulletin,* 5(19): 152–4.

Erskine, R. and Zalcman, M. (1979) 'The racket system: A model for racket analysis', *Transactional Analysis Journal,* 9(1): 51–9.

Goulding, R. and Goulding, M. (1972) 'New directions in tranactional analysis', in C.J. Sager and H.S. Kaplan (eds), *Progress in Group and Family Therapy.* New York: Brunner/Mazel. pp.105–34.

Groder, M. (1976) 'Guest editorial', *Transactional Analysis Journal,* 6(4): 365.

Holloway, W. (1973) *Shut the Escape Hatch, Monograph IV,* in *The Monograph Series I-X.* Medina, OH: Midwest Institute of Human Understanding. pp. 15–18.

James, M. (1974) 'Self-reparenting: Theory and process', *Transactional Analysis Journal,* 4(3): 32–9.

Kahler, T. and Capers, H. (1974) 'The miniscript', *Transactional Analysis Journal,* 4(1): 26–42.

Karpman, S. (1971) 'Options', *Transactional Analysis Journal,* 1(1): 79–87.

Lee, A. (1988) *Scriptbound.* Workshop presentation, Nottingham.

Mellor, K. (1980) 'Impasses: A developmental and structural understanding', *Transactional Analysis Journal,* 10(3): 204–12.

Osnes, R.A. (1974) 'Spot reparenting', *Transactional Analysis Journal,* 4(3): 40–6.

Perls, F.S. (1975) 'Group vs individual therapy', in J.O. Stevens (ed.), *Gestalt Is*. Moab, UT: Real People Press. pp. 9–15.

Roy, B. and Steiner, C. (1988) *Radical Psychiatry: The Second Decade*. Unpublished manuscript.

Schiff, J.L., Schiff, A.W., Mellor, K., Schiff, E., Schiff, S., Richman, D., Fishman, J., Wolz, L., Fishman, C. and Momb, D. (1975) *Cathexis Reader: Transactional Analysis Treatment of Psychosis*. New York: Harper & Row.

Steiner, C. (1966) 'Script and counterscript', *Transactional Analysis Bulletin*, 5(18): 133–5.

Steiner, C. (1971) 'The strokes economy', *Transactional Analysis Journal*, 1(3): 9–15.

Steiner, C. (1987) 'The seven sources of power: An alternative to authority', *Transactional Analysis Journal*, 17: 102–4.

Steiner, C. (1988) 'The pig parent', in B. Roy and C. Steiner (eds), *Radical Psychiatry: The Second Decade*. Unpublished manuscript.

Stewart, I. (1989) *Transactional Analysis Counselling in Action*. London: Sage

Stewart, I. (1996) *Developing Transactional Analysis Counselling*. London: Sage.

Stewart, I., and Joines, V. (1987) *TA Today*. Nottingham: Lifespace.

Tilney, T. (1998) *Dictionary of Transactional Analysis*. London: Whurr.

Ware, P. (1983) 'Personality adaptions: Doors to therapy', *Transactional Analysis Journal*, 13(1): 11–19.

Author Index

Subject Index